Say Goodnight, Gracie

Say Goodnight, Gracie

The Last Years of Network Radio

by JIM COX

McFarland & Company, Inc., Publishers
Jefferson, North Carolina, and London

Library of Congress Cataloguing-in-Publication Data

Cox, Jim, 1939–
    Say goodnight, Gracie : the last years of network radio /
by Jim Cox.
        p.   cm.
    Includes bibliographical references and index.
    ISBN 0-7864-1168-6 (softcover : 50# alkaline paper) ∞
    1. Radio broadcasting—United States—History. I. Title.
    PN1991.3.U6C69   2002
    384.54'0973—dc21   2002000142

British Library cataloguing data are available

Front cover art ©2002 PhotoSpin

Manufactured in the United States of America

McFarland & Company, Inc., Publishers
    Box 611, Jefferson, North Carolina 28640
    www.mcfarlandpub.com

To the Kentuckiana Radio Addicts,
a gentle, affable species
whose inexorable inquiry into past time
nets an extraordinarily gratifying pastime

Acknowledgments

Among the serendipities of digging into vintage radio are the not infrequent offers of assists that come my way from a myriad of fellow radiophiles. As I reflect on their kindnesses, I'm convinced that in their own way they are leaving something for future generations while augmenting—often substantially—such ongoing research with their time, their talent and the materials from their own radio collections that they so enthusiastically disseminate. I have been blessed with the devoted patronage of several individuals who might not comfortably produce words on paper but who are willing to share their possessions generously so others may benefit. A couple of illustrations should suffice.

One confidant almost never fails to inquire every time we are together: "Is there *anything* I can do for you?" He means it. As if the recorded and printed resources he passes along aren't enough, I *hear* the zealousness in his voice. It is *genuine*. Friends like this one are incalculable assets and I don't take that privilege casually.

Not long ago I was languishing over a dealer's table at an old time radio convention and happened upon two volumes that I realized could be indispensable in helping me to complete this book. I inquired of the attendant what he was asking for each work. When he responded, my heart sank for I was unprepared at that moment to part with such a hefty sum. We struck up a conversation and he asked my name. His expression soon changed; he was familiar with an earlier work of mine, having perhaps sold some copies. "In the interest of research," the gentleman replied, as if needing to justify his decision, he would sell the two books to me for less than what he was asking for the price of one.

"Let's just say it will be my little contribution to vintage radio research," he allowed. I could hardly contain my surprise and elation and thanked him profusely.

A sincere debt of gratitude for this volume is due to several OTR buffs who gave of themselves without strings attached. Among them: Henry Brugsch, Chris Chandler, Dennis Crow, Tom Hood, Warren Jones, Ted Kneebone, Bill Knowlton, Laura Leff, Chris Lembesis, Howard and Ron Mandelbaum, Ted Meland, Barry Mishkind, Charles Niren, Andy Ooms, Ken Piletic, James Snyder, Jim Wood and Stewart Wright.

A contingent of OTR newsletter editors continually inspires my exploration and I am grateful for their affirmation which arrives sporadically: Jim Adams, Jack French, Jay Hickerson, Ken Krug, Patrick Lucanio and Paul Urbahns.

I'm especially indebted to the members of the Kentuckiana Radio Addicts radio club for their unwavering encouragement. Bouncing ideas off this group from time to time, I find them quick to respond in a multiplicity of supportive dimensions.

The reassurance offered by my faithful companion, Sharon Cox, who incessantly indulges my obsession, is deeply appreciated.

Finally, there can be little doubt that OTR has been a lifelong passion with me—from the days I heard it broadcast live as network radio; and ordering my first tapes in the 1960s launched a fascinating pursuit that has never waned. I'm indebted to the fans who have preserved it for us and for future generations—as well as for the motivation they tender in my quest to dig deeper into a diversion that provides so much satisfying entertainment while requiring so little in return.

Contents

Preface

In the middle of the 20th century, most Americans drew heavily upon the only means of mass communications they had ever known: radio. Recognizing the potential it offered at its inception three decades earlier, they fell in love with the little contraption that could instantly bring the sound of the world to their doors. Humorist Will Rogers saw the possibilities, too. In 1926, at the formation of the National Broadcasting Company, he expressed what most Americans would probably soon be thinking: "Radio is too big a thing to be out of."

It was. From then until the late 1940s, when the medium's fortunes began to ebb, radio dominated every other venue available for keeping the nation informed and entertained. This volume reflects how most Americans, so highly dependent on their radios at the median of the 20th century, relegated aural communications to something perceptibly less than it had been within a single decade. The shift is presented within the context of a potpourri of economic and technological breakthroughs occurring in the postwar U.S. that significantly enriched both the pocketbooks and the lives of mainstream citizens.

There can be no question that most people were considerably better off materially in 1960 than they had been in 1950. During the 1950s many individuals had—for the very first time—sampled the good life. After that, few of them could ever be happy with anything less.

Network radio was a victim of the dawning of self-gratification and prosperity. As people achieved more, they wanted more. Television, the newest mass communications tool, was mesmerizing, and quickly supplanted radio in the lives of most ordinary folk. One by one the stars and programs vanished that had kept a nation glued by their consoles. A beam of light from a 13-inch horizontal screen suddenly became the focus of all eyes in parlors and living rooms across the land.

Yet despite what was to become the norm, during the 1950s radio continued to offer many hours of quality material to the millions who relished it. Drama, music, comedy, mystery, games, variety, audience participation, documentaries, sports, religion, public affairs and news— first-rate staples by which the aural medium had always been classified— abounded through late 1960. Even then there were still a few opportunities remaining for fans to recall how things used to be in radio's halcyon days.

Some well-intentioned historiographers, considering the golden age, have tended to disregard anything that survived on radio beyond the era when TV gained a foothold in the late 1940s. More perceptive authorities, however, agree that the final vestiges of the epoch truly occurred when CBS turned off the microphones for all but a handful of the long-running features it then carried. CBS was the last of the major chains to continue airing more than a modicum of vintage radio's traditional fare after the late 1950s.

"The day radio drama died," Friday, November 25, 1960, and the 48-hour period thereafter, have traditionally been acknowledged as the actual end of the golden age by most radiophiles. That timeframe is accepted in this book.

Network radio's goodies—beyond the news and public affairs features—didn't completely disappear even then. An additional chapter has been included in this work which offers a brief examination of network programming and practices in the years beyond 1960. This may well be new information to most readers. This author is confident that such a compendium has never been previously published, at least not in a single source, and certainly not to the extent it is provided here.

As noted in my earlier texts, I make no claim of infallibility. Every human effort has been made to produce correct data to avoid perpetuating falsehoods that sometimes creep into print and are subsequently repeated by others. Still, the discerning reader may discover an inconsistency here and there. Published accounts that proved to be unreliable were simply discarded in researching this material. Be assured that any mistakes you find are mine alone and are absolutely unintentional. The possibility of error weighs on me heavily; if such instances exist, the reader's indulgence is sincerely implored.

1

The Fifties:
An Introduction
to the Fading Days
of Radio's Golden Age

For everything there is "an appointed season ... a proper time for every project," the Holy Scriptures decree.[1]

For a vast majority of Americans, the 1950s literally became the "time of our lives"—exemplifying the best of all worlds, the best that many citizens had experienced to that point in their lives. A short summary will offer ample clues.

Having been through the downturn of a virtual total economic collapse followed by a decade of slow recovery, these inhabitants were suddenly thrust into the limitations and sanctions of yet another outbreak of global aggression. For the second time in less than a quarter of a century, international conflict threatened the very freedoms and independence for which their nation had been established. The loss of life stemming from that open hostility was greater among the peoples of the world than from any other combative period in history. The disruption at home, meanwhile, was counterproductive to an America that had embraced a strong work ethic and had produced the manpower, skills and industrialization that could make far-reaching contributions to all humanity, and not just themselves.

By the late 1940s, Americans were finally able to pick up where they had left off almost 20 years earlier. It was genuinely their "appointed season ... a proper time for every project." The promise of a new decade—the fifties—now offered at last the greatest prospects to get ahead in the lifetimes of nearly everybody. The spirit of optimism for many people, as it turned out, was well founded.

Success and even affluence abounded. A mid–1980s evaluation characterized the 1950s as "the centerpiece" of the longest cycle of capitalist expansion in history.[2] Set smack dab at the summit of a postwar economic boom that lasted more than a score of years, the 1950s witnessed an unprecedented prosperity in the lives of numerous Americans.

The gross national product, for example—the measure of the total output of the country's goods and services—shot up from a mere $285 billion in 1950 to $500 billion by 1960.[3]

Unemployment dipped to 4.2 percent by middecade.

Personal income doubled, and individual purchasing power jumped a whopping 30 percent.[4]

Yet the most impressive figure of all, perhaps, was that—across this decade—Americans amounted to but 6 percent of the planet's population while producing and consuming more than a third of its goods and services.[5]

Some years later a popular broadcast journalist would paint a tranquil, though blatantly austere portrait of life in America at midcentury:

> When World War II ended, the United States looked as it had looked in the 1930s. Very few civilian products were made during the war. When it ended, there were no new cars, people's houses and kitchens and bathrooms were prewar, the newspapers, magazines, and radio programs were largely unchanged. The look and feel of the countryside, of the big cities and small towns, was very much of the Thirties. At the beginning of the Fifties, America in the summertime was a country of ceiling fans, pitchers of icewater, and dusty roads.
>
> It took time in a country of 150,000,000 people to get new stoves, clothes, houses, and cars to everybody. And there was a great demand for new products, such as air conditioning, which was nonexistent in ordinary homes before the war. When the decade began, there were no self-service elevators, no direct-mail telephones, no computers, no credit cards, no transistor radios, no diet drinks.... All that had changed by the end of the decade, but when it began, it was a world in which the telephone operator said, "Number, please?" and the elevator operator asked you for your floor.

Before we got to the Fifties, we had lived in one kind of country. When the decade ended, we were on our way somewhere else.[6]

Yet, despite the better days ahead that millions of citizens eagerly anticipated, not all of the countrymen were so hopeful. Prompted by an escalating Cold War with the Soviet Union, a segment of the population had difficulty shaking the doldrums, being held hostage by increasing fears of a future stemming from the traumas of previous decades. For them, it was the country's darkest era since the earliest days of the Second World War.

A very real, very corporal conflict, meanwhile—one that would later be termed "the forgotten war"—promptly appeared on the horizon. In June 1950, President Harry S Truman sent U.S. troops to the aid of the South Koreans, then under siege by their northern counterparts in a Soviet-backed insurgence. Even with United Nations encouragement, however, the discord turned into a prolonged no-win debacle after Chinese Communists entered the fray supporting the North Koreans. U.S. involvement was questioned at home and abroad and the USA's perception as the world's peacekeeper was visibly reinforced. To Americans accustomed to unequivocal victory, three years later the war ended in total frustration without any decision.

There were other disorders that rocked the nation at the same time.

President Truman ordered a superbomb developed, one capable of dwarfing the destructive power of the atomic bombs used in World War II on Hiroshima and Nagasaki.

A former State Department official, Alger Hiss, accused of stealing government documents during the 1930s, was convicted of perjury.

Julius and Ethel Rosenberg were put to death, convicted of espionage; both were members of a mammoth spy ring. They had compromised the nation's security by supplying the Soviet Union with U.S. atomic secrets during World War II.

Beyond these incongruities, the period was also an inauspicious moment in the lives of the nation's minorities. Having not yet experienced the changes that were to benefit entire races following several key court-ordered edicts, many remained in abject poverty. Virtually disenfranchised, they were still unable to qualify as respected members of society in a land that was poised to achieve its greatest accomplishments.

By the end of the decade, however, America had definitely become a country headed somewhere else.

The 1950s witnessed dramatic changes in the way that Americans received their information, news and entertainment, which for so long had been vested almost exclusively in radio soundwaves. Radio had been the first means of instant mass communications that the nation had experienced. It emanated from the early 1920s and evolved in succeeding decades that were frequently dubbed "the golden age of radio."

Many had considered President Franklin D. Roosevelt (1933–45) as the first master of the medium. His ability to exploit the airwaves, making it appear as if they were his personal conduit, resonated particularly with millions of immigrants and poorer Americans and their offspring. Roosevelt's voice—warm, friendly and confident—was matched perfectly to the medium. His seductive "fireside chats" came across as visits with average Americans in their own homes.

By the early 1950s, however, it was clear that radio was about to be displaced by Americans' avaricious and ongoing quest for something new. Almost collectively, and rather quickly, the majority of listeners turned their backs on radio in deference to television, then just coming into vogue. They shifted their allegiances as nimbly then as they had shunned vaudeville for radio as their foremost amusement three decades before.

One reactionary claimed that the new decade that opened at the middle of the 20th century framed what was likely broadcasting's "most shameful, scandal-ridden ten years" in its altogether brief history.[7] Citing both audio and visual transmissions, he labeled the 1950s "the decade of fear and corruption." At least a half dozen extremes were cited, each tending to diminish the charms that had traditionally added an aura to the airwaves.

The first, simply branded as "McCarthyism," embraced one of the nation's great rationality lapses. It was named for the then junior senator from Wisconsin, Joseph R. McCarthy, who at midcentury was appointed chairman of a permanent investigations subcommittee of the Government Operations Committee. While McCarthy didn't create the mass paranoia that bears his name, he profited by it. He established a career, in fact, by ferreting out and banishing governmental insiders whom he accused of disloyalty to the nation. Spurred by a growing public scare of atomic attack and internal Communist aggression, McCarthy helped create an air of widespread mistrust and accusation. Few individuals openly opposed him for fear of being taken as traitors, sympathizers, Communists or—at the least—as un–American. (McCarthy gained some respected allies in broadcast journalism, incidentally, Fulton Lewis, Jr., and Walter Winchell among them. He also acquired some influential opposition in the industry, willing to take a personal stand against him: Raymond Gram Swing, Elmer Davis and eventually, the most authoritative voice of all, Edward R. Murrow.)

Closely welded to McCarthyism was "blacklisting," a concerted effort to ruin the lives of anyone identified with—or even suspected of being a member of, or favorable toward—Communist or fascist causes. In a role he obviously relished, McCarthy expanded his witch-hunt as he sought suspected subversives among the general population. Operating tenaciously and

Spurred by a growing public fear of atomic attack and foreign aggression, Sen. Joseph R. McCarthy (R-Wis.) (shown) fanned domestic suspicion and personal accusation in America in the early 1950s. A result was the blacklisting of individuals who allegedly held Communist or fascist sympathies, which destroyed the lives of many active professionals by simple innuendo. *Photofest.*

often without proof, he and his band of like-minded henchmen exposed, smeared and ruined the careers of thousands of artists, unionists, librarians, college professors, public school teachers, journalists, clergymen and further loyal, upstanding professionals and tradespeople.

Particularly successful were his punitive efforts in blacklisting members of the performing arts, including the legitimate stage, motion pictures and broadcasting. The latter category at that juncture consisted of a preponderance of radio actors, comedians, musicians, writers, producers and other performers and creative people in widespread disciplines. Employment opportunities evaporated for hundreds whose names were gathered, often on mere suspicion—with some of those gifted individuals never again to toil at the crafts for which they were well-suited. Nearly all became victims of ridicule and shame. Many lost more than their self-respect and livelihoods; spouses and families vanished from their lives. Some turned to alcohol and other drugs; some became chronically ill, physically or mentally or both, while others wound up on welfare. A few of them committed suicide. The madness of it all was incredible, becoming decidedly far less than the nation's finest hour.

It took four years, in fact, after the headhunting began for America's most respected spokesman of the times—the esteemed, forthright broadcast journalist, Edward R. Murrow—to throw down the gauntlet and cry "Enough!" (Murrow had gained the respect of the masses during his insightful reportage from European combat zones during World War II. He remained in high regard by most Americans during the postwar years, much as Walter Cronkite would become admired by succeeding generations as the nation's most trusted spokesman.)

Surprisingly, Murrow openly loathed TV for most of his life, lambasting it as "slumming" and rejecting it for himself and his revered radio protégés.[8] "If television and radio are to be used for the entertainment of all of the people all of the time," he demurred, "we have come perilously close to discovering the real opiate of the people."[9] Yet at great risk to himself and his network (CBS), Murrow personally challenged the fanatical, out-of-control McCarthy. One of the most important commentators in radio's history, Murrow—an engaging weeknight radio newscaster—earned his ultimate broadcasting triumph in television on that singular occasion.

On his weekly *See It Now* program on CBS-TV March 9, 1954, he went for the jugular. Using the Senator's own words, the newsman offered a masterful exposé of the tyrannical intimidation and innuendo that McCarthy employed against innocent victims. It took the famed Army-McCarthy hearings a few weeks later to finally bring the Senator down—the fractious, inconsistent, often inarticulate politician sparred with military officials over alleged espionage at a New Jersey base—but Murrow had plainly been a key in shifting the public tide from its near blanket endorsement of the Senator. (Murrow's contributions to that effort were so persuasive, wrote one media observer, that "the age of television news was born on the evening Senator McCarthy was exposed."[10])

By the end of that year (1954), McCarthy was finished. The U.S. Senate publicly humiliated him, censuring the lawmaker in a 67–22 vote for bringing "dishonor and disrepute through ... displays of contemptuous and insulting behavior" upon that body as well as "obstructing ... constitutional process." Our long national nightmare was over. Twenty-nine months later McCarthy, too, was dead, himself a victim of the ravages of alcohol abuse.

Unfortunately, there were several more broadcasting-related scandals in the 1950s.

A number of improprieties involving prominent industry figures, Federal Communications Commission officials and U.S. Congressmen surfaced in a late-in-the-decade inspection of regulatory agency practices. Several commissioners had abused their positions for personal gain. Some were double-billing both the government and the electronic media for reimbursement of travel expenses. Broadcasters, in the meantime, were rewarding FCC members with expensive trips and merchandise in exchange for favorable action surrounding contested station applications.

Furthermore, Congressman Oren Harris purchased an interest in a local broadcast outlet that had earlier been denied a power increase when it was requested of the FCC. That decision was suddenly reversed after Harris bought into the property—a highly questionable action. Harris soon left the Congress under appointment to a federal judgeship. In light of the investigation's discoveries, however, FCC chairman John C. Doerfer and commissioner Richard A. Mack were forced to step down. Some other government officials, including President Dwight D. Eisenhower's own assistant, Sherman Adams, also resigned in disgrace.

Yet another scandal of the era involved a secret pact that the president of the Mutual Broadcasting System, Alexander Guterma, made with Rafael Trujillo, the Dominican Republic's dictator, in January 1959. For $750,000, MBS was to put a positive spin on a specified number of news reports and commentaries to be aired each month so that they would be favorable to the Dominican Republic. However, a short time after closing the deal, the MBS president found himself mired in some commercial and legal dilemmas. The Dominican Republic blew the whistle on its arrangement, suing for the return of its capital. In the aftermath, suspicion settled over some legitimate programmers who might have fallen victim to other publicists just as one network executive had done.

Then there were the never-to-be-forgotten quiz show and payola indignities of the late 1950s.

In the former, several TV game shows with large giveaway prizes were rigged. Radio, as it turned out, was never involved. The reality only came to light when a few contestants began talking publicly. The careers of a dozen or more individuals who carried out the shenanigans to boost program ratings were destroyed. Ten persons who lied to a grand jury pleaded guilty to perjury. As a direct consequence, the huge cash giveaway programs vanished from the airwaves for decades.

In 1959, deals in which the producers of phonograph records were paying disc jockeys under the table to air their recordings were exposed to public scrutiny. In theory, if a top deejay on a major station aired a specific record often enough, the recording frequently became an overnight sensation among music purchasers. When a radio station received revenue for such commercialization—thereby deceiving the public in the process—the mayhem was termed "payola." Some of the nation's better-known deejays were caught in the quagmire and their services were terminated.

There were other difficulties that occurred in the fading days of radio's golden age which tended to both fragment and diminish the listening audience.

The rise of television was by far the most immediate, disruptive and insoluble crisis, and was at least an underlying root cause of several of the others. Radio had virtually been minting money since the early 1930s. By the 1950s, however, it would have to struggle to transform itself as it attempted to discover a viable new role of service.

The ability to see radio entertainers in the living room seemed a natural extension of the aural medium in a country that was obviously enchanted by new technology and its related electrical contraptions. As early as the 1920s developers assured Americans that television was on the way. By the middle of that decade one ambitious visionary predicted that within five years every home in the nation would maintain a device that would offer visuals of the programming people were then hearing.[11] While that didn't occur, *Variety* confidently updated the industry with a banner headline in its April 16, 1930, edition: "Television Near Ready."

Before that decade drew to a close, TV *did* arrive. The marketing of sets began in 1938, the same year that *Variety* published its first review of a visual program (May 1938). *Billboard* added TV reviews a year later.

And effective with its August 1939 issue, *Radio Mirror* optimistically renamed itself *Radio and Television Mirror*.

However, the optimism was short-lived. The research, production and distribution of receivers and transmitters was sidetracked by the intervention of World War II. The radio and television industries were swiftly converted to production for military purposes. Had it not been for that, TV would have confidently challenged radio in the early 1940s—and, almost assuredly, radio's golden age might have ended with the close of the 1940s rather than the 1950s. The potential for TV was never dismissed, however. As the war ended, manufacturers and the radio chains were anxious to reintroduce the tube to American consumers.

Television complemented radio in that many viewed it merely as an extension of the aural medium, ascribing to it such terms of endearment as "sight radio," "radio optics," "radio moving pictures" and "radio vision." The earliest visual features were often adaptations of major radio series or were quite similar in nature to existing radio shows. The newer medium's primitive offerings, therefore, weren't altogether unfamiliar to radio listeners.

The earliest example of the extraordinary influence of television was the spectacular rise of Milton Berle. Berle was the embodiment of an archetypical vaudeville slapstick comic. He flopped in radio but successfully burst onto TV screens in 1948. "The early history of television and the story of Berle's show were close to being one and the same thing," a witness to the period allowed. "The very success of Berle's show accelerated the sale of television sets; those Americans who did not yet own sets would return home after watching him at their neighbors' houses and decide that, yes, it was finally time to take the plunge."[12]

A textbook writer noted: "By 1948, radio had enjoyed the privileged status of an only child for 28 years. But in that year, a smarty pants kid, television, began to emerge as the dominant national medium."[13] A CBS vice president, Hubbell Robinson, Jr., succinctly compared the changing state of affairs to Custer's last stand: "Television is about to do to radio what the Sioux did to Custer. There is going to be a massacre," he warned.[14]

An important by-product of Berle's overnight rise in the public's consciousness was that his phenomenal popularity stirred other comedians into considering the new medium—including stars who had held back from making the jump from their comfortable radio digs. Berle

The early history of television and the TV show of Milton Berle (shown) were virtually one and the same. His slapstick comedy may have been difficult for some in aural audiences to connect with, but viewers readily absorbed it. The sale of millions of TV sets and transition of some of radio's most durable and revered comics to the tube resulted. *Photofest.*

proved to be as much a catalyst in attracting his peers as he was adept in gaining fans and selling TV sets. As several of his contemporaries witnessed his meteoric rise to fame, they aspired to a greater share of public acclaim for themselves. One by one, many of radio's most valued stars—who had been skeptical and reluctant to test the waters until they could see some evidence of the tube's magnitude—began making the transition to television. George Burns and Gracie Allen, Jack Benny, Red Skelton and a myriad of other funny people were among those soon leaping onto the bandwagon.

It can reasonably be argued that TV began to develop a large following only after several of the biggest names in radio began appearing on it, and when some of the largest advertisers in broadcasting reallocated their capital. By 1950 some of television's top-rated shows had arrived from the aural medium. One radio chronicler aptly surmised: "With such programming, what had begun as 'sight radio' began now to destroy its 'hearing-only' competition."[15]

One of the most telling signs that radio was in serious jeopardy occurred in mid–1949. *The Fred Allen Show,* which had long dominated a Sunday night half-hour time period over its 18-year run, abruptly left the airwaves forever. Ostensibly departing at the hands of a highly successful telephone quiz show (*Stop the Music!*) that competitor ABC had thrown against some of NBC's formidable Sunday night comedies, the Allen program was irrefutably caught in the shifting fortunes of radio.

A couple of radio historiographers went so far as to claim that "Radio actually died when *Stop the Music!* got higher ratings than Fred Allen."[16] Humorist Henry Morgan assured everybody that such an aberration drove "the final nail in radio's coffin."[17]

Allen wasn't sure whom to tag with his misfortune, so he tended to blame everybody. His acerbic ad libs and sharply pointed parodies had long attacked radio game shows, the genre that ironically did him in: "If I were king for one day, I would make every program a giveaway show; when the studios were filled with the people who encourage these atrocities, I would lock the door. With all the morons of America trapped, the rest of the population could go about its business."[18]

He took potshots at broadcasting executives, too, and left little doubt how he felt about TV, mounting a campaign to expunge it forever: "Television is a triumph of equipment over people, and the minds that control it are so small that you could put them in the navel of a flea and still have enough room beside them for a network vice-president's heart."[19] (The humorist was literally cut off the air for 35 seconds in April 1947 when he violated an NBC policy, telling a joke that poked fun at network vice presidents.) TV, he allowed, was "a device that permits people who haven't anything to do to watch people who can't do anything."[20] Finally, Allen offered this appraisal of the new medium: "When television belatedly found its way into the home after stopping off too long at the tavern, the advertisers knew they had a more potent force available for their selling purposes. Radio was abandoned like the bones at a barbecue."[21]

The comic's biographer claimed that his downfall could be attributed to a changing era. Declared Robert Taylor: "Allen's mordant, dark humor had worked when America was on hard times; as he mocked the successful and pompous, he had touched the right nerve in society. But as the country began to undergo unparalleled prosperity, people no longer wanted to make fun of success—they wanted to share in it."[22] Another reason, which Allen himself later admitted, was that shows like his had simply run on too long. "Even without the coming of television," he wrote, "the survey figures showed a gradual shrinking in the mass audience. The audience and the medium were both getting tired. The same programs, the same comedians, the same commercials—even the sameness was starting to look the same."[23]

Allen's departure from radio was only a start, and far from the "final nail" in the coffin. Radio's golden age would take another decade

The fall of Fred Allen left ominous clouds over radio. In 1950, the sagacious comedian (left) appeared on "The Colgate Comedy Hour" on NBC-TV in a reprise of his popular "Allen's Alley" sketch with radio denizens (l–r) Kenny Delmar (Senator Claghorn), Minerva Pious (Mrs. Nussbaum), Peter Donald (Ajax Cassidy) and Parker Fennelly (Titus Moody). *Photofest.*

to expire, succumbing to a slow and painful passing experienced by its dwindling corps of faithful listeners. Those stalwarts maintained that there was something in an aural transmission that could never be successfully duplicated by any visual means. The all-important ingredient, which was instantly displaced in TV, was *imagination*. In the theater of the mind, images were precisely etched on the listener's brain as perceived, never as a common picture affixed on a small screen. For all its worthy enhancements then, video could never provide that quality. Whether the fans realized it or not, that had to be a contributing factor in their reluctance to say "goodby" to longtime favorite shows and performers as, little by little, they departed from their long accustomed stands.

Lest the reader be misled, however, it must be clearly understood that television by itself wasn't the only culprit that determined radio's ultimate fate. The seeds of some of its most profound troubles in the 1950s were sewn in the years immediately following the Second World War, when a somber blow against the audio medium was struck. Let's digress for a moment to examine what was happening. Until then, commercial radio had been the nation's first and only unified source of communications and mass entertainment. Yet, in the postwar years, a media critic found an industry in disarray:

> Broadcasters had rallied behind the embattled flag. Government programs and announcements were dutifully aired; regular shows integrated patriotic themes into their scripts; and voluntary self-censorship was carefully and successfully carried out. But the cessation of the war left radio without purpose or direction, and in need of self-appraisal. Waging a crusade so intensely for so many years, by late 1945 radio personnel found it difficult to discover meaning in the new world.[24]

During 1945 and 1946, a protracted discussion concerning the prospects for radio's future appeared in the pages of *Variety*. The matter was of such import, creating such divergent opinions, that a couple of the medium's time-honored comedians, Eddie Cantor and Fred Allen, spoke openly on it, though taking opposite views. Cantor, on the one hand, called for broadcasters to be distinct. He saw that epoch as a time for a maturing radio industry to be daring and possibly even a bit audacious. But his contemporary, Allen, cautioned that radio was still in its infancy, still a problem child, and needed to focus on developing future performing and writing talent. FCC commissioner Clifford Durr, in the meantime, was lobbying for practical programming that could, if need be, rub listeners the wrong way. He was unsure that radio really had any idea of *what* people preferred. The editorial pages of *Life* and *The Saturday Review of Literature*, popular mass audience publications of the day, urged radio to consider a more eloquent approach for its choice of fare.

Several programming trends surfaced in the years immediately following the war. Some of them carried over to the next decade.

One was the resurrection of a quiz show craze that had been prevalent for a couple of years before America's involvement in the international conflagration. This was, without a doubt, the most popular expression of escapism then taking hold in network programming. By

1948 radio offered more than $7 million in cash and merchandise prizes on such shows. After the years of austerity, materialism simply validated its irresistibility to Americans at all levels. In unprecedented numbers, they tuned in, waited for the phone to ring and fantasized about being winning contestants.

Simultaneously, a number of top-rated comedy shows reverted to nontopical gags and clichés, a departure from their war-era practice. Yet satirists Fred Allen and Henry Morgan, who poked fun at such objects before the war, carried on at their usual pace. Top-drawer dramatic series transported the escapist theme further than ever, meanwhile, emphasizing it in tales of romance, mystery and horror.

In addition, the documentary, which would reach its developmental apex in the 1950s, got a foothold in radio's postwar era. For the first time, radio assumed a social accountability that it had tiptoed around in the past. The documentaries of the period explored issues like alcoholism, consequences of the atom bomb, juvenile delinquency and the Cold War.

Dishearteningly, there was inertia in broadcasting during this period, too. Of 108 network series that had been on the air at least a decade in 1950, a study revealed that a dozen of those had aired for two or more decades. Many people were calling for new voices, new formats and new shows. The postwar period was, as one critic put it, "the era of the doldrums." Despite this, radio continued without substantial changes. As a direct corollary, some of its fans were finding other places to spend their time. "It was," noted one observer, "a development from which radio broadcasting never fully recovered."[25]

A treatise focused on the early days of the radio networks and their operating methods will offer the reader substantial insights into how things "used to be":

> Perhaps the clearest indication of the importance of the networks ... was the increasing control that CBS and NBC exerted over their affiliates. Stations were bound to these networks for five-year periods, although the networks could end a contract after any single year. Mutual's one-year term for both sides was an exception.... Contracts assigned option periods each day to the network for its national commercial programming. CBS had the right to take all day, NBC most of the day,... and Mutual averaged four hours a day. Finally, stations legally could reject sustaining programs from the networks in order to air local shows, but rejecting commercially sponsored programs could jeopardize their affiliation.

The one-sided nature of network contracts was the result of relative strength. Local stations gave networks and national advertisers access to audiences in their communities. But networks had the advertising money to produce programs that stations needed to attract audiences. No single station could afford to put together programs that would be as popular as those of the networks.... Hence, the affiliated stations, even with regional coverage, needed the networks more than vice versa, and other stations always were waiting for a chance to affiliate.[26]

That was in the 1930s, and times change.

As the decade of the 1950s wore on, the local affiliates of the radio networks—many of them having been related to ABC, CBS, MBS or NBC for most of their commercial broadcasting existences—labored in unrest. Varied economic policies that affected their operations and over which they had little control were causing growing concern. The murmuring among themselves, while soft-spoken initially, would soon erupt into a groundswell of organized protest directed toward the networks' ownership. Most of their anxieties, and the affiliates' suggestions and demands, appeared to fall on deaf ears, at least in the beginning.

Yet in time the outlets gained the rapt attention of the web owners as a number of key stations—some powerful media conduits in the regions they served—threatened to suspend their longstanding ties with the national chains by becoming independents. The fact that this would break with tradition and result in discontinuing associations with venerable programming and scheduling that had long been favored by their most loyal fans appeared of little consequence. An apparent shift in priorities from the public goodwill to significantly increasing bottom-line revenues was obviously becoming more pronounced throughout the industry.

Growing numbers of major advertisers were pulling out of radio, leaving a large volume of sustaining (unsponsored) series in their wake. Early in 1951, first CBS, soon followed by NBC, reduced across-the-board commercial radio rates between 10 and 15 percent. ABC and MBS announced similar reductions. Even though radio's fees were being drastically cut for the first time in many years, trusted firms like Pillsbury, Standard Brands and Kellogg's—traditional mainstays that had long been invested heavily in radio—virtually left the medium altogether. (A major competitor, General Mills, had allocated as much as *half* of its $10 million advertising budget for the whole year to radio as recently as 1946!)

Such losses were of paramount importance to the national chains and to the regional station owners as well. The networks could hardly ignore forever the challenges that these local operators presented, especially as their vocal majority was augmented by a growing, almost feverish tenacity.

In due course, though quite reluctantly, the network chiefs gradually caved in, relinquishing to the stations an upper hand in several critical areas. (To its credit, CBS held out the longest, fending off banishing a large portion of its schedule to the Valhalla of old radio series until quite late in the 1950s and ultimately into the early 1960s.)

Assuming substantial clout from the previously impregnable networks—a power they had never possessed before—the affiliates could now boost their own incomes extensively by selling the bulk of their commercial time themselves. They would no longer depend so heavily on sharing in a portion of the trickle-down proceeds that had been previously realized from sales transactions generated by the national chains. To fill in relinquished network time, they developed local news and editorial reports, provided coverage of sporting events, added features and an endless parade of disc jockeys playing the top 40 record selections ad infinitum. The handwriting on the wall for the future of radio was becoming abundantly clear to any prognosticators daring to read it.

For pure economic greed, then, longstanding listener favorites were sold out, disappearing in wholesale lots as the radio webs divested themselves of some of their most popular talents and series. In so doing, they turned over increasingly greater amounts of programming time—and the lucrative advertising that accompanied it—to the local stations. It was a poignant epitaph for what for decades had been a singular, vital, seldom challenged entertainment and information form.

There were yet other factors contributing to radio's decline and signaling its eventual eclipse.

With a quartet of nationwide chains competing for a dwindling number of listeners, and sponsors pulling out altogether or placing the bulk of their advertising budgets elsewhere, the networks were reluctant to spend adequate sums to develop stimulating replacement series for those they were losing. To the contrary, the major chains (CBS and NBC) were rapidly shifting their vast resources—money that had principally been made in radio—to bankroll television's mammoth start-up costs, and to feed the tube's voracious appetite for revolutionary, exciting and sustained ventures. Thus an atmosphere that was increasingly opposed to innovative radio programming grew and grew. Radio was quickly turning into a castoff, worthy to finance the enterprise after years of testing ideas that did and didn't work, but sharing in few of broadcasting's rewards for its valued contributions. None of these developments substantially added to radio's ability to hold its current fans or to draw new ones.

Realizing that it would be difficult to support radio programming when sponsors left for television, broadcasters briefly considered the notion of direct audience support through pay radio. Under such a plan, listeners would be expected to kick in five cents a day—$18.25 annually— to hear shows that were devoid of commercials. The concept was placed on a back burner, however, when William Benton of Connecticut, founder of the advertising agency Benton and Bowles and one of the plan's strongest proponents, became a United States Senator. The idea was finally put to rest when it resurfaced only as a means to institute a home music service based on Muzak Corporation patents. There simply wasn't enough favorable response to go forward with the proposal.

Change was inevitable, of course, but some adjustments were drastic, contributing heavily to the perception that the aural medium really was no longer of enough import to be taken seriously. A number of radio executives tried every conceivable method they could think of to pare back spending on broadcasting's flagship medium. Not only did they severely trim talent costs, they reversed themselves on some of their own longstanding dictates that had been previously inscribed as sacrosanct.

Taping reruns of popular shows, for example, once an anathema at CBS and NBC, became commonplace by the start of the 1950s. The practice began quietly with such series as *The Bing Crosby Show* and Groucho Marx's *You Bet Your Life*, both of which not only aired taped reruns during the off-season but also ran prerecorded and edited presentations of *every* program in later time periods throughout the regular season. Other producers weren't about to sit idly by and let such developments go unchallenged, of course. Many of radio's weekly nighttime favorites—and an expanding list of daytime soap operas—were soon getting into taping their normal fare in advance.

An underlying incentive in this exploit, but one of considerable magnitude, was to cut production costs. For some programming, it could be accomplished by recording multiple performances back to back, a technique that is commonplace in syndicating game shows on television in the present day. A whole week's worth of a quarter-hour daytime radio serial, for instance, could be rehearsed and taped in only a few hours in a single sitting, freeing up studios, equipment, production personnel and talent. This also netted the by-product of allowing their professionals to take additional freelance assignments elsewhere on other days.

These circumstances combined had the obvious effect of continuing to displace radio as a vibrant, viable communications conduit. While radio's audiences were persistently depleted, the industry did little to stop the diminution, and seemed bent on encouraging it. In many minds, the persuasive message was that "radio doesn't matter much any more" as the medium increasingly turned into the industry's stepchild.

The soap operas, one of the most prolific and powerful forms of programming to go out across the radio airwaves, finally reached an ultimate conclusion on November 25, 1960, when the remaining quartet of daytime dramas still airing were canceled by CBS. In many ways, their abrupt departure signified the end of radio's golden age.

The fate of those ongoing narratives, which had fascinated homemakers over a period of three decades, could be applied to other genres facing extinction as radio rounded a sharp corner. An insightful historiographer of the aural medium characterized the prevailing situation:

> What was passing away was an era in American cultural history. What had begun in the 1920s as an experimental toy and a popular fad, had emerged in the next decade as the most compelling medium in communications. Recognized early by American capitalists as a profitable and strategic new industry, radio became an entertainment, informational, and artistic utility. Certainly, it was filled with commercialism. Certainly, too, it was shaped in part by sponsor and agency prejudices. But radio was still functional. To many critics it lacked esthetics.... Yet, radio from 1920 to 1960 mirrored the American civilization which it served. If it was commercialized, it was because the entire society was shaped by a capitalist, consumer economy with its penchant for competitive advertising and its advocacy of a business ethic. If it lacked grace and refinement, it was because radio served a democratic audience, a mixture of educational and economic levels which generally appreciated a belly-laugh more than a polite curtsey.[27]

The 1950s had been "an appointed season ... a proper time." When the decade ended, as a nation we were definitely on our way somewhere else.

2

The Early Years:
1950-1953

At midcentury, radio could be typified by national chains and sponsors and star-studded bills. A widely respected authority offered a laidback word-picture of the country's dependency on the aural medium in 1950:

> Leisure is important, ... radio is our main pastime. More than 90 percent of American homes have at least one receiving set. Millions have several. The average man and woman spend more leisure hours in listening to the radio than in anything else—except sleeping. The poorer and the less educated we are, the more we listen—and naturally so. For radio—cheap, accessible, and generous in its provision for popular tastes—has come to be the poor man's library, his "legitimate" theater, his vaudeville, his newspaper, and his club. Never before has he met so many famous and interesting people, and never have these people been at once so friendly and so attentive to his wishes. Even a President has repeatedly addressed him as a friend![1]

Alas, that portrayal of serene trust was about to be cruelly tested. As it turned out, an abrupt proliferation of new radio stations introduced between 1947 and 1950—all competing for waning audiences— and the astonishing escalation of television vowed that radio was going to have to make major changes, and quickly, if it was to survive and persist as a viable medium.

For some local stations the path of least resistance arrived in a form that was at least half as old as radio itself: the disc jockey, or deejay, show. As early as 1935 some independent stations had featured music-and-talk fare. By midcentury, others were converting to total deejay programming, frequently specializing in target segments of the listening audience. They were, therefore, able to sell commercial time to sponsors that found such focused sectors favorable to their businesses.

Multiple station owners Gordon McLendon of Dallas and Todd Storz of Omaha fostered a concept that was deftly referred to as Top 40, out of which evolved one of the more prominent entertainment institutions of the period. Aiming toward a youthful market—teenagers and early twentysomethings—their plan emphasized brief lag time, spread between recordings of single hits that were played on a turntable. The on-air framework was clearly marked by contests and singing identification jingles while the stations themselves were promoted far and wide via other media. In a brief while, Top 40 radio personalities acquired virtual life-or-death control over popular music recording artists and trade distribution systems.

By midway through the decade, rock 'n' roll thrust onto the American musical scene and many Top 40 stations concentrated on that new wave sweeping the country. Numerous markets fell under the spell of raucous, razzle-dazzle, rocking Top 40 stations while urbanized areas acquired as many as a quartet of Top 40 outlets. Their near fanatical, mostly pubescent audiences pushed those outlets to the top of the audience-ratings race wherever they appeared. Hard on the heels of rock 'n' roll's popularity, stations sprang up that were devoted almost exclusively to country and western or to folk music.

Eventually, when some stations fell short of their owners' optimistic expectations, industry insiders came to realize that success was not in mere Top 40 alone but in limitation itself. By the end of the decade those formats began to disperse into talk, news, ethnic variety, religion, contemporary hits, big band, beautiful music, country tunes and other realms of specialization.

Radio was changing for sure. The golden days were passing into the sphere of national folklore, whether anybody realized it or not.

Yet for all of the doomsday prophecies of the naysayers, who were writing radio's obituary at the start of the 1950s, NBC—broadcasting's oldest web—could be credited with introducing a trio of the most spectacular series on radio, all initiated during that decade. Such innovations reminded listeners that somebody at Radio City still cared.

One of those new programs would last but a couple of seasons. A second was also scrapped after just two years, but it made a comeback in a more polished form four years hence and stuck around for another three years. The epoch's crown jewel, however—appearing at middecade —continued to attract fans for nearly two decades, well after the golden age's extinction.

What were these diamonds in the rough?

Three guesses!

The Big Show and *Dimension X*, both of which debuted in 1950 (the latter series returning in 1955 as *X-Minus One*), and *Monitor*, premiering in 1955. This triumvirate wasn't the total cream of the crop in creative radio programming in the 1950s, but the three unquestionably offered some of the classiest and most innovative developments occurring in that decade. With their arrival came a new depth and stability to a medium that was rapidly being hurtled offstage while the remnant of a disillusioned, disenfranchised audience—still deeply enamored with radio— pondered disquietly among themselves: "What's happening?"

Many reviewers of that era of entertainment have cited *The Big Show* as the chain of the chimes' final leniency in stemming the tide against the new medium. (One sage mistakenly toasted it as "radio's last gasp," calling it "radio's final blowout," also its "last gaudy hurrah" and a "lavish last-ditch effort to reassert the primacy of radio."[2] Another wag acknowledged that it was easily "the last major attempt to tell audiences that radio was very much alive."[3] It may have been that, but there was to be another full decade of life left when *The Big Show* began.)

The web had an ulterior motive in creating its gigantic Sunday night spectacular, however, which was undoubtedly of far greater significance to NBC. Staving off the demise of a medium that was obviously in need of resuscitation and transfusion was purely a by-product of NBC's creative mind, and never the consummate intent. The flagrant objective—to anyone who thought about it for very long—was to inflict large doses of pain upon its old nemesis, the Columbia Broadcasting System, for what CBS had done to it only a short while earlier. To help the reader appreciate the dynamics impacting that environment, we temporarily digress.

Historically, the national radio networks had rivaled each other in their bids for programming, talent, sponsors and audiences. On the surface, they operated in a manner that generally might be perceived by outsiders as one enveloped in professional respect while sustaining a freewheeling competitive spirit. Beneath that façade, however, per-sisted a fierce and determined effort not merely to beat the competi-tion but to utterly humiliate it. Enterprising young executives, given to such unflagging pursuits, occasionally resorted to less than noble tac-tics to accomplish their ends. Their attempts were sometimes made at any price—whatever it took to achieve them.

By the late 1940s a heated rivalry, which had long been festering just beneath the surface, erupted among the major contenders. With a quartet of chains competing for fewer fans in an environment openly hostile to innovative programming, broadcasting's audio moguls reverted to a course that had been only faintly successful earlier. Pro-ceeding with a vengeance, they went after the stars and hit programs of other networks, seeking to transfer those prospects to their stables of talent in a concerted effort to improve their own ratings, increase their advertising revenue and embarrass the competition. In this regard, no one—but no one—surpassed CBS's owner-chairman, William S. Paley.

By 1949 he had wooed some of NBC's most venerated entertain-ers, including Amos 'n' Andy, Jack Benny, Edgar Bergen and Charlie McCarthy, George Burns and Gracie Allen, and Red Skelton. From ABC he was successful in capturing Bing Crosby and Groucho Marx (the latter host of the hit comedy-quiz show *You Bet Your Life*). Jour-nalists labeled such lightning-speed mayhem "Paley's Comet"[4] while a biographer more suitably depicted it as "the biggest upheaval in broad-casting since Paley bought CBS in 1928."[5]

It was indeed. For the first time in 20 years, in fact, CBS was lead-ing the radio audience numbers. Moreover, the net boasted complete sponsorship of 29 programs that it owned outright, a reversal of its prior circumstances. By the beginning of 1950, CBS owned 80 percent of radio's top 20 Nielsen-rated shows while rival NBC could do little but lick its wounds. Not the least among those atrocities was a $7 mil-lion loss in ad revenue in a single year, to say nothing of the departure of millions of its listeners!

CBS could move faster than NBC in raiding a rival network's tal-ent because broadcasting was the bedrock of the corporation's business. Broadcasting at NBC, on the other hand, was but a small portion of the far larger Radio Corporation of America. Despite that, NBC *was* able to take the situation comedy *Ozzie and Harriet* from CBS in 1948–49 for a year before that series moved on to ABC. And after a season at

When CBS owner-chairman William S. Paley pirated several major stars and shows from other chains, the press dubbed such robbery at lightning speed "Paley's Comet." Paley grins with some of the talent acquired in the deals that finally put CBS on top of the ratings heap: (l–r) George Burns, Paley, Gracie Allen, Mary Livingstone, and Jack Benny. *Photofest.*

CBS, that network's newly acquired *You Bet Your Life* shifted to NBC in 1950 where it remained for the rest of its broadcast run.

One should make no mistake, though: grave damage had already been inflicted on NBC, and several years would pass before the eldest network would regain the public standing it had enjoyed prior to the infamous CBS talent raids.

There are footnotes worth examining which reveal yet other possibilities for those outcomes, while offering valuable insights into radio's status at that juncture: Paley and RCA (NBC's parent firm) chairman, Brigadier General David Sarnoff, had both returned from World War II to pursue opposing obsessions—Paley, to master his chain's fate by controlling radio programming; Sarnoff, after years of imagination and experimentation, to turn TV into reality. Paley's talent raids and program development ultimately culminated in boosting CBS-TV. "He may have thought he was building radio," an incisive biographer allowed, "but his gut—the visceral, even primitive, love for stars and shows that figured in every move he made—was to give his fledgling television network an advantage Sarnoff would never match."[6]

The "legend" of Paley's Comet suggests that it grew out of a misconception. Some within the industry believed the CBS magnate was merely shoring up the web's horde of performers in order to switch them to the rapidly emerging tube. "Paley undertook the talent raids to strengthen radio, not to push into television," his chronicler fathomed. "The raids were designed to establish him, at last, as the undisputed leader—in radio."[7]

CBS president Frank Stanton confirmed it: "I never heard Bill talk about using the stars for television at all. For him in those days it was all radio. His postwar idea was simply to get control of radio programming. He never talked about television. He didn't see the light until well after the early days ... he didn't pick stars with any idea about leaping into television."[8]

A commercial journal went further: "CBS wanted to make sure radio audiences wouldn't go over to television by default. If CBS had the best entertainment and showmanship, it could keep a lot of its circulation *despite* TV."[9]

So intent was Paley on saving radio in the 1940s that, in reality, top aides were asked to support his position in whatever venues they appeared representing CBS. Paley hoped "to slow down the progress of television, trying to indicate the virtues which were uniquely those of radio,"[10] according to former publicist William S. Fineshriber, Jr. This became clear even to the competition: David Adams, an NBC executive and confidante of General Sarnoff, observed: "When TV was getting started, Bill Paley turned his back on it and thought there was money to be milked out of radio."[11]

Paley understood, inwardly of course, that TV was on its way. In the 1930s he attempted to postpone its arrival for as long as possible. In the 1940s and 1950s he was doing it again. For instance, nine semi-commercial television stations were on the air part time in this country when World War II ended, reaching about 7,500 households. Built by electronics manufacturer and NBC parent RCA, one such outlet was operated by CBS. Each of its telecasts was preceded with a baffling

While CBS chairman Bill Paley intensely supported radio at every turn, the network's president, Frank Stanton, pushed hard for television. In April 1952, Stanton (left) and CBS-TV president J.L. Van Volkenburg (right) examined drawings of CBS Television City, then under construction in Hollywood, the first such facility of its type in the world. *Photofest.*

message: "Good evening. We hope you will enjoy our programs. The Columbia Broadcasting System, however, is not engaged in the manufacture of television receiving sets and does not want you to consider these broadcasts as inducements to purchase television sets at this time. Because of a number of conditions which are not within our control, we cannot foresee how long this television broadcasting schedule will continue."[12]

    CBS's Stanton understood Paley perhaps better than anyone: "Bill did not want television. He thought it would hurt radio. It was also a question of money.... He didn't see any profit in TV at all. Bill was concerned about the bottom line, that we couldn't afford television, that it was too costly."[13] CBS had made a comprehensive study of TV's potential. It discovered that, whatever its ultimate value, the tube faced "seven lean years"—a desolate spell of enormous capital expense with paltry yields. Paley pondered: "Why starve for seven years when you can continue to feast on radio profits?"[14] While NBC's Sarnoff never denied the probability of some lean years, he was convinced that the potential of the new industry—and Americans' right to enjoy it—justified television's risks and investments. He had told the *New York Times* in 1945 that TV would be a billion-dollar industry within a decade. As it turned out, that figure was surpassed several years earlier.

When CBS's Stanton was budget planning for television for the first time in 1947, he urged Paley to participate. The chairman begged off, feigning an overloaded calendar. He wouldn't be a party to anything that smacked of displacing radio. "Radio was CBS's best hope," he was totally convinced.[15] Fortunately for radiophiles, it would take the chairman a little time to overcome that attitude.

Let us return to those innovative programming concepts that NBC introduced in the 1950s.

To counteract the erosion of listeners, advertisers and talent flowing out of radio, and to instigate payback time for the Columbia Broadcasting System, NBC derived a glitzy format featuring some of entertainment's most compelling stars—and flung them before a live audience for an hour and a half on Sunday night. *The Big Show*—which debuted November 5, 1950—was just that, big, and aired directly opposite some of the major headliners that had so recently departed from NBC. If the fans hadn't known that radio was a dog-eat-dog business before, they certainly should have realized it then.

The Big Show was a super-spectacular variety showcase that drew upon a hefty coterie of mega-name performers. Guests on a typical broadcast might include Ethel Merman belting out Broadway standards and the comedy of Jimmy Durante, interspersed with slices of dramatic narrative adapted from major theatrical plays. Comic Fred Allen regularly contributed to the writing and the dialogue.

Among others occasionally turning up were Fanny Brice, Ralph Bunche, Eddie Cantor, Mindy Carson, Jose Ferrer, Judy Garland, Portland Hoffa, Judy Holliday, Bob Hope, Danny Kaye, Frankie Laine, Peggy Lee, Paul Lukas, Groucho Marx, Edith Piaf, Ezio Pinza, June Powell, George Sanders, Gloria Swanson, Danny Thomas, Margaret Truman,

NBC Radio's *The Big Show* (1950–52) with hostess Tallulah Bankhead was considered by some cynics to be the medium's last gasp, an attempt to stave off the inevitable demise of radio. Regularly appearing on the 90-minute glamour showcase were (l–r) orchestra conductor Meredith Willson, Portland Hoffa, Bankhead, and comic Fred Allen. *Photofest.*

Rudy Vallee, Ed Wynn—almost everyone, in fact, who wasn't already committed to TV or CBS or nailed down elsewhere. It was all delivered into homes from the expansive stage of the Center Theatre, adjacent to NBC's Radio City in New York.

Presiding over this extravaganza was one of the first ladies of theater in times past: basal-toned actress Tallulah Bankhead, who patronizingly explained that she accepted radio offers "only when poverty stricken," yet took credit for saving the medium from its grave, dubbing herself "Queen of the Kilocycles."[16] Yet she could hardly make time for extended radio series earlier, having triumphed onstage in *The Little Foxes*, *The Skin of Our Teeth*, *Private Lives* and more plays in both New York and London. Self-indulgent and good-humored, she claimed to be "the foe of moderation, the champion of excess."[17]

On the downside of what had been a stunning career, Bankhead was presented weekly as "unpredictable" mistress of ceremonies of *The Big Show*. The legendary Alabama-bred thespian sprinkled her verbal exchanges with a trademark dahhhling delivered in thick Southern drawl. (One scribe pounded her "husky dirty laughs," convinced "she sounded outlandish and a little scary."[18] Fred Allen remarked that she possessed a voice "like a man pulling his foot out of a pail of yogurt."[19]) She'd conclude each week's mammoth broadcast with a vocal rendition of "May the Good Lord Bless and Keep You" as Meredith Willson conducted a 44-piece orchestra and 16-voice chorus. Willson often played her stooge: "Thank you, Miss Bankhead, sir," he'd concede, following her weekly salutation to the maestro.

The show was penned by a corps of inspired scribes under the tutelage of head writer Goodman Ace. Ace had been both actor and dialoguer for one of radio's earliest humoresque successes, *Easy Aces*, and was later to script Perry Como's TV shows. Once again, two industry well-knowns announced the series—Jimmy Wallington and Ed Herlihy—and all of it was produced and directed by another pro, Devere Joseph (Dee) Engelbach, whose credits included similar posts on *The Chamber Music Society of Lower Basin Street*, *The Hallmark Hall of Fame*, *The Radio Hall of Fame* and *This Is Nora Drake*.

To insure the program's triumph, NBC supplied exorbitant sums, certainly by audio standards. It budgeted *The Big Show* at an unprecedented $100,000 per week—"real TV money," *Newsweek* magazine sneered. For the series' second season launch the web flew the entire cast to London and Paris for two weeks of gala broadcasts and publicity stunts. The European press wasn't impressed, unfortunately, alluding to "90 minutes of bad jokes, tuneless songs, witless dialogue, soapy compliments, and onion-under-the-nose emotion."[20]

The American press, on the other hand, was ecstatic from the start. Reviews tended to glow: "...a perfectly wonderful show—witty, tuneful, surprisingly sophisticated and brilliantly put together ... one of the fastest and funniest ninety minutes in memory."[21] Even decades later it was still championed: "*The Big Show* was a wonderful program.... (It) offered every week a knockout lineup of talent."[22]

Yet its ultimate fate was recorded as a dismal failure when—after two seasons—*The Big Show* had made little dent in the ratings of its formidable CBS competition. NBC pulled the series from its schedule on April 20, 1952, after losing $1 million on the venture. Writing the program's obituary, a newspaper reporter offered a veiled tribute, saying it was "good enough to make one wish he could have seen it."[23] A contemporary reviewer hinted that "the growing popularity of *The Ed Sullivan* Show on television" was the show's nemesis.[24] But a radio historiographer may have assessed the situation aptly: "*The Big Show* had its moments, but *The Jack Benny Program* rolled along on CBS, as consistently brilliant and funny as ever. The moral, perhaps, is that brilliance and genius cannot be bought, that a buckshot approach never works, and that most good things come finally from a single inspired source."[25]

Tallulah Bankhead, incidentally, died in New York City December 12, 1968. She was 66.

A postscript to the talent raids previously discussed will be interpretive. General David Sarnoff, the RCA chairman, attempted to compensate for the losses NBC suffered by generating new programming, *The Big Show* being the linchpin. In all he spent $1.5 million on such ventures, though none of them developed enough audience appeal to equal what was lost to the competition. Licking his wounds during a subsequent stockholders' gathering, Sarnoff admonished: "Leadership built over the years on a foundation of solid service cannot be snatched overnight by buying a few high-priced comedians. Leadership is not a laughing matter."[26] While he could have readily upped the ante and probably retained some of the stars and shows that NBC lost, on principle Sarnoff was deeply opposed to buying his way. A biographer contended simply "he was wrong," based purely on dollars and cents.[27] Privately, an NBC insider suggested: "The General got himself involved

David Sarnoff (shown), chairman of RCA, parent firm of NBC, took an active role in guiding the oldest web through radio's golden age. Outwardly, at least, he reacted graciously to NBC's loss of talent to CBS: "Leadership built over the years on a foundation of solid service cannot be snatched overnight by buying a few high-priced comedians." *Photofest.*

emotionally in what was a problem in cold business. He resented the attitude of the performers whom, after all, we had helped build up into stars. He felt, I think, that they were being disloyal.... Some of us thought of talent simply as a marketable commodity, that's all. In the final analysis we have had to accept the star system and to live with it."[28]

The second of NBC's most significant radio debuts in the 1950s (responsibly classified a "landmark science fiction series"[29]) was originally titled *Dimension X*, aired initially on April 8, 1950. While X wasn't the first science fiction thriller (it was preceded for a few weeks by a rather nondescript MBS anthology, *Two Thousand Plus*), its impressive reception ushered in a wave of technological fare. The genre unquestionably became established as one of radio's late but most potent audience draws.

John Dunning, who chronicled much of radio programming history, placed radio's inception in a relevant progression of events. In so doing, he supported the theory of radio traditionalists that the theater of the mind is far too complex to be limited to a mere picture-box.

The vast and fertile S-F field had been curiously neglected for the entire 25-year history of the medium. Fantasy had been relegated to such kiddie epics as *Flash Gordon* and *Buck Rogers*, with such occasional hybrids as NBC's *Latitude Zero* (1941). Occasionally an S-F story might appear on the mainstream series *Escape or Suspense*, and in July 1950 CBS and Wrigley's Gum carried three episodes of a Chicago-produced fantasy series, *Cloud Nine*, which contained the work of Jack Finney and others. But until *Dimension X* arrived, radio left the deeper reaches of the universe unexplored.

The appearance of *Destination Moon* in movie houses helped make 1950 the year of S-F on radio. *Dimension X* rose to the task, proving that radio and science fiction were ideally compatible. The series demonstrated (though it would take the perfection of television to prove it) that adding a picture to a story of vision, illusion, or myth does not automatically enhance things. The tube is too small, the props too artificial (no matter how ingenious or technologically advanced) to compete with the landscape of the mind. For its time, *Dimension X* was a wonder.[30]

A wonder indeed.

Host-narrator Norman Rose opened the show cold: "Adventures in time and space ... told in future tense! Dimension X ... X ... x ... x ... x ... x..." The organ came up with a swelling thump, merged with drumlike rolls and cymbals and combined with the theremin, an electronic musical device whose striking pitch and tone set the narratives into a haunting milieu.

Dimension X offered somber imaginative phenomena based on stories by prominent authors (Ray Bradbury, Robert Heinlein, Fredric Brown, Ernest Kinoy, George Lefferts, Robert Bloch, Isaac Asimov, Kurt Vonnegut and more). "As network radio headed into its final decade, the caliber of writing not only got sharper, and bolder, but in many ways more adult," an observer noted. *Dimension X* "provided more consistently intelligent science fiction than Hollywood movies did."[31] Many of its tales, in fact, were adaptations of works appearing in *Astounding Science Fiction*, a leading pulp forum of the species.

Superior writing was not the only attribute making this new venture appeal to listeners' ears, however. Strong casting of seasoned New York actors added appreciably to the high watermark. Among them were Art Carney, Jack Lemmon, Santos Ortega, Joan Lazer, Jack Grimes, Mandel Kramer, Everett Sloane, Joan Alexander, Jan Miner, Claudia Morgan, Bryna Raeburn, Ronald Liss, Larry Haines, Ralph Bell, Evie Juster, Jackson Beck and Joyce Gordon. Aside from that, futuristic musical scores were written for *Dimension X* while as many as three sound effects specialists were regularly assigned to the show. Significant echo effects were derived by broadcasting from a mammoth studio that was two stories tall.

While the show aired live for 13 weeks, it was taped after that. The mostly sustained series continued through September 29, 1951, having faced the difficulties presented by an erratic scheduling formula. It was often shifted between Friday and Sunday nights on NBC's schedule and deleted for long periods, including a 19-week disruption in early 1951. This undoubtedly took its toll on maintaining a consistent following and almost certainly figured in its early demise.

Fortunately for the fans who, by that time, had become enthralled with radio science fiction, it returned under a new moniker at mid-decade, squeezing out another three years of astronomical plots. We shall encounter its extension, *X-Minus One*, at the proper interval.

Suffice it to say that *Dimension X* had set in motion a new sphere of adult-oriented dramatic fare, heretofore untried in any serious extent during radio's previous decades. The fact that the series was so successful should have suggested to programmers and advertisers that there was plenty of lifeblood left in the medium, and a ready audience for it. Regrettably, most of that fell on deaf ears. The caretakers of this public trust, it appeared, were doing little more than eagerly anticipating the day they could pull the plug and turn out the lights forever. Some things simply didn't make sense.

The third major NBC contribution in the 1950s, *Monitor*—the network's sprightly weekend magazine, which arrived in 1955 and stuck around for nearly two decades—will be examined later. Without any doubt, it was the most noteworthy, durable and innovative programming development of the entire decade.

The radio western was habitually relegated to youthful audiences until the late 1940s and early 1950s. The juvenile fare that dominated the airwaves on MBS and ABC shortly before sunset on weekday afternoons typically included several idealistic adventures set in old West locales. Operating within an environment that focused on unrestrained adolescence, such features were characterized by secret identities, action-packed chases and athletic heroics. Among them were *Red Ryder*, *The Cisco Kid*, *Sky King*, *Straight Arrow* and *Tom Mix*.

During this period CBS introduced yet another genre that more advanced listeners caught up in radio were swift to embrace: the adult western. A handful of noteworthy series resulted, exhibiting a combination of mature plot, fuller human characterization and intelligent themes executed to critical dramatic standards. Often their subject matter seriously explored violence and sex, premises that would have been totally bizarre if included in their juvenile predecessors. The real-life environment of ripened fictional tales was suitably explored:

> The most impressive aspect of the adult programs was the aura of social doom which pervaded their stories. Mirroring fears in the minds of listeners living in a nation tense with internal Cold War conflicts and external military threats, these series created a social environment in which the line between civilization and barbarity was uncertain, and where heroes were indispensable. Whether they were bona fide law men, military officers, mercenaries, or simple do-gooders, it was apparent that these champions were the principal forces protecting nascent American civilization from the savagery which surrounded it in the wilderness.[32]

The realistic western had first emerged in literature, and was offered to filmgoers in 1939 in *Stagecoach* starring John Wayne. By 1952 it had achieved a marked degree of sophistication as witnessed in cinema's *High Noon* featuring Gary Cooper.

CBS attempted to initiate its new concept with *Hawk Larabee* starring first Elliott Lewis, then Barton Yarborough as Hawk (1946–48). The leads and parts were so frequently rotated among the actors, however (and several other cast changes occurred almost routinely), that the effort was only mildly successful. For over two decades the fans also tuned in to hear the venerated *Death Valley Days* with Jack MacBryde as the Old Ranger, subsequently replaced by Robert Haag as Mark Chase under the revised moniker *Death Valley Sheriff*. (The dual package ran from 1930 to 1951.) But their series fell short in providing the stark realism of a grown-up narrative. One misplaced elucidation argued that "*The Lone Ranger* [which we will meet again and explore in depth in this volume in a more apropos setting] may have been the first adult western."[33] The fact is that that ageless epic transcended the generations, appealing to people of all time periods.

There can be little doubt that the true radio adult western and granddaddy of the breed was inaugurated under the moniker of *Gunsmoke*, which premiered on CBS April 26, 1952. Later in that decade CBS was to add *Fort Laramie* with Raymond Burr as cavalry captain Lee Quince (1956) and—in 1958—a trio of advanced cowpuncher capers: *Luke Slaughter of Tombstone* with Sam Buffington in the title role, *Frontier Gentleman* with John Dehner as reporter J. B. Kendall, and a radio

Defining the adult radio western and setting standards for others to follow, *Gunsmoke* was conceived by producer-director Norman Macdonnell (left). For two years he and writer John Meston plotted the mature epic of the old west. Polished actor William Conrad (right) played the marshal of Dodge City for the series' full run (1952–61). *Photofest.*

version of a new TV hit, *Have Gun, Will Travel*, with John Dehner as the soldier of fortune Paladin. In the interim, NBC introduced a couple of adult westerns of its own, *The Six-Shooter* starring Jimmy Stewart as plainsman Britt Ponset (1953) and *Dr. Six-Gun* with Karl Weber playing the gun-toting Dr. Ray Matson (1954).

    With the exception of *Have Gun, Will Travel*, none but *Gunsmoke* lasted for more than a season, despite the growing interest in such entertainment by fans. A transition series between the comic-book qualities of radio adventure shows and the graphic realism of early 1950s plays, movies, and TV, the transcribed *Gunsmoke* was to air once or twice weekly for nine-plus years.

    The fact that it appeared at a time when Americans were, by and large, turning off their radios and turning on their TVs, categorically blunted its potential. Despite that, *Gunsmoke* became so popular with radio lovers that CBS even carried it for several months beyond the outer limits of the traditionally accepted end of radio's golden age. When the series was discontinued with the 480th episode, broadcast on June 18, 1961, it had already completed the sixth of a 20-season run on CBS-TV, during which it became one of the most genuinely beloved dramatic series ever televised.

Without reservation, *Gunsmoke* defined the adult western genre and set a lofty standard for all other entries that attempted to follow it. Cited as the style's "highest achievement,"[34] it was properly identified as "a classy western, with more mature plots, writing, and characterization than almost anything on radio."[35]

There had to be reasons for the unparalleled radio success of *Gunsmoke*. Indisputably, they were its brilliant directing, writing and casting.

Producer-director Norman Macdonnell was the guiding hand in its development. He had proven his abilities already as director of CBS's popularly chilling *Escape* adventure anthology (1948–49, 1950–52, 1954). He also held a similar capacity on the sentimental omnibus narrative *Romance* in the summer of 1950. For two years he and writer John Meston plotted a truly mature radio classic to be set in the old West.

The skilled craftsman Meston, himself a CBS story editor at the time, would almost single-handedly pen many of the scripts for radio's *Gunsmoke*. Otherwise he contributed heavily as head writer, giving direction to a cadre of skilled artisans who shared his and Macdonnell's views of a saga where every sound added to the story line. The drama was set in Dodge City, Kansas in the 1870s, which was proclaimed "a suburb of hell," an outpost on the prairie that Marshal Matt Dillon had come to repress.

The principals in the cast—a quartet of accomplished thespians—remained intact for the full length of the radio run. These veterans had appeared in sporadic and long-running roles on numerous preceding series. There was the distinctively gravely voiced William Conrad as Matt Dillon, "the first man they look for and the last man they want to meet"; Parley Baer as the townsman and Matt's faithful sidekick, Chester Proudfoot, who evolved into a full-fledged deputy on TV; Howard McNear as the crusty old Doc (Charles) Adams, who on radio was given to strong drink at inopportune moments; and Georgia Ellis as Kitty Russell, the saloon gal who also took in customers—though never so stated—as a prostitute. Eventually, quietly, she emerged as Dillon's love interest.

In addition, a company of radio's most gifted professionals surrounded them. These actors were heard in occasional episodes playing character parts, enhancing the show's quality even more. Among them: Harry Bartell, John Dehner, Virginia Gregg, Joseph Kearns, Jeanette Nolan, Vic Perrin, and Lawrence Dobkin.

John Dunning gives his readers a collage of the contributions that made *Gunsmoke* so expedient:

> The show drew critical acclaim for unprecedented realism…. When Dillon and Chester rode the plains, the listener heard the faraway prairie wind and the dry squeak of Matt's pants against saddle leather. When Dillon opened the jail door, the listener heard every key drop on the ring. Dillon's spurs rang out with a dull clink-clink, missing occasionally, and the hollow boardwalk echoed dully as the nails creaked in the worn wood around them. Buckboards passed, and the listener heard extraneous dialogue in the background, just above the muted shouts of kids playing in an alley. He heard noises from the next block, too, where the inevitable dog was barking.[36]

Sound technician Ray Kemper, who was responsible for many of the background noises heard on *Straight Arrow*, *Suspense* and *Have Gun, Will Travel*, acknowledged years later: "Of all my sound effects days, *Gunsmoke* was my joy."[37] With such import given to the sound effects in the passage quoted, could there be any wonder why Kemper felt that way?

When talk of a TV series began, the radio cast was auditioned but bypassed in favor of James Arness (Matt), Dennis Weaver (Chester), Milburn Stone (Doc) and Amanda Blake (Kitty). John Meston was engaged to carry on the tradition he had begun in scripting the radio epic. Weaver eventually claimed he despised the role he played as Chester. Parley Baer, who performed it for nine years on radio, seemed satisfied. The idea was later advanced that the part that became the apex of Baer's professional life had—to his TV successor—become "a limiting, confining trap, like the picture tube itself."[38]

Bill Conrad, on the other hand, took his loss of the leading role to Arness quite personally, staving off interviews for a while. While he would later be given the chance to direct some of the episodes on the tube, for a spell he slipped into obscurity. Eventually he reappeared in TV guest slots while acquiring several voice-over roles in the medium that had little use for a middle-aged, pudgy, balding, mustachioed actor.

They finally found some starring roles for him on the tube anyway: as the portly detective *Cannon* on CBS-TV 1971–76, and as a tough district attorney in *Jake and the Fatman* on the same network in the late 1980s. Cannon died in North Hollywood, California, on February 11, 1994, at the age of 73.

Dunning reflects on the caliber of this important drama in dual mediums: "There would always be champions of radio vs. TV, and among radio people *Gunsmoke* is routinely placed among the best shows of any kind and any time. That radio fans considered the TV show a sham was due in no small part to the continued strength of Meston's [radio] scripts."[39] To that, it must be added that—while some radio addicts may have felt like that—certainly not all did. In addition, many were happy that "their" adult western increased in favor with audiences across two decades, often dominating the TV ratings. As for *Gunsmoke* the radio show of the fifties, its nearly invincible stature and substantial entertainment value fostered a new breed of program during vintage radio's waning years.

Radio historiographer Fred MacDonald adequately assesses the species of the radio adult western:

> In American popular culture the western has had immense success. It was an irony, however, that radio did not develop the genre fully until creative broadcasting was in ebb. Several reasons help account for this condition. Among them were the reluctance of sponsors to underwrite a western for primarily adult audiences, network economics which mitigated against sustaining series, the lack of creativity among script writers who chose to remain with proven formats rather than experiment, and the general inertia in radio programming which over the decades created patterns of imitation and variation rather than produce the widest possible range of shows for listeners' tastes. When the mature western did appear, its full impact could not be calculated. By this time statistical ratings were low relative to the figures earned by programming in the 1940s. Many adult westerns also appeared on Saturdays [*Gunsmoke* being one of those], a day not intended to attract an optimal audience. And by the 1950s, a growing number of Americans were viewing television and were oblivious to innovations in radio drama. Nonetheless, the adult western enjoyed popularity and respect with those who still cared for innovative radio programming.[40]

The detective drama is one of the most gripping and celebrated forms of creative expression in American popular culture. Traditionally it has experienced wide-ranging success in radio, literature, film and television. In the aural medium, such fare achieved the good fortune of not only being attractive to listeners but also being inexpensive to produce. Star-studded series like *The Jack Benny Program* and *The Bing Crosby Show*— with their large casts, live orchestras and guest celebrities—were budgeted at $40,000 per week in 1950. Nevertheless, most mysteries at that time could be produced for something in the neighborhood of $4,000 to $7,000.

Admittedly, not often did the detective series acquire the high numbers that the Nielsen or Hooper ratings systems logged for those renowned music and comedy programs. No matter. The cheaply produced dramas delivered more listeners per advertising dollar than did shows claiming far more prestige. In 1950, according to *Variety*, the average evening mystery series attracted 267 households per dollar spent. Meanwhile, musical-variety programs drew only 215 households while general dramas pulled just 187. Comedy-variety shows garnered 163 households and concert music features settled for a mere 123. While the detective programming may have been a bargain basement sale in the perception of some within the industry, at the start of the decade, its sponsors nonetheless considered it a strong buy.

Another programming trend occurring in this epoch was the inauguration of several sophisticated detective series. Police dramas like *Broadway Is My Beat* with Anthony Ross as detective Danny Clover (1949–54), *Dragnet* starring Jack Webb as detective sergeant Joe Friday (1949–57), *The Line Up* featuring Bill Johnstone as police lieutenant Ben Guthrie (1950–53), and *Twenty-First Precinct* including Everett Sloane, James Gregory and Les Damon at varying times as captain Frank Kennelly (1953–56), were instructive, albeit foreboding productions giving their listeners straightforward, though dismal, examinations of law enforcement in metropolitan settings.

Private investigators like *Yours Truly, Johnny Dollar* with many of New York's finest thespians in the namesake role—Dick Powell, Charles Russell, Edmond O'Brien, John Lund, Bob Bailey, Bob Readick and Mandel Kramer (1949–54, 1955–62)—and the criminal-tracking journalist Randy Stone on *Night Beat*, which featured actor Frank Lovejoy (1950, 1951–52), offered their fans heroes who operated within a strictly adult environment.

Of all of these, *Dragnet* and *Yours Truly, Johnny Dollar* were clearly the most influential as well as the most memorable. MacDonald offers a clear picture of some of the distinctive features that set apart their innovative styles.

> While crime had been an anti-social activity in earlier detective formats, the hallmark of the emergent Neo-Realistic format was its emphasis upon crime as a symptom of deeper social sickness. The likable personalities that dominated ... gave way to a group of disillusioned, embittered men who reluctantly went about their professions. These characters usually expressed an abusive tone when dealing with others.... They also articulated a general disdain for most of the positive symbols of civilization and social order.... These programs emphasized ugly crimes investigated by brutalized detectives existing within a depressingly grim environment.[41]

There were other anomalies surrounding these dramas.

To listeners, the nation's largest metropolitan areas, including New York, Los Angeles, Chicago and others, were nothing less than immoral cesspools. They appeared to have little more than a handful of disheartened public servants and private eyes to protect them from pure angst.

A disdain for wealth that had not been previously accentuated turned up in many of these dramas. The detectives were compensated for bringing criminals to justice, so it wasn't a denunciation of capital as such. Their scorn, instead, was focused on the affluent who often tended to buy privilege with their gain.

While earlier audio detectives appeared to demonstrate integrity and respect in their quest to right civil wrongs, the sleuths of the neo-realistic era flaunted a kind of halting crudeness themselves. Persistently drawn into conflict, they functioned in a vacuum within the lapses of social failure and criminal behavior. In doing so they clearly performed their tasks in mechanical, often repetitious fashion.

Nontraditional themes were inserted into the story lines of these dramas. On *Broadway Is My Beat*, anti–Semitism and juvenile delinquency were addressed. Abandoned kids, children running from home, drug addiction and female juveniles posing for pornography turned up in *Dragnet* tales. Attacks on police officers, contract murders, muggings, strangling the elderly and political retribution were typical fare on *Twenty-First Precinct* and *The Line Up*. None of these topics would have been covered in depth on most crime series before this time.

Unquestionably, *Dragnet* starring Jack Webb as Sergeant Joe Friday

Elevating police drama to a level it had not previously enjoyed, *Dragnet* was the most credible series of the genre in the 1950s. As of late 1952, assisting Sergeant Joe Friday in apprehending criminals in L.A. was a new partner, officer Frank Smith. Ben Alexander (left) played Smith while Jack Webb (right) was Friday for the full run. *Photofest.*

was radio's most influential police drama in the 1950s. When it first appeared on NBC on June 3, 1949, it pioneered for its millions of fans a realism in a detective series that they had never previously experienced.

Webb was no newcomer to radio audiences or to this line of programming: on two occasions he had emerged in the title role of the private eye feature *Pat Novak for Hire*, initially on ABC's West Coast network (1946–47), and for 19 weeks on ABC (February-June 1949) as *Dragnet* was being readied and launched. A former clothing salesman, Webb took bit parts in radio and film and was a technical advisor for the movie *He Walks by Night*. In 1954, he starred in *Dragnet*, the feature film. He took the radio show, which lasted through February 26, 1957, to TV on January 3, 1952, where it became still more popular. It continued through September 1959, returning for an added few years from

January 1967 through September 10, 1970. Having been a hit on radio, the Webb-directed *Dragnet* was later proclaimed "the most successful police series in the history of television."[42]

In the role of Sergeant Joe Friday of the Los Angeles Police Department, Webb robotically displayed a cool, calculated temperament. True to neorealistic form, the drama projected a fraudulent society defended by committed but dispirited cops, and limited by the vastness of imperfection. Set in a semidocumentary style, it stressed precise references to numbered regulations in the police code. With frequent intrusions of extraneous material, the drama seemed quite real. Its chief interrogator, Friday, became something of a believable hero to fans. He was ultimately as much a part of the police force as any real-life officer, a quality that was absent in most earlier crime presentations.

Webb died at the age of 62 in West Hollywood, California, on December 23, 1982.

The fact that the changes exhibited in the more urbane detective dramas failed to appear until the last decade of network radio is likely the result of several phenomena that arrived together. For one thing, audiences in the postwar era had become more sophisticated themselves. They were by then accepting of—and they even eagerly anticipated—pragmatic trends in entertainment forms, including film, literature and broadcasting. The radio neorealistic detective was a generous approximation of both its print and celluloid antecedents. Audiences approved of sleuthing that was no-nonsense and got down to business; this was an overt departure from earlier aural presentations and people loved it.

Television, of course, had a major bearing on all that was happening in entertainment at the time. Now more than ever TV was becoming widely understood to be radio's greatest foe. Serious radio defenders within broadcasting's ranks continually sought alternatives to add impetus to the industry's first medium and dampen video's ability to ravage radio's audiences. Instituting certain new styles of programming, like the sophisticated detective dramas, was an attempt to cope with the erosion of both fans and sponsors caused by TV. Such developments would not have been necessary much earlier, of course, nor might their listeners have been as receptive to such striking changes as they were at midcentury.

Another factor in the welcome received by the realistic crime dramas was a growing discontent with the repetitiveness inherent in the traditional formats. As Fred Allen pointed out, "The audience and the medium were both getting tired. The same programs ... the same commercials—even the sameness was starting to look the same."

Finally, the fact remained that as long-running music and comedy shows with headliners in their names (Benny, Crosby, et al.) began to draw larger audiences on the tube than on radio—eventually pulling out of the original medium—the major chains scrambled to fill some of the voids they left. A few innovative producers saw what might be their final opportunity to air something of lasting quality and significance. The reality-based dramas were among their few creative efforts introduced in the 1950s.

One of the most unnerving consequences of the McCarthy blacklisting mêlée (discussed in depth in chapter 1) was that broadcast employees were asked to sign statements reflecting their individual allegiance as U.S. citizens. The illegalities of such requests, especially as they are viewed from a vantage point at least 50 years later, are positively mind-boggling. Without question, it was a flagrant violation of the workers' civil and constitutional rights. The fact that Communist party membership in this nation was legal made it still worse. Even CBS chairman William S. Paley, upon reflection, admitted: "My own feelings for personal privacy are so strong that I am astonished that I could have tolerated the invasion of privacy that even our mild questionnaire required. Yet, the more I reflect on this, the more I see that CBS, too, was caught in the crosscurrents of fear that swept through the whole country."[43]

NBC had implemented such an occupational proviso only a short time earlier. CBS, considered the most tolerant of the national chains, capitulated to an incessant pressure that it, too, was receiving from its sponsors. (Right-wing journalists frequently tagged CBS "the Red network" and "the Communist Broadcasting System.") In late 1950, therefore, CBS rolled out a loyalty oath of its own, and mandated that all its 2,500 staffers complete it. In the summer of 1951, an expansion was ordered to include a sizable cluster of New York freelancers who were then steadily working for the corporation as the result of a potent surge of original programming. The CBS "questionnaire"—the web didn't refer to the document as an "oath"—interrogated the staffers at just three points:

1. Are you now, or have you ever been, a member of the Communist Party, USA. Or any Communist organization?

2. Are you now, or have you ever been, a member of a Fascist group?

3. Are you now, or have you ever been, a member of any organization, association, movement, group or combination of persons which advocates the overthrow of our constitutional form of government, or of any organization, association, movement, group or combination of persons which has adopted a policy of advocating or approving the commission of acts of force or violence to deny other persons their rights under the Constitution of the United States or, of seeking to alter the form of the government of the United States by unconstitutional means?

Any responses in the affirmative resulted in asking for the names of all such organizations, dates of membership and details of activities. Participants could also add their personal clarifications. A keen observer of the era documented these unparalleled circumstances:

> Most performers signed and went on to their jobs uncaring or oblivious to the fact that a small piece of their guaranteed liberties, the freedom of political belief and discussion, had been chipped away. For others, it set off a wave of fear or righteous indignation or both. Who, they asked, is the Columbia Broadcasting System to question my allegiance to my country? Who is CBS to ask me to protest my innocence about something of which there is no reason to suspect me?... Particularly disturbing for those who had been or still were members of a listed organization was that CBS made no provision for a hearing or for the right of appeal.[44]

The entire phenomenon was, in effect, McCarthyism in microcosm, and the whole industry took its cue from CBS. If artists appeared on CBS, they had discernibly passed muster. "CBS and blacklisting became synonymous," noted a report for the Fund for the Republic a few years later. "The refusal of Paley and [CBS President Frank] Stanton to take a stand against the vigilantes did no honor to them or CBS," wrote one critic. "Not only were they unwilling to jeopardize profits, they feared antagonizing the FCC [Federal Communications Commission] and the Congress, which were controlled by forces sympathetic to blacklisting. Although they knew that the supposed Communists and fellow travelers posed no threat whatsoever to the nation, Paley and Stanton found it expedient to hire only those who were politically neutral. It was easier to go along than to fight."[45]

At the same time, NBC was engaged in a similar witch-hunt. Stanton explained: "There was cross-checking between NBC and CBS ... a sharing of information."[46] David Adams, a former NBC vice chairman, recalled that "NBC had a blacklist that I tore up toward the end of the McCarthy era."[47]

As already intimated, it was one of broadcasting's darkest hours. When it ended, Paley insisted, "We didn't have a blacklist."[48] In that, just as in the reality that television was a force to be reckoned with, the chairman simply ignored the preponderance of evidence to the contrary.

There can be no doubt that during World War II CBS had built a reputation as a superlative, impregnable news organization. Reporting from the foxholes and front lines wherever a battle raged, the network gained respect from many millions of listeners dutifully waiting by their radios at home for an accurate assessment of what was happening abroad. They got it daily, and CBS's reputation soared. So impeccable was it, in fact, that key U.S. government officials—including a number in the White House, the Central Intelligence Agency and the Pentagon's Joint Chiefs of Staff—began their workday with transcripts of the morning CBS *World News Roundup*. The truth was, nobody came even close to achieving that kind of status. "We all felt that we worked for the best broadcast news organization in the world, that there was nobody who could touch us," declared CBS newsman Robert Pierpoint.[49]

When the war ended—fully realizing its earned preeminence in this all-important category—the network wasn't about to do anything to undermine its extraordinary prestige for integrity, objectivity, immediacy and disclosure. CBS chairman Paley continued to support the contributions of a crack team of seasoned journalists in the postwar era, comprehending what an esteemed entourage of this magnitude could deliver in both audience and revenues. He saw to it that news continued to be highly visible at CBS, and provided unlimited resources to maintain the web's leadership in gathering and producing informational programming.

No one can argue that Edward R. Murrow was the powerhouse that drove CBS's preeminent news-building organization, however. His calm, terse voice, tinged with an echo of doom, delivered world news at pivotal moments in the nation's history. Before and during the war years this distinguished journalist gathered a cadre of professional newspeople about him. Their names became household words in American homes and their voices instantly recognized by people tuning in to overseas reports.

Affectionately dubbed the "Murrow Boys," these 11 individuals—including one woman—were identified in a compelling treatise by Stanley Cloud and Lynne Olson: Mary Marvin Breckinridge, Cecil Brown, Winston Burdett, Charles Collingwood, William Downs, Thomas Grandin, Richard C. Hottelet, Larry LeSueur, Eric Sevareid, William L. Shirer and Howard K. Smith. Of these, Collingwood, Downs, Hottelet, LeSueur, Sevareid, and Shirer were hired by Murrow, served alongside him during the war, and became his devoted friends and respected colleagues. Ultimately, their pride and sense of being a breed apart would lure a salient new peer group of correspondents to CBS.

"When CBS was really riding high in news, it wasn't because of ratings. It was because of the reputation of the Murrow Boys, because of the Murrow legacy," Pierpoint, who was outside that inner circle, acknowledged.[50] Colleague Daniel Schoenbrun confirmed: "For a few brief years, the Murrow team was nonpareil. There was CBS and then the others.... While it lasted it was dazzling."[51]

Egbert Roscoe Murrow, who would be persuaded by Paley in 1946 to fill the slot of network news and public affairs vice president, was born in 1908, the son of a simple dirt farmer at Polecat Creek, North Carolina. Raised there and in Washington state alongside two brothers, Murrow learned the value of hard work early, developing skills as a lumberjack. (He changed his first name to Edward when his peer loggers kidded him about his given name.) Murrow majored in speech at Washington State College. Following graduation he was employed by student organizations, which allowed him to travel to Europe several times, expand his global horizons and establish new contacts. He applied to CBS in 1935 and was hired that September as director of talks. He was dispatched to London as the web's European director 19 months later.

As Murrow's capabilities were revealed, his stature grew rapidly within CBS, and he was soon considered the network's chief overseas correspondent. His 1940s postwar salary of $112,000, then the highest ever paid to a newscaster, was eclipsed by the $250,000 he received when two TV programs—See It Now, a documentary, and an at-home celebrity interview series, Person to Person—were added to his show repertoire. Meanwhile, he continued airing a quarter-hour news commen-

No one could argue that Edward R. Murrow (shown) was the powerhouse that drove CBS's preeminent news organization in the 1940s and 1950s. The respected newsman surrounded himself with a cadre of first-rate professionals who gave eyewitness accounts of World War II and subsequent major events at home and around the globe. *Photofest.*

tary on CBS Radio weeknights at 7:45 P.M. Eastern Time. His trademark signature is still recalled by legions of fans: "Good night, and good luck."

Murrow remained a major factor in news operations at CBS (one critic called him "the godhead of radio and TV network news"[52]) until 1961, when he was tapped by newly elected President John F. Kennedy to head the U.S. Information Agency.

As 1950 approached, the CBS news enterprise made a momentous decision to bring several of its popular foreign correspondents together before a studio microphone. They discussed where the world was, halfway through the 20th century, and where it appeared to be headed. Their conversation was moderated by none other than Ed Murrow, assisted by Eric Sevareid. A Murrow Boy, Sevareid was destined to reach even greater feats in later years in televised news journalism.

Thus, on January 1, 1950, for three-quarters of an hour, a handful of noteworthies engaged in a freewheeling, scholarly exchange on the precarious state of global affairs at midcentury. Although Murrow fielded the questions and summarized it all at the program's conclusion, he turned the spotlight on his correspondents, allowing them to bask in the glow that he might have reserved for himself alone. It spoke volumes about why they admired him so deeply.

This was a program well received by audiences and critics. "I thought that the broadcast was one of the most distinguished I had ever heard," said Bill Paley in a note to Murrow, copies of which he distributed to all the participants. "[Their remarks] sounded like pieces which might be written 50 years from now by top historians," he allowed, "certainly not by guys who have lived through most of the period."[53] It went over so well, in fact, that the web decided to air a similar year-end roundup discussion every year, titling it *Years of Crisis*. For the next 11 seasons these correspondents gathered for what became an annual event on an afternoon between the Christmas and New Year's holidays. Cloud and Olson, who documented all of these occasions in their book, characterized the affair as "a significant national event," contending that "the conversation was absolutely brilliant."[54]

Most of the Murrow Boys maintained a personal rapport with their mentor but not with each other. The annual roundups reminded them of their unique status, which they all treasured; that they were a band of brothers and had always been so.

That formidable fraternity shared opinions on many subjects, not the least of which was television. In a word, they were "hostile," during its infancy at least. Before they were broadcasters, they were scribes. Radio to them was but another way of conveying the printed word, a substantive expansion of the printing press itself. TV had absolutely nothing to commend it: at that time the Murrow Boys earned far more from sponsored radio newscasts than they could have hoped to gain from the tube. They despised the lights, cameras, makeup and other show business trappings that TV required, too. Schoenbrun explained, "In radio, you threw a switch and you spoke."[55] TV required a whole entourage working together. One of the Murrow Boys' number, Howard K. Smith, acknowledged: "We felt it was kind of unmanly to go on TV and perform, just as it was in an earlier era somehow unmanly for newspapermen to go on radio."[56] Executive producer of *60 Minutes*, Don Hewitt, CBS-TV's subsequently durable newsmagazine, added: "Radio was for adults and television was for children.... I sort of think they may have been right."[57] Hewitt could well have spoken volumes.

Murrow, who protested, "I wish television had never been invented" and was labeled "an evangelist for radio,"[58] starred in perhaps the most provocative documentary series in TV history. Introducing the weekly *See It Now* on CBS-TV on November 18, 1951, Murrow explained: "This is an old team trying to learn a new trade." (The show was an outgrowth of radio's *Hear It Now* [1950–51]), which producer Fred W. Friendly referred to as "pictures for the ear," and which was a magazine of sorts. It covered news events of the previous six days in the voices of the newsmakers themselves, either by transcription or live interviews. It won a Peabody Award for outstanding journalism and inspired similar series on rival networks, ABC's *Week Around the World* and NBC's *Voices and Events*, though neither acquired the preeminence of the original they imitated.

At a time when Murrow and his compatriots continued to fool themselves that radio—and they—would forever lead the pack, Cloud and Olson observed: "Walter Cronkite was coming up fast on the outside."[59] The heyday of the Murrow Boys and their domination of broadcast news was drawing to an inevitable close. When the era passed, most Americans would gain their headlines and commentary from a new source of electronic journalism, television. While there would always be a place for radio news, it would never command the dependency it had in years gone by.

White performers and executives ran the industry during the golden age of radio, and for the most part their black counterparts seldom achieved equal prominence or remuneration in that epoch. There were some exceptions, but most Negroes were prevented by their limited training, education, experience and opportunity from reaching the potential that their white brother and sister broadcasters enjoyed.

Programming wasn't specifically intended to appeal to black audiences, either. Successes actually appeared to lead to segregated broadcasting as all-black programs and stations lost sight of the more idealistic integrated possibilities. A healthier balance was achieved while the decade progressed as black music emerged through rhythm 'n' blues and rock 'n' roll. There was a need for all-black programming, of course, just as there was a demand for broadcasts explicitly tailored to other ethnic groups. Keeping such programming from becoming permanently segregated was a major challenge, however, during the early 1950s.

The significantly smaller incomes that blacks customarily received at midcentury was often cited as a major reason for the absence of trends that would focus on the black consumer. "Once the sponsors realize the Negro's purchasing power is great, programs will be designed to appeal to Negroes," a CBS West Coast research director asserted.[60]

Some industry officials were disturbed, however, by the inequities between the races and took up the cause to benefit black listeners and artists. NBC, for one, engaged the Philadelphia public relations firm of Joseph V. Baker Associates, with strong ties to the black society. By October 1950 agents of the National Association for the Advancement of Colored People and the National Urban League were talking sporadically with the top brass of both NBC and its parent body, the Radio Corporation of America. The purpose of their discussions was to remove stereotyping from the content of NBC programming while launching concerted efforts to hire more employees of color. Following the group's third conclave, in early 1951 NBC issued a revised code of Network Standards and Practices that included this statement:

> All program materials present with dignity and objectivity the varying aspects of race, creed, color, and national origin. The history, institutions and citizens of all nations are fairly represented.... Defamatory statements or derogatory references expressed or implied, toward an individual, nationality, race, group, trade, profession, industry, or institution are not permitted.[61]

Subsequently, in January 1952 Jackie Robinson, who had broken the color barrier in baseball only a short time earlier, was named to direct community activities for WNBC, the chain's flagship outlet. Inaugurating a policy of "integration without identification," NBC also permitted black performers to appear in nonblack roles for the first time. As 1952 drew to a close, the network announced that black talent had doubled in appearances on NBC Radio (to 1,540 performances) over the previous year, including musicians, groups and individuals.

The Negro population in New York City increased by 63 percent in the decade ending in 1951, a research study that was commissioned by local radio outlet WLIB revealed. In addition, investigation across the nation determined that, while incomes in typical white American households doubled, incomes in average black American homes tripled at the same time. Further studies suggested that high percentages of employable blacks were working, and black high school and college enrollments soared.

Perhaps predictably, executives in local radio markets were dutifully impressed by the release of such figures, and many of them took steps to cultivate the potential offered by black consumers. While only four U.S. radio stations included programs specifically for black members of society in 1943, by 1953 a total of 260 stations were doing so, attracting both national and regional advertisers.

By the end of 1953 the value of the black marketplace was estimated at $15 billion, a strong incentive for numerous stations to switch from all-white to all-black formats. Within a short while the escalating factors that came to bear on the black marketplace reached a zenith in American radio, and permanently altered the framework of the industry.

In an introspective collegiate textbook on broadcasting, Leslie Smith states that—as far as radio advertising went—"The last good year for network sales was 1948."[62] Citing a 4.5 percent increase over 1947, Smith maintains that this happy circumstance was followed by a dozen years of shrinking sales. The pattern of decrease, in fact, was interrupted only once. Network billings ultimately fell about $100 million during the period. (More optimistically, *Variety* reported in September 1949 one chain's president, Niles Trammell, boasted to affiliates of his network: "NBC goes into the fall season in radio with only five evening half-hour periods between 8 and 11 p.m. for sale.... In the daytime, NBC is sold out solid, Monday through Friday, with the exception of one 15-minute strip."[63])

In what Smith calls "a bad time for radio," the nation was just entering a phase of economic recession. Typical local station and network billings were diminishing while at the same time network audiences were plummeting. Network affiliation was seen as an obstacle by some stations. While tinkering with new formats and appealing to minority interests and preferences, some of them also aggressively pursued untapped retail sources in their quests to sell commercial time. Revenues increased as a result.

For their part, in the meantime, networks dropped their bans on using recordings and taped matter while adding a few disk jockey features that became immensely popular. In an effort to increase listenership, they also implemented telephone quizzes like *Stop the Music!* hosted by Bert Parks and *Sing It Again* with emcee Dan Seymour. Such shows offered cash and merchandise prizes to listeners who could answer simple questions. But little came of it. Network series continued to be canceled, sometimes without replacements.

Oh, dear! What could the matter be? Leslie Smith offers a singular answer: "The problem was a horde of loud, vulgar, squat, ugly, one-eyed monsters that invaded America's homes and mesmerized the inhabitants therein for hours at a time. To make matters worse, the public willingly invited these monsters into their living rooms, and they multiplied like rabbits. Far-seeing science fiction writers had been predicting their arrival for years, and now here they were—television receivers."[64] Even the erudite president of Boston University, Daniel Marsh, was overheard to suggest: "If the television craze continues, we are destined to have a nation of morons."[65]

As early as 1946 a *Variety* headline queried whether TV was "Radio's Frankenstein?" The notion of TV as a monster persisted, and was explored in depth in *Variety*'s September 29, 1948, edition. Only a few months hence, NBC president Niles Trammell predicted that "within three years, the broadcast of sound or ear radio over giant networks will be wiped out."[66]

Apparently, most web executives didn't agree, citing TV's escalating costs as a supreme detriment. "They felt that television would grow slowly enough to make a gradual radio-to-television transition during the 1950s."[67] Said a research report issued in 1949: "We seriously doubt that television will ever become a truly nationwide medium (as compared with present radio patterns and service) if it has to depend on the economics of advertising alone."[68] But the public's interest in and advertiser fascination with television, as well as the impatience of radio executives to make a mark in the new medium, left network radio "a dying operation" by 1950.[69]

That year more people were watching TV than were listening to radio in several major metropolitan centers in the Northeast and in Los Angeles. Research strongly indicated that when more video stations and sets were in use, radio would crumble. Doomsayers predicted that when urban areas became inundated with television, radio could hope for no more than 15 percent of the prime time audience.

Since 1947 television had been growing at lightning pace. Sales of receivers soared while station license applications swamped the Federal Communications Commission. A total of 108 stations were already on the air but only 24 cities claimed two or more outlets. Networks were then patched together for major events like heavyweight fights and the World Series. At best, the nation's TV map was a spotty business. The FCC quickly determined that it was going to receive more TV applications than there would be channels available. As a consequence, in 1948 that federal regulatory body, acting with the concurrence of the Truman administration, ordered a six- to nine-month waiting period before completing further requests. But the issues evolving from the operation were so complex that the freeze was allowed to remain intact for 42 months, until July 1, 1952, when the processing resumed.

In the meantime, the extension of the coaxial cable to the West Coast, which was completed on September 10, 1951, greatly augmented a surge in the nation's TV expansion. (Until then the majority of sets were situated in saloons. Programs were often aimed directly at such patrons—wrestling and ladies with large bosoms on variety shows—according to John Chancellor, who later became a major news presence for NBC-TV.)

Nearly half of the sets in American homes by 1949 were in New York City. Most of the rest were located in Philadelphia, Washington, Boston, Chicago, Detroit and Los Angeles. The networks had stretched their grasp from New York to Washington, D.C., in 1946, on to Boston in 1947, and to the Midwest in 1949. But in 1951, for the very first time, coast-to-coast television became a reality. The same year that the coaxial cable system was completed, more Americans watched television between the peak three hours starting at 9 o'clock at night than listened to radio. "Television," advised comedian Fred Allen, "was already conducting itself provocatively, trying to get radio to pucker up for the kiss of death."[70]

In the 30 months immediately following the lifting of the freeze, 308 new TV stations signed on the air. The number of TV sets in use across the nation swelled from 190,000 in 1948 to 32.5 million by 1955, touching 65 percent of all American homes. Station revenues in the same period improved from $6.2 million to $372.2 million, an increase of 6,000-plus percent. (NBC had lost money on TV at its start, but by 1950, with sales of telecast time tripling, the tide had turned completely.) By 1952 the industry was taking in $41 million in profits. That was mere chicken feed: total network billings vaulted from $2.5 million in 1947 to $308.9 million by 1955, or up 12,250 percent. Could there be any doubt about where most Americans were turning for entertainment and information—and where the networks wanted them to be?

> Americans had already begun to adapt their habits to accommodate their favorite programs. Studies showed that when a popular program was on, toilets flushed all over certain cities, as if on cue, during commercials or the moment the program was over. Radio listenership was significantly down. People went to restaurants earlier. Products advertised on television soared in public acceptance. Book sales were said to

be down. Libraries complained of diminished activity. Above all, television threatened the movie business. By 1951, cities with only one television station reported drops in movie attendance of 20 to 40 percent.[71]

Respected media analyst Charles Siepmann offered his followers a more optimistic interpretation, at least as it affected the aural medium halfway through the 20th century:

> It seems almost certain that, of all the media, radio will be the hardest hit. There are prophets of disaster who foresee its total displacement by television. There will be a temporary disequilibrium but, once the present craze is over, subsequent adjustment to a more normal pattern of behavior seems possible.... Radio will continue to hold a number of trump cards. As we probe the distinctive attributes of radio and television and their relation to the needs and circumstances of the consumer, we discover grounds for the belief that radio's days are far from numbered....
> Both self-interest and public interest now seem to require that radio study how to win back the audiences it has lost through default of service, and to build audiences it has hitherto considered not worth courting. Lesser majorities of taste and interest than that for entertainment are still capable of providing advertisers with a rich reward for their investment.[72]

Shifting patterns within broadcasting would continue to create major changes for radio throughout the 1950s and the years immediately beyond. While Siepmann's confidence was well intended, it was also misplaced. Perhaps he could not anticipate the hidden factors at work against a resurgence of the audio medium, or conceptualize the phenomenal acceptance that television was about to receive.

By the end of 1953, even members of Murrow's Boys who had held the strongest disdain for TV began to acknowledge that it had totally eclipsed radio as the dominant broadcast news system. Howard K. Smith, Richard C. Hottelet, Daniel Schoenbrun and Bill Downs as well as Robert Pierpoint had all come to the conclusion that radio, for their purposes, was dead and that the future belonged to television.

Soon even CBS's Bill Paley was finally coming around, albeit reluctantly. Despite the reality that, until 1950, CBS Radio's advertising revenues continued to grow, within a year of TV's initial black ink Paley embraced the newer medium unconditionally, as if he was realizing its potential for the first time. Radio's most eloquent defender had been won over to the opposition. The days of the elder medium were surely numbered now.

There were multiple attempts in the golden age to introduce regional radio networks. Their members, often serving in markets with basic similarities, sought to achieve parallel goals and opportunities and to provide common services that would offer a competitive advantage to their listening audiences beyond what they could expect to achieve as mere independent operations.

Many of these regional networks and the stations in them were affiliated with one or more national networks and carried their programs. By 1941 some 20 provincial linkages existed, 14 operating in single states and six covering greater territory. (Comprehensive details of such organizations, their call letters, locations and dates of individual membership—beyond what is substantiated in a fairly brief account below—may be found in *Telecommunications: Special Reports on American Broadcasting, 1932–1947* [Arno Press, 1974] edited by Christopher H. Sterling, and in *Stay Tuned: A Concise History of American Broadcasting*, 2nd edition [Wadsworth Publishing, 1990] by Sterling and Kittross.)

There were a half-dozen principal players among the smaller networks: the California Radio System, organized in 1936 by the McClatchy and Hearst newspaper chains, which began with six stations in the Golden State; the Yankee and Colonial Networks, originally a 17-outlet Northeastern joint affiliation formed in the 1930s; the Don Lee Broadcasting System, founded in 1928 when an entrepreneur linked two stations, one in Los Angeles, the other in San Francisco, that initially led to ties with CBS, then—together with the Colonial Network in 1936—into affiliation with the Mutual Broadcasting System, thereby making MBS a national network for the very first time; the Pacific Broadcasting Company, incorporated in 1937 with a four-station hookup in Oregon and Washington, also airing Mutual and Don Lee programming after Don Lee joined MBS; the Michigan Radio Network with eight stations in the Wolverine State tied together in 1933 also featuring programs originated by Detroit's WXYZ—one of that network's owners was George W. Trendle, the enterprising creator-owner of *The Lone Ranger* and other series emanating from the studios of WXYZ, a station he also owned; and the Texas State Network, a 23-member chain established in 1938 to serve the Lone Star State, also affiliated with MBS.

Some other established associations, although possessing less influence, included the Arrowhead Network (Minnesota), the Empire

State Network (New York), Inter-City Broadcasting System (Northeast), Pennsylvania Network (Pennsylvania), Texas Quality Network (Texas), and Virginia Broadcasting System, Incorporated (Virginia).

Late in radio's golden age the Liberty Broadcasting System surfaced as one of the more lively and controversial ventures among these regionals. Begun as a single Texas station by entrepreneur Gordon McLendon in 1948, Liberty's programming was to rely heavily on recreating sports presentations through odd combinations. Using wire service reports of ongoing major-league baseball games, the chain adapted recordings of sound effects aired at the same time and causing listeners to think they were tuning in to actual play-by-play descriptions of live games. Of course, various baseball clubs controlled the rights to such broadcasts and in time a legal quagmire over these breaches was to strongly contribute to the web's undoing.

In the meantime, Liberty was soon feeding both baseball and football games to more than 80 outlets across the Southwest. By mid–1951 as many as 400 stations were deriving both their news reports and sports competitions from Liberty, the network by then having amassed a rather formidable and competitive news staff. But it all began to unravel when McLendon added a Texas oilman of conservative bent to his staff who simply annihilated the news bureau. At about the same time, the operation was thrust into litigation initiated by several ball clubs. Business was suspended in mid–1952 as a consequence. Subsequent attempts to revive the web went nowhere since the ex-affiliates had become independents or initialed deals with major national radio chains.

When Liberty folded, the heyday of the regional networks had definitely come and gone. They would never again wield the influence that they did, in limited quarters, during network broadcasting's earlier decades; nor would they have the organizational structure.

It seems appropriate to introduce yet another deviation from the discussion presented heretofore about radio transmission: frequency modulation or FM. This may have impacted the major networks only minimally on the surface, yet it was instrumental in how millions of listeners received their aural communications. Seen as an alternative to the static that interfered with reception on amplitude modulation (AM), FM was the ultimate life's work of an enterprising American innovator, Edward Howard Armstrong (1890–1954). His discovery was first patented in late 1933, yet by 1941 only 18 commercial stations had been licensed to operate on the FM band in the U.S.

While the number of FM outlets increased steadily throughout the 1940s to a peak of 733 commercial and 48 educational ventures by 1950, the number of AM stations climbed, too, reaching 2,086 by 1950. FM, therefore, comprised only 35 percent of the total commercial radio operations in America at midcentury. In addition, from that point on—throughout the fading days of the golden age—FM's numbers would spiral downward rapidly, descending to a low ebb of 530 commercial and 125 educational facilities in 1957. Conversely, there were 3,008 AM stations by then. At that point, FM's commercial radio share was but 17.6 percent of the total, about half of the percentage it occupied just seven years earlier.

Why the dramatic changes?

The key was lack of revenue. Advertisers, still spending in AM radio with many by then placing vast sums in television, couldn't see the benefit of merely adding more radio—radio that was often lacking in prestigious network affiliations and programming and that neglected pockets of listeners in out-of-the-way places far from limited broadcasting sites. Another negative factor coming into play was that few Americans owned FM receivers or still more expensive AM-FM combination sets. There weren't many FM operations, in fact, that could even produce data for prospective advertisers on how many in their audiences were able to receive FM. Most FM stations were merely duplicating the programming of their sister AM stations, in the meantime, giving FM audiences—such as they were—free bonuses. The handful of stations that didn't reproduce AM schedules were often characterized as "fine music" channels, but their low percentage of listeners hardly drew many sponsors. Finally, the mass giveaway of FM time was a near-fatal blow to the few independent FM outlets trying to sell commercial time.

While total FM revenues never reached $1 million until 1948, at no time earlier or in the years just ahead could the FM industry be considered even close to the financial break-even point. In the early 1950s, then, unable to augment a system that had obviously peaked, and was then in decline, broadcasters cut their losses, shedding more than 200 FM commercial stations. They would concentrate on more lucrative AM radio and television ventures. The bottom line was understood then as well as it is today.

In regard to AM's phenomenal growth following World War II—which seldom stalled for many subsequent years—relaxing the engineering standards required for station licenses by the Federal Communications

Commission encouraged the debut of many more AM outlets. As small stations went on the air in hamlets and villages, and more stations sprang up in urban areas, the number in service leaped to 3,500 by the end of the golden age. Almost half of those were restricted to daytime broadcasting only, however. The limitation prevented them from conflicting with stations that shared the same frequencies, as radio waves travel greater distances at night.

A straw in the wind during the 1950s was an increase in the number of simulcast programs. Popular radio shows went to television while continuing to broadcast the aural portion of their video features on radio. Listeners, meanwhile, grew increasingly exasperated by bewildering studio audience laughter or unexplained references that could only be understood by the eye. A couple of astute analysts concurred: "Many of these programs gave the impression of waiting for the time when they could abandon radio completely."[73]

A few shows airing on both radio and television went the second mile for their hearing-only audiences, however. When *The Guiding Light*, which had been broadcasting its weekday melodrama on radio since 1937, added a video version in 1952, sponsor Procter & Gamble paid to have dual productions of the same scripts staged each day. The cast would tape a sound adaptation every afternoon for the following day's radio broadcast. Action requiring visual interpretations could be revised or edited out. Then the cast would report to TV studios in another facility early the next morning for blocking and rehearsing that day's live video performance. This drama continued on both mediums for four years, until 1956 when only the telecasts were retained. *The Guiding Light*, at the time this is written, is well into its seventh decade on the air.

Another development that surfaced at about the same time as television was stereocasting. While the concept wasn't new—there had been laboratory experiments with stereophonic sound as far back as the start of the 20th century—some AM stations, particularly those playing classical music—attempted dual-outlet AM stereocasting. One station broadcast the left channel, another the right. Such broadcasts, initially airing in the early 1950s, almost always featured live music as few sources for taped or recorded stereophonic music existed. (Stereo records weren't in widespread use until 1958.) The national networks saw a new niche here, however: that same year NBC broadcast its *Bell Telephone Hour* stereophonically, and ABC stereocast *The Lawrence Welk Show* by combining AM radio and television. It was obviously a fad whose time had come.

Trends like these were transpiring in the periphery of network radio during its final years. But they would become supremely important to Americans as their listening habits were dramatically altered following the close of the golden age. Those transformations will be vigorously explored when we arrive at that spot in our progressive inquiry.

As noted already, a number of extraordinary new ventures and genres surfaced or became firmly entrenched in radio in the early years of the 1950s. They included the introduction of a more advanced approach to drama in crime, western adventure and science fiction tales. There was also a glitzy star-studded extravaganza, *The Big Show*, which was branded radio's final attempt to stem the tide as its shorelines gradually ebbed out to sea.

The Steve Allen Show, which premiered on CBS in 1950, introduced an extraordinarily talented young comic and composer to a nationwide audience. Allen was to have a colossal impact on a wide spectrum of American entertainment in the fifties and following decades.

Several other shows making network debuts during this period filled voids as some of radio's perennials left the air. Among the new, with their networks and initial years in parentheses, were: *The Halls of Ivy*, featuring Ronald and Benita Colman (NBC, 1950); *Hopalong Cassidy*, with William Boyd (MBS, CBS, 1950); *Live Like a Millionaire*, hosted by Jack McCoy (NBC, 1950); *Mark Trail*, with Matt Crowley (MBS, 1950); *City Hospital*, featuring Santos Ortega and later Melville Ruick, and Anne Burr (CBS, 1951); *Meet Millie*, starring Audrey Totter and later Elena Verdugo (CBS, 1951); *Wild Bill Hickok*, with Guy Madison and Andy Devine (MBS, 1951); *The Woman in My House*, a Carlton E. Morse production and the only open-ended soap opera premiering in the 1950s to continue for five or more years (it aired eight-plus years) (NBC, 1951); *My Little Margie*, starring Gale Storm (CBS, 1952); *Whispering Streets*, radio's last closed-ended (complete in one episode or in a five-part story line) daytime serial airing five or more years (it also lasted eight-plus years) (ABC, 1952); and *The Crime Files of Flamond*, featuring Arthur Wyatt (MBS, 1953).

One of the more innovative programming creations of this period was a laid-back, satisfying six-hour weeknight marathon of soothing recorded melodies called *Music Till Dawn*. Hosted by disk jockey Bob

Hall, it originated at midnight over New York's WCBS on April 13, 1953, and spread to other CBS-owned and -operated outlets in metropolitan centers like Chicago, Los Angeles, and Dallas. Sponsored by American Airlines, the series became an institution in itself, airing nightly for almost 17 years.

Another of radio's most prestigious and durable contributions to the American listener, which substantially raised the level of understanding and appreciation of the fine arts in millions of households, achieved a milestone during this period. *The Voice of Firestone*, featuring classical musical selections, instituted its series of weekly visits on December 3, 1928. It aired on the same network (NBC) at the same hour (8:30 P.M. ET) on the same day (Monday) for the same firm (Firestone Tire and Rubber Company) for more than a quarter of a century. Beginning in 1948 the program was simulcast on both radio and television.

On the occasion of its 25th anniversary on the air, celebrated with a live hour in dual mediums on November 30, 1953, the maestro of *Firestone*, Howard Barlow, once again held the baton, conducting orchestra, chorus and dancers. Six popular semiregulars appeared, singing the familiar tunes that had altered the perceptions of highbrow music of many in its vast audience, including Jerome Hines, Robert Rounseville, Eleanor Steber, Rise Stevens, Brian Sullivan and Thomas L. Thomas. The distinguished basal modulation of announcer Hugh James, who for many years literally was the "voice" of Firestone, introduced the artists and their selections. The themes, "If I Could Tell You" and "In My Garden," both penned by Mrs. Harvey S. (Idabelle) Firestone, Sr., introduced and concluded the celebration of the long musical tradition that was this venerable series.

Some other legendary performers—several members of the Metropolitan Opera Company—who appeared frequently on the *Firestone* broadcasts and whose names, as a result, were instantly recognized in many American homes, included: Franklyn Baur, Eugene Connelly, Nadine Connor, Richard Crooks, Vaughn DeLeath, Nelson Eddy, Eileen Farrell, Igor Gorin, Lois Hunt, Dorothy Kirsten, George London, Christopher Lynch, Lauritz Melchoir, James Melton, Patrice Munsel, Ezio Pinza, Gladys Rice, Cesare Siepi, Beverly Sills, Margaret Speaks, Gladys Swarthout, Lawrence Tibbett, Helen Traubel and Dorothy Warenskjold.

On the show's 25th anniversary, Hugh James acknowledged that the august series was the oldest coast-to-coast network program on the air. He also noted that it was the first commercially sponsored musical program to be televised and the first of its genre to be broadcast simultaneously on radio and TV. During a commercial break he introduced General David Sarnoff, the RCA chairman. Sarnoff paid tribute to the late Harvey S. Firestone, Sr., founder of the sponsoring firm, who stated at the close of the initial broadcast 25 years earlier: "I hope this program has been a wholesome feature in your household." Sarnoff affirmed that that hope had been "fully realized" for a quarter of a century. Concluding, he praised "a fine American family and a great American business organization, the Firestones," and expressed "our appreciation to their significant contributions to the prosperity and the culture of America."

The series Firestone engendered continued on the air a total of 35 years, albeit on ABC in its last few seasons. It was finally withdrawn from ABC Radio on June 10, 1957, and from ABC-TV on June 16, 1963. Several years later a Japanese conglomerate purchased the company that bore the Firestone name. In 2000, the latter fell on hard times as millions of its flagship products were recalled, creating a financial and public relations nightmare. In late summer that year the *New York Times* speculated that the grand old tiremaker, and its revered moniker, could ultimately fade into oblivion as a final consequence. It seemed, for all who had experienced *The Voice of Firestone* and made it a welcome guest in their homes for so many decades, like an unthinkable incongruity.

Not surprisingly, a number of the powerful dynamics we have encountered already coalesced to mournfully impact the audio medium in the period 1950–53. The unfortunate result was that scores of respected, durable series disappeared from the dial in wholesale lots during this time. A number of those shows were longstanding favorites of radio audiences. An attempt is made here to list some of the more prominent series, classified by when they departed from the airwaves. The years in parentheses following their titles indicate when they premiered on a national network or in syndication.

1950: *Blondie* (1939), *Bride and Groom* (1945), *County Fair* (1945), *A Date with Judy* (1941), *Doctor I.Q.*, *The Mental Banker* (1939), *Ethel and Albert* (1944), *The George Burns and Gracie Allen Show* (1932), *The Goldbergs* (1929), *Here's Morgan, aka The Henry Morgan Show* (1940), *The Jimmy Durante Show* (1933), *Jimmy Fidler in Hollywood* (1934), *Leave It to Joan,* aka *Joan Davis Time*, et al. (1943), *Ladies Be Seated* (1943), *Lassie* (1947), *The Light of the World* (1940), *The National Barn Dance* (1924), *Today's Children* (1933).

1951: *The Adventures of Sam Spade, Detective* (1946), *The Adventures of Superman* (1940), *The American Album of Familiar Music* (1931), *The Baby Snooks Show* (1936), *David Harum* (1936), *A Day in the Life of Dennis Day* (1946), *Death Valley Days* (1930), *The Fat Man* (1946), *Jack Armstrong, the All American Boy* (1933), *The Life of Riley* (1941), *Portia Faces Life* (1940), *Quick as a Flash* (1944), *The Saint* (1945), *The Southernaires Quartette* (1930), *Straight Arrow* (1948), *The Tom Mix Ralston Straightshooters*, et al. (1933), *We Love and Learn*, aka *As the Twig Is Bent* (1941), *We, the People* (1936).

1952: *Against the Storm* (1939), *Big Sister* (1936), *Big Town* (1937), *The Chamber Music Society of Lower Basin Street* (1940), *Duffy's Tavern* (1940), *I Love a Mystery* (1939), *The Lanny Ross Show* (1929), *Lone Journey* (1940), *Mr. Chameleon* (1948), *Mr. District Attorney* (1939), *The Mysterious Traveler* (1943), *The Screen Guild Theater* (1939), *The $64 Question*, aka *Take It or Leave It* (1940), *The Story of Mary Marlin* (1935), *The Strange Romance of Evelyn Winters* (1944), *Ted Mack's Original Amateur Hour*, aka *Major Bowes' Original Amateur Hour* (1935), *Valiant Lady* (1938).

1953: *The Aldrich Family* (1939), *Archie Andrews* (1943), *The Bob Hawk Show*, aka *Thanks to the Yanks* (1942), *The Cavalcade of America* (1935), *Club Fifteen* (1947), *Give and Take* (1945), *Grand Slam*, aka *Irene Beasley Songs* (1943), *The Hallmark Hall of Fame*, aka *Hallmark Playhouse* (1948), *The Horace Heidt Show*, aka *The American Way*, et al. (1932), *The Judy Canova Show* (1943), *Meet Corliss Archer* (1943), *The Quiz Kids* (1940), *The Red Skelton Show* (1939), *Smilin' Ed's Buster Brown Gang* (1944), *Tarzan* (1932), *This Is Your FBI* (1945), *Victor Lindlahr* (1937), *Your Hit Parade* (1935).

A couple of species remained virtually unscathed throughout these years, however. One could be predominantly classified as musical presentations, the other as news programming.

For much of radio's history a host of melodic features—some perceived as highbrow entertainment, others as mainstream vocal and instrumental amusement or focused on diverse interests—were broadcast over the nation's four major networks. In a few cases some subsequently appeared on other hookups. At least a score of such accepted fare continued late into the golden age: *The Bell Telephone Hour* (1940–

58), *The Bing Crosby Show*, et al. (1931–57, 1960–62), *The Boston Symphony Orchestra* (1933–57), *Chicago Theater of the Air* (1940–55), *The Cities Service Band of America*, aka *Highways in Melody*, et al. (1927–56), *The Dinah Shore Show*, et al. (1939-55), *The Frank Sinatra Show*, et al. (1942–58), *Grand Ole Opry* (1925–present), *Hawaii Calls* (1935–75, 92–present), *Lombardoland, USA* and earlier series headlined by band-leader Guy Lombardo (1927–57), *The Longines Symphonette* (1943–57), *Luncheon with Lopez* and earlier series under the baton of orchestra leader Vincent Lopez (1928, 1933–56), *The Metropolitan Opera Concerts* (1931–present), *The Metropolitan Opera Auditions* (1935–58), *The NBC Symphony Orchestra* (1937–54), *The New York Philharmonic Orchestra* (1927–63), *The Salt Lake City Mormon Tabernacle Choir* (1929–present), *Sammy Kaye's Sylvania Serenade* and earlier series conducted by orchestra maestro Sammy Kaye (1938–56), *The Vaughn Monroe Show*, aka *The Camel Caravan* (1942, 1946–54), *The Voice of Firestone* (1928–57).

Such tuneful gems continued to retain devoted fans throughout their air lives, most of them remaining fully sponsored until their network runs ultimately came to an end. Musical entries in the program logs frequently could be easily distinguished from their radio peers because they often tended to remain in place considerably longer than some other programming genres. A music critic underscored their importance: "The annals of broadcasting now confirm that the music-makers of that significant period contributed perhaps more to the success and popularity of the medium than any other group of entertainers. Indeed, America's vast listening audiences proclaimed that the most memorable and magical moments of radio were the musical gifts from an amazing and mighty music box."[74]

On another tack, most of those frequent, familiar, seemingly inde-fatigable voices that conveyed current events across the decades stayed by their stuff in the waning days of radio. Whether they were respon-sible for communicating mere headline reports or in-depth commen-tary and analysis of daily or weekly happenings, they could be counted upon to deliver the goods. Among the more prominent names that Americans relied on in the latter days of the golden age—all of whom were on the air for at least five years with their own programs, and some for more than 25 years—were the following newscasters, commenta-tors and analysts, together with their most durable network identifi-cations:

ABC: Martin Agronsky, Edwin D. Canham, Elmer Davis, Don Gardiner, Paul Harvey, George Hicks, Quincy Howe, Walter Winchell.

CBS: Douglas Edwards, Allan Jackson, Larry LeSueur, Edward R. Murrow, Lowell Thomas, Robert Trout.

MBS: Cecil Brown, Bob Considine, Bill Cunningham, Cedric Foster, Gabriel Heatter, Robert F. Hurleigh, Fulton Lewis, Jr.

NBC: Morgan Beatty, Alex Dreier, Pauline Frederick, H. V. Kaltenborn, Henry J. Taylor, John W. Vandercook.

A postscript seems appropriate. One of these electronic news journalists—ABC's Paul Harvey—first went on the air nationwide on December 3, 1950. On December 3, 2000, at the age of 82, he was still before his weekday microphone, continuing to do what he loved best. It was a record unparalleled by any newsman before him; quite possibly, it might never be exceeded.

Finally, a travesty of sorts occurred in ABC's daytime programming in the 1951–52 radio season. That chain had deliberately abandoned most vestiges of soap opera in 1942 (it was then still known as the Blue Network), in one stroke deleting the seven serials it was airing at the time. Subsequently, in the next nine years it made only one attempt to reverse that calculation, adding *Sweet River* in 1943–44 for a few months. Then, nothing.

Perhaps by the 1950s, the fact that NBC and CBS were continuing to be successful in holding a contingent of listeners with their daytime dramas was not lost on ABC: seeing its daytime audiences ebb and flow elsewhere, the web decided to get back into soap opera production in a major way. To do it, it initially acquired one of NBC's strongest serials, *When a Girl Marries*, during the summer of 1951. At the same time it revived two previously aired feminine favorites, *Lone Journey* and *The Strange Romance of Evelyn Winters*. That fall they were joined by a quintet of returning washboard weepers, all formerly established series that had left the air a few years earlier: *Against the Storm, Joyce Jordan, M. D., Marriage for Two, The Story of Mary Marlin* and *Valiant Lady*.

It was too late, however. The ABC brass had badly miscalculated.

Fans of long-established favorite dramas that continued to air without interruption over the years weren't ready to switch to competing entries. In addition, of course, by then, new ones were beginning to surface on television. ABC's ratings-building ploy was a pure disaster. By June 1952 seven of the network's eight dishpan dramas were gone forever. Only *When a Girl Marries* survived. A final attempt to introduce another open-ended soap opera in 1954, *Ever Since Eve*, also failed—it lasted just eight months. ABC's glory days as a soap opera perennial broadcaster were history.

On the other hand, dramas airing on the rival networks continued to retain a valid body of listeners. CBS and NBC programmed a combined 27 quarter hours of daytime dramas in the 1950–51 season, and that number was holding firm in the 1953–54 term. Thus, a breed that had traditionally prevailed in weekday programming for more than two decades continued to dominate the final days of radio's golden age. It was confirmation enough that the people who were creating the programs and those who were hearing them were still markedly on the same wavelength.

The historians of electronic media have ascribed a myriad of picturesque epithets to entertainer Arthur Godfrey, who was to have more impact on both radio and television than any other single performer during the early 1950s.

Godfrey, "radio's one-man show,"[75] was labeled "as close an approach to a one-man network as radio and television ever produced."[76] Cited as "one of the best-loved men in America,"[77] he was, notwithstanding, variously endorsed as "the most important man in America,"[78] "the most recognized man in America"[79] and "the most powerful man in broadcasting."[80] Possessing "radio's longest continuous career,"[81] the old redhead was called "the original and ultimate infotainer."[82]

While he would be "deified and discarded"[83] during an on-air professional life that stretched from the 1920s to the 1970s, he was also recognized as "the greatest salesman who ever stood before a microphone"[84] and "radio's most trusted pitchman."[85] Ultimately, some would consider him "the greatest communicator of the century."[86]

A contemporary biography of his life notes that "most Americans alive today don't know the name Arthur Godfrey."[87] Unlike the same era's Lucille Ball, Milton Berle, Jackie Gleason and Ed Sullivan whose TV efforts have been recalled again and again, Godfrey's shows weren't transportable. Largely aired live, wandering and scriptless, they—and their star—acquired "no place in the public eye or in the public mind."[88]

In his prime, however, Godfrey—more than any other performer—ruled the broadcasting airwaves, with a CBS vice president singularly assigned to the one showman. In 1953 Godfrey, by then heard and seen by 80 million Americans weekly, was personally responsible for contributing 12 percent of his web's annual revenues. The total was a tidy $27 million for CBS, while he lined his own pockets with a cool million plus. On the air he often claimed that he paid the network's expenses for the day before CBS chairman Paley awoke every morning.

Actually, no single individual before or since Godfrey has come even close to raising 12 percent of a network's revenues. All the while Godfrey did it in a manner contradictory to longstanding commercial delivery methods that had been in use since radio's incubation: to that time, addressed to no one in particular, sponsors' messages would be offered in a stuffed-shirt style that frequently began, "Ladies and gentlemen...." Godfrey dispensed with the formality, a technique he adopted after lying in a hospital bed for four months in late 1931 while recovering from a near-fatal vehicular accident. Returning

Impacting radio and TV in the early 1950s more than anybody else, Arthur Godfrey (shown) had a fondness for doing things right—and wrong. The old redhead had the public eating from his hand while he attracted more ad revenues to a network (CBS) than anyone thought possible. Yet a self-destructive fault exacted a heavy toll on his popularity. *Photofest.*

to the microphone—rather than seeing a vast faceless audience—he recognized a single listener as his challenge: his role was to convince that individual to buy the commodity he advertised. Godfrey chatted as if he was carrying on a conversation in a living room and not over the air. He revolutionized commercial delivery and scores of sponsors signed on for his programs.

In his prime, Godfrey would eventually fill the CBS Radio and TV airwaves for up to 15 hours per week with live entertainment from his four programs. Since commercial broadcasting began in the 1920s, no single performer before or after him has even come close to commanding that much time and prestige. His fans developed a passionate following for his shows, while hopeful advertisers signed up on waiting lists for slots to open up so they could sponsor him. Yet, life takes funny turns at times, and the electronic media's super genius was about to shake the very foundations of his extraordinary success.

Despite all the positive things that can be said about Arthur Godfrey and his momentous contributions to radio and television at mid–20th century, his idle backfence chitchat belied a ferocious ego. One should make no mistake: he was the supreme authority concerning everything in his world, and all were at his command. When his wishes weren't precisely followed he became angry, made snap decisions (some of which he later regretted) and sometimes reacted in impish ways that accentuated his unbridled power. His clout and ego together eventually alienated many within the broadcasting industry.

At the outset, he claimed his shows had no stars beyond himself, and thus suggested there was little need for his employees to sign contracts or acquire agents. All "the little Godfreys" worked at the pleasure of their mentor and could be summarily dismissed at will. When he perceived that one had gotten out of line he might totally ignore that individual on a given day, not calling upon him for a scheduled vocal number. Working without a script, he'd conveniently drain all the airtime with jousting or allow others to perform extra vocals. To add insult to injury, he'd dock a miscreant's pay for failing to appear on the show.

Such a mean streak became even more pronounced as time went on. While most of it stayed beneath the surface and the public knew none of it, the seething vitriol burst to the surface on October 19, 1953, when Godfrey—disturbed over a perceived lack of humility in singer Julius La Rosa—fired him while *Arthur Godfrey Time* was on the air nationwide. It was the start of a long good-bye for Godfrey for the public reacted swiftly, audibly and overwhelmingly negatively. His popularity fell dramatically and he was never able to recover it. CBS was at that very juncture considering adding a Saturday morning show to Godfrey's impressive holdings but nixed that idea at once. In an orgy of self-destruction, Godfrey persisted in dismantling what had been one of the greatest performing triumphs in the history of broadcasting.

La Rosa's abrupt departure was followed by the most amazing string of self-defeating acts ever witnessed in the profession. Longtime band-leader Archie Bleyer was fired a short time afterward. More than a dozen other "little Godfreys" would, in fact, be sacked in due time. Exclaimed a radio biographer: "What might have been an isolated incident stretched into six years of bitchy, bickering strife."[89]

Years later Julius La Rosa acknowledged that, while he never hated Godfrey for firing him and would always be grateful to him for the help he gave his career, his former tutor simply "wasn't a nice man."[90]

Godfrey's temper flared in other ways, adding to deteriorating relations with the press. On January 7, 1954, he got into trouble for buzzing the tower at the airfield at Teterboro, New Jersey, when he was denied access to a runway he preferred. For six months his pilot's license was lifted as a result of that violation.

In discussing Godfrey's *Talent Scouts* showcase of up-and-coming artists, author John Dunning hit the nail on the head in reference to the great showman's diminishing career which began with the firing of La Rosa: "*Talent Scouts* is Godfrey at his best—wisecracking, rambling, then rushing through the spot to get the last act in. The temptation is strong, listening to these [shows], to think of Godfrey as a decent man who lost his way."[91]

The inauguration of President Dwight D. Eisenhower at the start of 1953 coincided with even better times for most Americans. The stalemated Korean War, which had dragged on for three years, concluded with an armistice treaty that was signed that summer. About the same time new optimism and unparalleled prosperity were fueled by a reduction in apprehension associated with the lingering Cold War. All of this signaled what was to be the start of the *nifty fifties*, as the period was tagged, a period later celebrated in the movie *American Graffiti* and the TV comedy *Happy Days*. While set in the early 1960s, they offered an abundance of music and memories taken directly from the previous decade.

During 1953 the U.S. turned out two-thirds of all the world's manufactured goods. Although Ike couldn't be credited for all or even most of this economic boom, it occurred on his watch, and like him, the sudden affluence Americans enjoyed stemmed primarily from the Second World War. The war had largely devastated the industrial revolution in Europe and Japan for a while, yet it actually proved beneficial to U.S. plants that were left unscathed and called upon to expand rapidly. Simultaneously, the priorities of war production spawned an enormous pent-up demand for manufactured consumer goods during the postwar era, commodities like vehicles, household appliances and television sets.

The enactment of the G.I. Bill of Rights was yet another of the war's outcomes that was favorable to many U.S. citizens. That bill stoked the economic fires even more, creating an upwardly mobile group of educated and ambitious vets. Nearly half of the 13 million individuals who served in the nation's armed services in the war benefited from the bill's generous provisions of financial assistance to study in schools of higher learning.

Despite signs to the contrary, the prosperity the nation was enjoying extended into radio in at least some quarters. In 1950 newsman Walter Winchell, for example, signed a lifetime contract with ABC assuring him at least $10,000 weekly as long as he was mentally and physically able to air his quarter-hour Sunday night radio broadcast. If he became incapacitated, he was still guaranteed $1,000 a month. Not bad by 1950s standards.

In the same time frame the nation was humming the number-one tunes on the hit parade, broadcast weekly on radio, including "Goodnight Irene," recorded by Gordon Jenkins and the Weavers in 1950; Patti Page's "Tennessee Waltz" in 1951; Johnnie Ray's "Cry" in 1952; and "The Song from Moulin Rouge," an instrumental number featuring Percy Faith's Orchestra in 1953.

On the political front, in September 1951 Senator William Benton (D–Connecticut) proposed that a limited portion of broadcast time be assigned without charge to responsible candidates for federal office to reduce their campaign costs. It's a reform that, a half-century later, has never been implemented.

For those working in the radio industry, a question that lingered during the period was: What will it take for the aural medium to survive? As insiders came to rapidly understand, there would be no easy answers to that one.

3

The Middle Years: 1954-1956

CBS owner-chairman Bill Paley wasn't the only one in broadcasting who championed radio for a prolonged period of time, although he may have been its most viable, visible, vocal proponent. Paley desperately hoped—against insuperable odds—that radio would thrive, albeit alongside a newer medium that was gaining rapid favor in U.S. homes.

David Sarnoff, RCA's chairman, for all his avowed intentions of bringing television to the forefront of American entertainment, maintained a healthy respect for the industry's initial link, too. He even went so far as to profess that radio would not die because so many homes were equipped with receivers.

General Sarnoff's statement simply doesn't hold water. Just because so many homes were equipped with radios, there was absolutely nothing to say that the passion many listeners had developed for an exclusively aural transmission would remain undisturbed, perpetuated forever. According to *Variety*, in late 1955 only 786,000 households tuned in to a radio series during a typical evening, although 46.6 million American homes had at least one radio.[1] In retrospect, Sarnoff's thought could hardly have convinced even the most militant idealist. Given evolving circumstances, there was plainly no way things could continue as they had.

Radio must change if it was to regain any hope of success. It had experimented for some time with several new forms, including science fiction tales, a hard-hitting approach to crime, and the launch of a more urbane western drama. It had also attempted a 90-minute variety show-case that ultimately flopped. However, even that had substantiated that there was still an interest, a potential and a creativity (the last a tad in decline) that lingered in a medium that so recently had occupied a fundamental quarter in American domiciles.

Now, facing a new social environment, radio *had* to find a balance or perish. To be viable, it must derive new economic measures while cultivating supplementary programming styles, to discover what its function for the future was to be. There could be no question but that TV was the ominous threat mandating such swift changes.

The ratings figures released in 1955 merely validated a point probably understood by almost everybody then connected with the industry: radio had lost its primary audience and must be transformed if it was to remain feasible—and certainly so if network programming was to continue. In the mid–1940s, NBC president Niles Trammell had mused thoughtfully, urging the aural medium to find "a niche where it can best serve the public."[2] By the mid–1950s, do-or-die time had arrived. A venerated historiographer concluded: "Radio on the network level was now a supplementary, secondary entertainment source. To survive, it had to do better those things which television could not do."[3] To that, he solemnly added: "Despite ... creditable achievements, radio as heard since the early 1930s was dead."[4]

The funeral, of course, was off a spell. For at least five years, radio's confirmed addicts would have lots of opportunity to mourn the corpse. There were times when the networks would seem almost tolerant toward the medium that had made them billions of dollars. Conversely, at other times the webs appeared that they couldn't care less about the original enterprise. On such occasions they reduced its funds for experimentation, dropping shows that were costly to produce. The money that had been made in radio was often diverted to television, where nearly everybody sensed the future of broadcasting was headed.

In spite of all of that, network radio would make a solid effort to hold its head up in dignity and self-respect in the mid–1950s, if nothing more than for public appearances' sake. As it transpired, radio encountered eroding levels of advertisers, audiences and—in some cases—affiliates. Where it seemed absolutely imperative to do so, the national chains *did* pour money into some sinking ships. They totally underwrote a number of sustaining series (those without paid commercial sponsorship) to maintain a complete program log when sponsors pulled the plug. They sometimes did likewise when substitute series were added to fill the voids created by departures of longstanding listener favorites.

Through various means, the chains took pains to minimize any ambivalent thinking that their listeners might be developing concerning the fate of network radio's future—and its mounting possibility of extinction. Occasionally they employed surreptitious methods as they went about their tasks. The goal was to keep audiences believing everything was hunky-dory, whether it was or not. No slip of the tongue, no intimation whatsoever that radio as the fans had known it as far back as the 1920s was living on borrowed time, an enormous vacuum approaching rapidly. They would attempt to fool all of the people all of the time.

When the end came, millions of the faithful, suddenly dispossessed, would literally cry out in anguish. Many would vent their anger at the networks in heedless outrage. It would all be to no avail. But that time was not yet. The full realization of a catastrophe-in-the-making wouldn't occur until 1960.

In the meantime, how did the networks hide the inevitable?

One technique was to pretend that radio would continue forever. On programs that were commercial-free, or were only partially sponsored, an ebullient CBS spokesman might inform the fans of one show what type of jam the insurance investigator with the huge expense account would find himself in during that week's episode of *Yours Truly, Johnny Dollar*. Interlocutors for the other webs simultaneously verbalized similar plugs for their own shows.

With a trace of jauntiness in his voice, the announcer would conclude the piece of unpaid commercial copy he was then reading with a typical reminder like this: "You'll always find action and adventure when you keep your radio tuned right here to the stars' address ... CBS." No hint, of course, that the series on which he was appearing *right then* might be in jeopardy, or possibly the one he was promoting—or that half the chain's schedule could be yanked at any moment to satisfy scores of clamoring affiliates who were demanding that network programming be drastically curtailed.

No notion like that, until one day when time ran out for a soap opera (or, pick a breed) and a common advisory was inserted near the end of the final show: "This concludes the present series of *Young Widder Brown* broadcasts."

No explanation of what happened to the characters that legions of housewives, in that case, had been following for years. No word until then that anybody was about to pull the rug from under much of the fare that the webs had been airing for nearly three decades. It made no sense, of course, but in fact that's the dismal end that many programs—and their fans—were left to wrestle with.

There will be more on this subject later.

By the mid–1950s, network radio was proceeding along in a kind of guarded, unspoken optimism. Not even all of those who suspected the true facts would acknowledge them. Some astute individuals inside and outside the industry were realizing by middecade that radio couldn't go on forever—not in the form they had known, anyway. The sad thing was that the few who could have done something to preserve it, even on a reduced scale, weren't taking very many steps to insure or prolong its life.

One of the innovative actions that network radio *did* pursue in the 1950s, alluded to already, helped stave off the demise a little while longer: a move toward participating or multiple sponsorship of various programs. Since radio's inception, single or—at the most—dual advertisers underwrote almost all commercial programming. Even the names of the sponsors were often incorporated into the titles of the shows they purchased: e.g., *The Johnson's Wax Program with Fibber McGee and Molly*, *The Lucky Strike Program starring Jack Benny*, *The A&P Gypsies*, *The Clicquot Club Eskimos*, *The Voice of Firestone*, *Oxydol's Own Ma Perkins*, *Smilin' Ed's Buster Brown Gang*, *The Lux Radio Theater* and scores of others. As the good times rolled toward an end, though, and sponsors of many years began transferring their advertising dollars elsewhere, radio had to quickly find a way to pay its bills—or be extinguished. Even then radio's ability to compensate for its disadvantages with innovative thinking allowed it to continue without serious interruption.

In the past radio had acted almost as a common carrier, distributing programs produced or controlled by advertising agencies and often having only a limited say in series' content or scheduling. In the mid–1950s, however—by the time many of the major program sponsors had siphoned off much or all of the funds that had traditionally flowed into radio—a concept practiced on a limited basis near the close of the 1940s was recalled and executed to a much greater extent.

By the middle of the fifties, the networks were offering cooperative (dual arrangement) or participatory or multiple sponsorships for vast numbers of programs. Under the plan an individual feature, which might have been underwritten by a single firm for years, theoretically could have as many as a dozen sponsors by middecade. Not all of those advertisers would appear on the same broadcast, mind you, but perhaps as many as three could.

The reader should be aware that the commercials in those days were at least 60 seconds in length and often longer. Ten-second sound bites acceptable in broadcast advertising today hadn't arrived during radio's golden age, thus fewer commercial messages were aired.

The numbers were less for another reason, too: a 30-minute program broadcast in prime time typically offered a sponsor about three minutes to air its messages, based on Federal Communications Commission policies then in effect. Daytime programs, on the other hand, could squeeze in at least three minutes per quarter-hour, still a far cry from the prolonged, seemingly endless commercial distractions carried by most stations 50 years later. Listeners back then never realized they had it so good!

In participatory advertising, when General Motors, for instance, dropped a long-running series that it had sponsored (and may have owned) from the program's inception 20 years earlier, the show might continue with multiple sponsors. The network carrying the show would sell segments of it to several sponsors whose combined advertising dollars would underwrite the full expense of the series. Actually, advertisers could also purchase local spots within certain programs, adding substantially to their ability to be flexible and creative with their spending. As a result of these options, if all the commercial spots in a show were filled, a network likely suffered no financial loss.

A favorable by-product of the participatory trend was what it did for firms that were not in the top tier of global and national commercial enterprises based on their annual revenues. For the first time ever, participatory sponsorship allowed smaller organizations—often medium-sized corporations without the resources to underwrite expensive weekly or daily radio productions—to reach vast numbers of listeners with their messages. They could do so at a fraction of what it would cost them working independently, too, which many couldn't afford in the first place. Partnership deals permitted noncompeting products and services to be advertised on shows that continued to draw respectable audience sizes, resulting in a winning environment for sponsors, networks and listeners. Making these changes, or signing for half-time cooperative

sponsorships, allowed numerous network productions to carry on continuously for several more years.

Another outgrowth of these changes directly affected the relationships of the advertisers, their agencies and the networks. The sponsors were, in effect, relinquishing much of the control they had
possessed over a given program's content and scheduling, in some cases
for the first time in commercial radio's history. With many of them no
longer interested in owning the shows on which their products were
advertised (program rights were often sold or transferred to their originating networks) they maintained far less say-so in who could appear
as guests on their programs, or whether a series might be preempted
for an occasional event the network might prefer to air. Yet for many
factors, chief among them reduced expense, dual or multiple sponsorships often made economic sense for advertisers—and gave increased
control to the networks over schedules and content.

A study of 317 features and their sponsors still being aired by the
four major national networks at the start of 1956 showed the following
divisions:

• 188 series (59.4 percent) sustained by their networks.
• 74 series (23.3 percent) underwritten by a single sponsor.
• 55 series (17.3 percent) underwritten by cooperative or multiple
sponsorship.

While the last group at first appears small by comparison, two of
the series included in the multiple sponsorship category (*Monitor* and
Weekday) accounted for nearly 46 hours of programming per week, a
significant chunk of network radio's entire broadcast schedule. The
time filled by these multiple-sponsored services greatly skewed the balance in the results.

Furthermore, the sustaining features included major segments of
programming where production costs were minimal, particularly in the
categories of musical offerings, public affairs forums, religious talks and
discussions on a myriad of additional topics (health, business, education, finance, gardening, cooking, homemaking tips, and so on), plus
news programs. Such features often aired for a quarter-hour or less and
many of those were heard weekly, not daily, decreasing the status of the
sustainers.

For a spell, then, radio successfully practiced one-upmanship in regard to its losses of durable advertisers. At least a few in the industry were nevertheless working tenaciously to safeguard it from the morass that appeared to be hell-bent on sucking it under.

Arthur Godfrey, still the king of daytime radio variety programs (though admittedly a categorically tarnished celebrity by the mid–1950s), fell further from grace in his apparent bid to self-destruct. As if the Julius La Rosa debacle in 1953 closely followed by the dismissal of long-time bandleader Archie Bleyer wasn't enough, by 1955 Godfrey seemed to thrive on firing some of his most faithful and publicly admired pro-tégés. On April 15, 1955, he pulled the rug from under nine regulars: the Mariners quartet, who had been with him for the heyday of his radio and television runs, Hawaiian singer Haleloke, vocalist Marion Marlowe, and three longtime writers—Charles Horner, Preston Mileas and Charles Slocum.

Displaying a cavalier attitude about performers, the public and particularly the press, Godfrey—on one of his nationwide morning broadcasts—called columnist Dorothy Kilgallen "a liar" and referred to TV host Ed Sullivan as "a dope." By October 1955, he had discharged Larry Puck, the coproducer of *Talent Scouts*, who had married Marion Marlowe the previous June. (An unambiguous Godfrey policy had long forbidden romantic fraternizing among the shows' staff.) Godfrey ter-minated the services of announcer George Bryan and musical conduc-tor Jerry Bresler on his *Talent Scouts* show, too. The following day singer Lu Ann Simms was let go from his other shows (*Arthur Godfrey Time* and CBS-TV's *Arthur Godfrey and His Friends*).

A Godfrey biographer observed: "He was appallingly lacking in tact and professionalism when it came to managing change or working with the press."[5] All his radio and television audiences were rapidly depleting. At a time when radio was being extinguished on other grounds, Godfrey paid no mind to the fact that his personal habits were irrefutably making enormous contributions to the slippage.

In the meantime, and on a more positive note, at about this same time the Negro radio market was gaining striking recognition. Whether this could be directly linked to the Supreme Court's historic 1954 deci-sion disallowing segregated school systems nationwide is open to ques-tion. That judgment became a watershed in changing the country's perception of various ethnic groups, and the practical issues of race relations.

The ruling was followed in 1956 with another by the same body in which segregation at all public institutions of higher learning was banned. Segregation was also declared unconstitutional in public transportation in 1956. Millions of American citizens, from that era forward, would begin to individually rethink the positions they had clung to all of their lives in regard to racial awareness, sensitivity and separation.

In January 1954 the National Negro Network commenced service on radio with the debut of *The Story of Ruby Valentine*, a weekday serial featuring actress-songstress Juanita Hall, and jointly sponsored by the Pet Milk and Philip Morris companies. The soap opera was an outgrowth of two others aired previously: *As the Twig Is Bent*, which began in syndication in 1941, and *We Love and Learn*, which evolved from it in 1942. The new web also developed other short-lived series, including *The Life of Anna Lewis*, with Hilda Simms in the title role; *It's a Mystery, Man*, starring Cab Calloway; and planned a fourth serial to star gospel vocalist Ethel Waters.

Broadcast Productions, a Chicago firm, attempted to introduce Jesse Owens in a radio series that also appealed to African-Americans. At about the same time an outfit known as Negro Radio Stories sought to present a quartet of added daytime dramas featuring all-black casts: *Ada Grant's Neighbors*, *My Man*, *Rebeccah Turner's Front Porch Stories* and *The Romance of Julia Davis*. Clearly, radio was exposing black audiences to opportunities never before witnessed.

In March 1955 ABC presented its first all-black network series, *Rhythm & Blues on Parade*. African-American host Willie Bryant conducted the interviews while introducing all-black entertainers. The trade paper *Variety* took note that the network called on one of its black TV cameramen to be the show's audio engineer, safeguarding the show as 100 percent black.[6]

Only the year before, radio executives had assessed the Negro market and found it to be worth $15 billion.[7] With figures like those, if radio's golden age had lasted much longer, Rochester, Beulah and Birdie would have likely found higher-paying occupations! In addition, by the mid–1950s announcers and program and technical assistants of color were already on the job in several major markets, including stations owned by the networks. It was an auspicious trend during the seminal stages of a civil rights-minded era.

An experiment by ABC Radio in 1954 proved prophetic, yet carried far greater meaning than anyone could have then imagined. Seeking to offer its listeners flexible programming that would augment

Americans' increasingly mobile lifestyle, on the weekends the chain introduced a five-minute newscast hourly. ABC's fortuitous measure was to become a threshold in broadcasting that would influence all four webs in that decade; the innovation still affects surviving network radio in the contemporary period. The impact of these news updates will be considered in enhanced detail later.

As the mid–1950s approached, the winds of change were blowing swiftly on several fronts, and an America accustomed to ballads and big bands at the start of the decade was about to be inundated with its newest export to global entertainment—rock 'n' roll—blasted from radios and jukeboxes across the land. Station WINS became the first in the Big Apple to succeed with a rock 'n' roll format, a format that was to carry far beyond the confines of Manhattan.

It began when WINS hired a popular rock DJ at Cleveland's WJW, Alan Freed, also called "Moondog." Freed began to turn the youth in metropolitan New York and—via syndication in 60 other markets— onto rock 'n' roll on September 6, 1954. He presided over a one-hour weekday afternoon show at 4 o'clock and a three-hour follow-up at 11 o'clock nightly. Eighteen months later, in March 1956, CBS added a 30-minute Saturday night teen bash to its television schedule that it called *Rock 'n' Roll Dance Party*. Freed and musician Count Basie cohosted. The series featured teen idols, luminaries like the Drifters, Fats Domino, Joe Turner, and the Moonglows.

By all accounts Freed was one of the medium's future breed of true "stars" in thousands of towns, large and small. While *American Bandstand* had been on local TV in Philadelphia since 1952 and was destined to have even greater influence on a youth-oriented culture, it didn't arrive before a national TV audience until August 1957, about a year and a half following Freed's launch.

A postscript is in order: On June 2, 1958, Freed switched from WINS to WABC in New York when the former station suspended him temporarily for provoking a riot in Boston during a local rock 'n' roll extravaganza. Shortly, he also signed with WABD-TV (soon renamed WNEW-TV) to host *Alan Freed's Big Beat Party*, an hour-long weekday afternoon dance marathon that was to rival *American Bandstand* locally in the environs of New York. Freed may have become a victim of his own success, though.

In late November 1959 he was fired by both the New York radio and television outlets for refusing to sign a statement that he hadn't received payola (inducements from recording companies to play certain records). In a moment his fame and fortune evaporated; the foundation he had established would be left to others to build on.

The hit parade was a strong indicator of the nation's rapid progression toward a more boisterous musical blend—1954's favorite was the simple ballad by songstress Kitty Kallen, "Little Things Mean a Lot." Bill Haley and the Comets followed in 1955 with "Rock Around the Clock." Swivel-hipped Elvis Presley hit the big time with the number one tune in 1956, "Don't Be Cruel." A completely loose, amorphous youth culture was on its way. It would surely drive yet another nail in the coffin of an exclusively aural amusement and information communication system that the nation had embraced since the advancement of sound wave technology.

One of the saddest obituaries written in broadcasting during this era was for George Heller, who gave most of his professional career to raising the compensation of industry employees. For 18 years he guided the American Federation of Radio Artists (by then, the American Federation of Television and Radio Artists). He left an organization of 33 locals and a national membership exceeding 18,000. The *New York Times* acknowledged: "George Heller ... was fiercely devoted to the economic well-being of performers on the air; all are in his debt. His fairness, his patience and good humor won him the respect of network executives as well. Mr. Heller was an able labor leader; he was also a fine human being."[8] George Heller was 49 when he died May 30, 1955.

If the mark left by television in the early years of the 1950s impacted radio's fortunes more than any other single factor—resulting in the erosion of audiences and advertisers, the transfer of several longstanding personalities to the tube, a strong bent toward sustaining features, an executive staff with diminished interest in audio quality that drastically curtailed the resources for it, and a few affiliates beginning to rumble restlessly—the mid–1950s could be largely characterized by the departure of copious durable shows, several of blockbuster levels, as a direct yield of the trends established in the early years of the decade. Shows long entrenched in the American entertainment psyche began to topple like dominoes. Some weren't simply disbanding, however. Instead they were concentrating their efforts on the tube.

A handful of exceptional premiers in this period indicated that radio was not totally dead. Still, such features were few and far between, compared with the amount of programming they were replacing.

It was unquestionably a defining moment in radio's brief history.

In practice, in the perception of millions of newly converted tele-philes, the aural medium gave them no substantive reason for further attention. The remainder of its dwindling audience was left to cope with frequently shifting schedules, to deal with replacement series that were often inferior by earlier standards, to encounter reduced options for superlative drama and comedy—both of which had been hallmarks of radio's golden age—and to acquire a sinking feeling of being sud-denly dispossessed by something that had quietly slipped in during the night and whisked away their major entertainment resources. Their conviction would become even more pronounced as the seasons pro-gressed.

Herewith, let us recognize a few samples of those truly notewor-thy features that had steadfastly characterized radio's adherence to ster-ling quality.

A pair of series in separate genres that departed the airwaves dur-ing this era convincingly attained such high standards that they were unmatched by any potential rivals. For western adventure, none equaled the epic proportions of *The Lone Ranger*, a radio dramatization that appealed to all ages. In silver screen reproductions, no series acquired the excellence of the *Lux Radio Theater*. Both shows were broadcast for 21 years and were widely esteemed for their consistent superiority vir-tually every time out.

The Lone Ranger was the bedrock upon which a radio production empire sprang. Conceived in the mind of George W. Trendle, the myth-ical knight on a shining white steed replaced criminal activity with jus-tice while he and a faithful Indian companion, Tonto, spread peace to the settlers of the old West. Theirs was the genesis drama of a line of so-called juvenile tales that included *The Green Hornet* (1938–52) and *The Challenge of the Yukon* (1947–55). The trio was beamed across North America from the tower of Detroit's WXYZ, a CBS station (originating as WGHP) where Trendle had become managing partner in 1930. By 1934 this operation was to be instrumental in forming the Mutual Broadcasting System.

Sensing enormous promise, and having in place a radio repertory company and large musical library, Trendle led the station to pursue the route of independency in 1932 and generate its own programming. Fran Striker, a writer then living in Buffalo, New York, came to his attention at about that time. Trendle shared with Striker an inspiration he had earlier conceived: to develop a fictional narrative of the western plains that would center on a do-good figure that would be admired far and wide. It was the start of a personal relationship that was to continue for decades, and resulted in the character who would represent the antithesis of greed and hate as early Americans advanced westward.

Their hero would become, in millions of homes across the land, a symbol of righteousness representing moral and ethical decency to which every individual—young and old—might aspire. While the series might be randomly labeled as juvenile-oriented, a sector of its audience would always be adults who were transfixed as easily as preadolescents by the magnitude of this unblemished heroic character.

The Lone Ranger burst onto the air on January 31, 1933, to the theme of Rossini's *William Tell Overture*, a composition that this drama would soon come to immortalize. To this day anyone who followed the series on radio or television (it was on ABC-TV from 1949 to 1957) cannot help but recall the masked man—who traveled incognito to amplify his honorable pursuits, riding the white stallion Silver as the music resounded—and the stirring words of its best known narrator, Fred Foy: "Nowhere in the pages of history can one find a greater champion of justice. Return with us now to those thrilling days of yesteryear. From out of the paths come the thundering hoofbeats of the great horse Silver! The Lone Ranger rides again!" They were followed by the ranger's shout: "Let's go big fella! Hi-Yo, Silver! Hiiiiii!" Sidekick Tonto commanded his own mount: "Getumup, Scout!"

Tonto, incidentally, was fond of grunting discriminating epithets. He'd report to the masked man, for instance, on an hombre they had previously encountered: "Him go to town, Kemosabay," he'd say, employing the pet Native American moniker he had adopted for the ranger, which meant "faithful friend." Or he'd introduce himself to a stranger as "Me ... Tonto." One wag noted that the red man "could never get his pronouns straight no matter how long he was exposed to the Lone Ranger's impeccable English." All of this might have been remedied, of course, "if only he could learn to change *him* to *he* and *me* to *I*, but then he wouldn't have sounded 'Indian' enough."[9]

The formidable pair rode together against lawlessness thrice weekly, playing to 12 million listeners every week. Reportedly working 14 hours daily six days a week, author Striker not only turned out 156 scripts annually but also 365 daily comic strips, as well as a dozen juvenile novels. He also wrote over 30 episodes for a couple of *Lone Ranger* movie serials. "Trendle and Striker deserve some kind of posthumous literary recognition for their inspired creation," a critic protested.[10]

The part of the masked man was successively played by George Stenius (1933), Earle Graser (1933–41) and Brace Beemer (1941–54), with John Todd as Tonto throughout the run. The voice of Beemer, formerly an announcer for the series, who stepped in to fill the void when Graser died unexpectedly, is readily recalled by millions of fans as the Lone Ranger. (Beemer was furthermore cast in the role of Sergeant Preston in *The Challenge of the Yukon* during that series' final season on the air ending June 9, 1955.) The WXYZ repertory company, with a contingent of well-trained radio actors, regularly appeared in the plots of all three of that station's famous dramas. Home audiences instantly recognized many of their vocal intonations.

New episodes of the famous horse opera, copied but never transcended, bit the dust on September 3, 1954, although transcribed repeats aired through May 25, 1956. Then *The Lone Ranger* vanished as suddenly as it had appeared. In its wake it left a generation of adventurers imbued with the noble ideals that had profoundly contributed to the nation's moral fiber, who wondered what became of the masked man to whom they were so devoted.

The Lux Radio Theater, in the meantime, evolved from a mediocre anthology of the Broadway stage into "the most important dramatic show in radio."[11] Beginning on October 14, 1934, as a Sunday afternoon series, it focused on New York theatrical productions with an occasional inclusion from the West Coast. It would never have achieved the distinction to which it ascended, however, had it continued very long in that vein. With ratings falling, talent fading and the show facing quick extinction, it was totally revamped in late spring 1936 and its venue shifted to Hollywood. There it originated live, expensively produced adaptations of many of filmdom's major commercial motion picture releases.

On most occasions these ventures would feature original theatrical stars playing in the roles that may have made them famous, thus highlighting already luminous careers. If an actor weren't available, a substitute—often of equal fame—would accept a part. Introduced by hosts John Anthony (1934–35), Cecil B. DeMille (1936–45), William Keighley (1945–52) and Irving Cummings (1952–55), the show drew a large studio audience every week. Announcers included Melville Ruick, John Milton Kennedy and Ken Carpenter.

Hailed by one wag as "the most important dramatic show in radio," *The Lux Radio Theater* offered one-hour adaptations of premier Hollywood films during most of the series' long run (1934–55). Screen actors Charles Farrell and Janet Gaynor star in a recreation of *Seventh Heaven* on the Hollywood sound stage before a live audience. *Photofest.*

Lever Brothers underwrote the performances throughout a 21-year run on behalf of Lux toilet soap, "the beauty soap of Hollywood's most glamorous women." While the series was broadcast on three different networks before it finally left the air on June 7, 1955, the years from 1936 to 1954, in which it maintained a lock on the 9 o'clock hour on Monday night on CBS, easily constituted its heyday. During this period the show's fortunes shifted, its ratings increased, everybody wanted to be in its live audience, and major film stars and production houses jockeyed for the exposure to be gained on *The Lux Radio Theater*.

In addition to the film stars broadcasting from the Music Box Theatre on Hollywood Boulevard (later the Vine Street and Huntington Hartford Theaters and finally the Doolittle), the cast and crew typically included 50 members plus a 25-piece orchestra. The stars (usually two or three of them) fetched fees of $5,000 each while the host commanded $2,000 weekly. Supporting actors normally earned $133 weekly, better wages than in any other radio show in Hollywood, one report noted.[12] Lever Brothers dispensed $20,000 or more per show, yet obviously saw positive results from its investment in strong sales of soap bars "just like nine out of ten film actresses use."

The success enjoyed by *The Lux Radio Theater* profoundly shaped the future of broadcasting in America, too. When the floundering series shifted its locale and emphasis from Broadway to Hollywood, the move precipitated a wholesale exodus of radio production to the West Coast. The networks reasoned that they would be close to the film colony's glamour and name recognition there. With some having taken adversarial positions earlier, the stars were now cooperating with radio, many for the first time. Soon the most revered programs in the medium originated from the Hollywood network studios. The prospects were bright. A single series had impacted its industry, making it "the most important dramatic show in radio"—for more reasons than one.

Radio comedy's popularity across the years, averred philosopher Fred MacDonald, could be attributed to two conditions: the exciting and humorous personalities of the comedians themselves and a therapeutic necessity for laughter.[13] These comics were distinctive characters who acquired a rapport with their audiences, each broadcast attempting to renew that relationship. While they had scrupulously rehearsed their scripts, their individual wit, warmth, spontaneity and identification with their audiences made them champions of their profession. They achieved their preeminence, MacDonald suggested, "because they had good material, they knew how to tell a joke, and above all, they were funny individuals."[14]

Radio comedy prospered because people needed to laugh, too. "In the world of increasing stress and complexity that has characterized the United States in the twentieth century, humor exercises a cathartic, healthful value as it has allowed harried people for a short while to laugh away personal tensions," noted MacDonald. "In general, radio enjoyed its greatest popularity during a time of unprecedented uncertainty within the nation."[15] Several momentous forces at work in America during radio's golden age were cited: wars, economic collapse, urbanization, increased competitiveness, technological displacement, and religious reevaluation.

A 1946 survey revealed that comedy shows were the most popular form of radio entertainment programming then with 59 percent of listeners claiming humor as their preferred evening diversion. In such an environment, comedians became the most acclaimed entertainers in broadcasting.

While radio comedy didn't fade away during the 1950s, it "ceased to be relevant to American society."[16] Many reasons have been given in an attempt to explain its decline on the air. Some believed there was a lack of new talent while others suggested that it was repetitive and had become dull. It was television, however, that was the factor undermining it most.

A pair of America's greatly beloved wits brought their extended radio runs to an end in the spring of 1955. Bob Hope and Jack Benny, who tickled the nation's funnybone for more than two decades, had—with at least some trepidation—entered television with their heretofore audio buffoonery a few years earlier: Benny in 1950, Hope in 1949. Both persisted in radio, however, the medium that had established them with millions of devoted allies. For decades this duo attracted audiences that could be envied by all but an elite handful of radio comics including Fred Allen, Edgar Bergen and Charlie McCarthy, Fibber McGee and Molly, and Red Skelton, and a few favored crooners—Bing Crosby certainly comes to mind.

In 1942-43 Hope's show won an almost unbelievable 40.9 rating. Five seasons earlier Benny's popularity had soared, allowing him to broadcast on dual nights every week while reaching a combined high of 44.8. For 20 seasons he destroyed his competition with double-digit figures. But despite such heady success, by the early 1950s many sound

The most beloved comic of radio broadcasting—whose career is still tracked by legions of admirers—was Jack Benny. His mock collapse at the violin was one of his show's long-running gags; he confounded his violin teacher while providing nonstop hilarity for his audience. Ultimately Benny (shown) lasted an unprecedented 33 years in dual mediums. *Photofest.*

lovers began drifting elsewhere, leaving former idols to fend for themselves, and those fading radio stars feeling like guests of honor at a wake.

Benny could well be voted the most beloved comedian of the golden age to have stood before a microphone. The unbridled passion some Americans still harbor for him is little short of monumental. Surprisingly, many weren't even born by the time of their hero's death in 1974. A new generation is now laughing tumultuously at Benny's antics by listening to audiotapes or watching videos of the comedian's remarkable 33 years in broadcasting.

For 23 of those years—all but the first two at 7 o'clock on Sunday night—a vast cross-section of the nation's citizens chortled over his weekly half-hour routine. (The same timeslot was reserved for him on three competing networks: "one of the few constants we could rely on in a rapidly changing world," noted Milt Josefsberg, a Benny writer.[17]) For 15 years—five of them overlapping his radio era—Benny appeared on TV. The legacy he left in dual mediums is one unequaled in the annals of comedy broadcasting.

A native of Waukegan, Illinois, Benny was born on Valentine's Day in 1894. He began his journey into show business at the age of six when his father presented him with a fiddle. While becoming a maestro of the instrument, he used it effectively as a foil in sketches on his program, to the great consternation of a frustrated violin teacher. His "ineptness" became one of a series of long-running gags that his audiences adored.

In the 1920s Benny played the vaudeville circuits. As a Broadway headliner in 1932, he was invited by journalist Ed Sullivan to an interview on Sullivan's quarter-hour radio show. Benny was so refreshingly funny that he was immediately offered his own show. *The Canada Dry Program*, his initial radio effort, debuted on May 2, 1932, on NBC's Blue network. He followed it by headlining *The Chevrolet Program*, *The General Tire Show*, *The Jell-O Program*, *The Grape Nuts and Grape Nuts Flakes Program* and *The Lucky Strike Program*. Benny's shows, while popularly and collectively referred to by listeners as *The Jack Benny Program*, invariably reflected the names of his sponsors.

Following the infamous 1948–49 talent raids on NBC's stable of comics by CBS chairman William S. Paley, Benny moved to CBS on January 2, 1949. (One should recall that Paley's raids netted for CBS such top-flight figures as Amos 'n' Andy, Bing Crosby, Red Skelton and more; it made that web the one to beat in TV's embryonic era. Unquestionably, however, "The biggest prize of all was Jack Benny," wrote a radio critic. "He had been at the top of his profession for so long that he was a true statesman, respected everywhere."[18])

Dwindling audiences finally possessed CBS to pull the plug on the taped radiocast of the durable Benny comedy series, effective with the May 22, 1955, airing. Chronicler Anthony Slide noted that it was the 924th radio broadcast. Following in the footsteps of a contemporary, Bob Hope, Benny's last gasp on radio hadn't yet been heard, however: from October 28, 1956, through June 22, 1958, CBS repeated *The Best of Benny* in his hallowed Sundays at seven half-hour.

Throughout much of the run the cast included actress Mary Livingstone (who in real life was Mrs. Jack Benny), along with Irish tenor Dennis Day, portly announcer Don Wilson, Benny's valet Rochester (played by actor Eddie Anderson), mythically "inebriated" bandleader Phil Harris, and comical linguist Mel Blanc.

Benny didn't require of his writers that he be given all of the funny lines; the ensemble he gathered onstage was allowed to shine instead of playing stooges who merely rotated around a single individual. Years later a Benny wordsmith, George Balzer, recalled: "He had complete respect for everybody.... He was easy to work with, always ready to listen and never insisted on doing anything if there was someone who didn't feel it was right."[19]

Sketches might involve something as simple as visiting Benny's neighbors, the Ronald Colmans, who in the scripts held halting disdain for him; or going to a department store to return a gift. The plots were seldom elaborate or complicated; the interaction of the cast along with a series of running gags made them intensely hilarious. Benny was played as the most miserly human being who ever lived—a factor interwoven into virtually every show. (In real life he was the antithesis of this characterization, reportedly one of the most munificent individuals in the industry. "In real life he wasn't cheap, not ever in any way, shape or form!" his daughter attested. "I can't imagine a man more generous and thoughtful than my father."[20]) He also clung to the age of 39, seldom revealing his true years beyond that one.

The president of the International Jack Benny Fan Club, Laura Leff of San Francisco, affirms that the simplest, yet most complete, description of the comedian is probably the one that adorns his grave: he was "a gentle man."

Benny was slow to embrace TV. In 1946, four years before he went on the video air with his own show and while wetting his feet in a 45-minute tube special, he informed a reporter: "Hold off television! Science be damned! Long live radio!"[21] For years he was guarded about the visual medium; some critics thought he was seldom comfortable in it and frequently cited references to his fondness for radio.

Radio's most popular comic in history, Benny clearly understood TV for what it was:

> By my second year in television I saw the camera was a man-eating monster. It gave a performer a close-up exposure that week after week threatened his existence as an interesting entertainer. I don't care who you are. Finally, you'll get on people's nerves if they get too much of you. I don't care how wonderful or handsome or brilliant or charming you are—if the public gets too much of you, they'll be bored. Given that kind of magnification combined with intimacy that's characteristic of television, the essence of a comedian's art becomes inevitably stale. The audience gets to know you inside and outside. Your tone of voice, your gestures, and your little tricks, the rhythm of your delivery, your way of reacting to another performer's moves, your facial mannerisms—all of these things, so exciting to an audience when you are a novelty, soon become tedious and flat.[22]

With a quarter-century to his credit in radio, Benny believed people loved him in a different way. "I came at them gently—quietly, through their ears. I suggested subtle images to them, picture jokes. I was like a friendly uncle, a slightly eccentric, mad uncle—now [with 15 years in TV] I became something too much. The television camera is like a magnifying glass and you can't enjoy looking at anything blown up for too long."[23]

One radio historiographer conceded:

> It wasn't that Benny was bad on TV, he just wasn't as purely or as quintessentially Jack Benny. His movie parodies tended to rely on costumes, often with Benny in a dress or some other outlandish, unBennyesque getup; he had a latent zany streak that he indulged on TV. Whenever Benny appeared in a make-believe guise ... he was never as funny, but audiences by then laughed because it was Benny....[24]

From the video beginnings the media critics claimed Benny offered little visual appeal. Said a biographer: "It contrasted with the magic of radio listening when Benny could create an imaginative show of an inestimable appeal."[25]

Despite that, Benny (who doubtlessly was the *quintessential* comedian of all time!), outlasted all of his radio comedy peers except one—Edgar Bergen, whose show aired for a year beyond Benny's, and all but one of his TV contemporaries, Lucille Ball. Benny was distinctive even after he was gone!

A duo of beloved humor series, including one with the last major comedian still on radio in a strikingly atypical sitcom, said their farewells in 1956 after long runs.

The Edgar Bergen and Charlie McCarthy Show featured ventriloquist Bergen playing himself and impersonating an irrepressibly mischievous wooden dummy with whom Americans of all ages fell in love. McCarthy was decked out in top hat and tails and carried a monocle. The inseparable twosome initially appeared on December 17, 1936, as guests on Rudy Vallee's *Royal Gelatin Hour*. By the following spring Vallee's sponsor (Standard Brands) had signed Bergen and McCarthy for their own half-hour show. They were around almost continuously until time finally caught up with them on July 1, 1956.

Another "couple" that left the security of "regular" employ in 1956 made their first radio appearance on a Chicago station in 1924. Jim and Marian Jordan—through almost a score of reincarnations—finally evolved into their most familiar characterizations, *Fibber McGee and Molly*. They occupied permanent NBC timeslots from April 16, 1935,

The residents of 79 Wistful Vista kept the laughs coming as their neighbors dropped in on them in *Fibber McGee and Molly* each week, often creating uproarious mirth with simple exchanges. Jim and Marian Jordan (shown), whose professional careers spanned nearly four decades, portrayed the twosome. Their show held a single half-hour NBC timeslot for 21 years. *Photofest.*

through March 23, 1956. Beyond that, from June 1, 1957 to September 6, 1959, their amusing vignettes (cleverly branded "Just Molly and Me") were broadcast five times each weekend on *Monitor*.

The Jordans were natives of Peoria, Illinois, who drifted into radio after a stint in vaudeville. This married couple's first permanent work in the new medium was in singing commercials, a mission acquired in 1925. A couple of years later they performed as *The Smith Family* on Chicago's WENR, a sort of Caucasian answer to *Amos 'n' Andy*. In 1931 they met Don Quinn, an ex-cartoonist who was then writing radio scripts. The trio collaborated on *Smackouts*, a sketch about a grocer "smackout" of everything. Though their success was limited in that venture, their next one—in which Quinn created the characters of Fibber McGee and Molly—brought them fame and fortune that lasted a lifetime. "Jim and Marion [sic] Jordan were not exactly identical to Fibber McGee and Molly," noted a chronicler of the medium, "but the line that separated them was thin and wavering. It was Don Quinn who molded the Jordans into the McGees with his masterful scripts."[26]

In one sense the McGee show wasn't a sitcom at all. Rather, action evolved from the slightest provocation, often beginning in their home at 79 Wistful Vista and sometimes never leaving it. The couple might be poring over a photo album or trying to decide how to stop a leak in the kitchen sink. On one occasion McGee spent the half-hour laboring over a manual typewriter, employing the hunt-and-peck system while writing Hollywood's next smashing spectacle for movie-goers: "The Story of the Typewriter."

His outrageous fabrications for many listeners called to mind a daytime counterpart, crackpot inventor Lorenzo Jones, whose hairbrained concoctions seemed just as delusional to matinee audiences. "Behind every great man there stands a woman" someone said. For these two eccentrics there were, fortunately, Molly McGee and Belle Jones, whose feet were planted solidly on terra firma. They could, after all, interject a measure of reality and stability into the far-fetched schemes that their mates consistently dreamed up.

Whatever the McGee shows' premise for a given week, listeners could be certain that a parade of townsfolk would ring the doorbell at 79 Wistful Vista. Adding to the story line, each visitor recounted his or her own opinions or added disquieting tales. At varying times "regulars" who could be anticipated to put in a three-minute exchange with Fibber and Molly included domestic helper Beulah (who soon spun off into her own series), elitist Mrs. Millicent Carstairs, Greek restaurateur Nick Depopoulous, erudite and cantankerous rival Doc Gamble, windy neighbor Throckmorton P. Gildersleeve (who also spun off into his own series), vote solicitor Mayor LaTrivia, wise-cracking Mr. Old Timer ("That's funny, Johnny, but that ain't the way I 'heered' it ... one feller sez tu th' other feller, sez..."), inquisitive tow-headed Teeny ("Hi mister!, Hi mister!, Hi!"), highbrow Mrs. Abigal Uppington, announcer Harlow Wilcox as himself (referred to as "Waxy" by McGee because their conversations invariably dissolved into commercials for longtime sponsor Johnson's Wax products), weather authority Foggy Williams and henpecked husband and bird-watcher Wallace Wimple ("Hello folks").

Each one was highly predictable and many of the show's running gags were based on that. Doc Gamble never missed an opportunity to trade barbs with McGee on *any* topic; the two seldom expressed a civil thought while addressing one another. Wallace Wimple consistently thought up ways to get something over on his "big old fat wife Sweetieface" without being put in the doghouse for his indiscretions. Finally, Teeny, the whiny adolescent from next door, annoyed McGee with her constant questions when he was occupied in deep thoughts elsewhere.

The largest guffaw getter of the series, however, occurred when someone opened the closet door at the McGee home each week. Everything it held back fell to the floor with about a 12-second bong-bang-boink-thud and finally a tingle at the end. The live studio audience, anticipating it, dissolved into raucous laughter as soon as somebody placed a hand on that doorknob. By the time the gag ended, even though it happened weekly for more than a decade, the studio had erupted into pandemonium. McGee often muttered: "One of these days I've got to get that thing cleaned up!" He never did, and the listeners at home and in the studio loved it.

Fibber McGee and Molly, which began in 1935, was an indispensable part of NBC's primetime roster, remaining there through June 30, 1953. It maintained a lock on the 9:30 P.M. half-hour on Tuesdays for more than 15 years. From October 5, 1953, through March 23, 1956, the show aired in quarter-hour segments every weekday morning. Then the McGees continued their witty exchanges on *Monitor* for a couple of years beyond that, until Marian Jordan became too ill to continue. They expected to sign for three more years when Marian died on April 7,

1961. Jim Jordan, who later remarried, lived in semiseclusion there-after, and died at 91 on April 1, 1988. It was appropriately April Fool's Day.

Their antics couldn't have been easily transferred to television, of course. Aside from the closet door escapade, few of their routines were adaptable to a visual medium. In 1949 Jordan told a reporter: "We pio-neered in radio, but we aren't as ambitious as we were 25 years ago, so we'd rather sit back for a while and let the young blood do the ground-work."[27] For decades they were comfortable in an aural setting. They came along during a slower pace when people simply wanted a good laugh at the end of a day of labor and cares. While the show was highly conventional, Americans got a kick out of it for more than 20 years.

Of four salient teenage situation comedies—*The Aldrich Family* (1939–53), *Archie Andrews* (1943–53), *A Date with Judy* (1941–50) and *Meet Corliss Archer* (1943–56)—all had disappeared by 1953 except *Archer*, which drew the genre's last laugh. A generation of adolescents had grown up with those four and their familiar figures and pretense.

The departure of *Archer* signaled the end of radio family crises in which anxiety-laden, pimple-faced central characters dealt with the pecu-liarities of being young. All of it was exaggerated, of course—nobody's family acted like that in real life—yet it provided models that emulated many of the experiences that teenagers were expected to encounter. Given that perspective, the teen comedies offered a rewarding, endur-ing contribution that legions of listeners thrived on.

Radio comedy, for nearly three decades a fundamental of mass entertainment, lost its meaning to a culture that was progressively becoming TV-obsessed. As radio inescapably revisited its original frame-work of talk and music, its role as a source for widespread humor dis-appeared. Yet the heritage it left is noteworthy. The following assessment appears to capture the strategic legacy of broadcast comedy:

> Comedians had revived radio in the early 1930s, and in the process made it one of the most effective antidotes to mass despair and the Depression.... While it was reassuring to millions that most of the suc-cessful comics of television in the 1950s had their roots deep in the his-tory of broadcasting, it was disappointing to some that the imaginative realm of humor created by radio was gone. Radio comedy had served its audiences faithfully as companion, advisor, model, and entertainer. Its passing into irrelevance in the 1950s signaled the end of a distinct era in the history of American civilization.[28]

A quartet of America's favorite radio sleuths who had spellbound millions with their deductive ingenuity and who premiered at least a dozen years earlier faded from the airwaves in 1955—three of them within the same week, as CBS sought to apply a tourniquet to its hemorrhaging listenership. *Mr. Keen, Tracer of Lost Persons*; *Mr. and Mrs. North*; and *Casey, Crime Photographer* departed the week of April 18. Over at Mutual *Nick Carter, Master Detective* was gone by the end of summer.

All four aired from New York and provided golden opportunities for some of the East Coast's most seasoned radio actors. It was not uncommon to hear familiar voices as supporting players every week on any of these programs. Sometimes an actor might appear on multiple series during the same week. That's how talented thespians earned their livelihoods, meeting qualifying standards and expectations of the industry and—as a result—plying their craft frequently. Some turned their abilities into a comfortable living. Those who weren't successful or determined were soon looking elsewhere.

Mr. Keen, Tracer of Lost Persons, easily the most durable and perhaps the best remembered of the four, found his last cold-blooded killer on April 19, 1955. The "kindly old investigator" was one of the longest-running gumshoes in broadcast history, debuting on the Blue network on October 12, 1937. The series was launched as a thrice-weekly quarter-hour serial. From its start, Keen conducted his most "widely celebrated missing persons cases." That description remained throughout the long run even though its focus shifted a half-dozen years later. (The haunting refrain of "Someday I'll Find You" persisted as the show's theme even after the premise was significantly altered.)

Instead of searching for people who disappeared from their homes, families and jobs—intentionally or otherwise—Keen searched for murderers who had finished off a relative, a former lover, a business associate, or an acquaintance who could make trouble for the culprit. These half-hour tales on CBS, beginning Thursday night, December 2, 1943, opened with a brief vignette during which the murder of the week was committed. Someone close to the victim subsequently visited Keen's office to beg for his help in solving the homicide. Keen's interview with several potential suspects followed. At the end, he unraveled the mystery with minimal logic, often through coincidence, slips of the tongue, and twists of fate. The simplest clue might expose a killer. Surprisingly, such reasoning appeared well beyond the reach of the deductive powers of professionally trained law-enforcement officers.

"Saints preserve us, Mr. Keen. It's a weapon!" observes partner Mike Clancy, played by James Kelly (right), to Mr. Keen in *Mr. Keen, Tracer of Lost Persons.* Each week, Philip Clarke, cast as Keen in this 1950s photograph, took from his files "one of his most widely celebrated missing persons cases," then tracked down a cold-blooded killer, always exposing him at the close. *Photofest.*

Keen performed his work alongside a bumbling colleague, Mike Clancy, whose Irish brogue quickly separated him from other members of the cast. At least weekly this thick-headed buffoon made some startling revelation that astonished only him, seldom the audience. In his most telling line, he'd allow: "Saints preserve us, Mr. Keen! He's got a gun!"

Mr. Keen—who appeared to have been born without a first name—could break all the rules that everyone else was subject to in a murder investigation:

(1) He visited crime scenes that should have been cordoned off from all but the police, examined objects there with disregard for possible fingerprints, and even removed articles at will from the scene.

(2) He didn't have to report conversations with suspects and any knowledge he'd gained to investigative authorities.

(3) He bypassed search warrants, forcing illegal entry into victims' or suspects' homes or businesses while in search of clues that the police might have overlooked.

(4) In the end, he arrested those he fingered as killers, notwithstanding the fact that he had no power to do so. "We usually work along with the police" was the prime justification given to anyone inquiring of Keen and Clancy's involvement in a murder case.

Bennett Kilpack played the tracer of lost persons for most of the run. Philip Clarke succeeded him and near the series' conclusion was followed by Arthur Hughes, who was then simultaneously completing a 23-year stint in the title role of *Just Plain Bill*. Jimmy Kelly was the notorious bull in a china shop, Mike Clancy. James Fleming and Larry Elliott were the drama's durable announcers, often speaking on behalf of the Whitehall Pharmacal Company, a division of American Home Products Corporation (for Anacin pain reliever, Kolynos toothpaste and "many other fine, dependable pharmaceutical products"). Dialoguist Lawrence Klee penned most of the later scripts.

A five-night-a-week serialized version ran at 10 o'clock on CBS from May 24, 1954, through January 14, 1955. CBS again aired the drama in a half-hour self-contained format at 8:30 P.M. Tuesdays in its final weeks on the air.

This detective melodrama produced by Frank and Anne Hummert, the moguls of matinee, who also created *Just Plain Bill*, maintained a fascinating allure that kept millions of listeners coming back for more. Perhaps it was the intrigue of trying to guess which of a handful of suspects had the superior motive and opportunity for eliminating the victim and who was telling the truth. It might have been the simplicity of Clancy's character, of course, in which he failed to "get" the obvious, inquiring: "Mr. Keen, do you mean...?" The "boss" (Clancy's appellation for Keen) would laboriously point out what everyone else invariably knew. Or possibly the real draw was the benevolent charm and soft persuasion of the "kindly old investigator" himself. It never really mattered. Armchair detectives thrilled to such contrived inquisitions for

18 years. It was a sad day in Sleuthville when this whodunit vanished forever.

When CBS completed its detective house cleaning in the spring of 1955—still quite obviously committed to radio drama and attempting to sustain an audience for it while trimming the talent and production costs—it traded some of its longstanding private eyes for others, like *Yours Truly, Johnny Dollar*. The show was then a quarter-hour serialized narrative that was inserted into the schedule five nights a week.

Dollar was a respected member of the aural gumshoe coterie, having debuted in 1948. CBS hoped that—by programming it on a nightly basis—just maybe it would supplant those negative pangs the die-hard fans would experience in the departures of *Keen*, the *Norths* and *Casey*. It must have worked: the *Dollar* drama hung on to September 1962 (by then in closed-ended, half-hour episodes), still a couple of years beyond the traditionally accepted demise of the golden days. As such, it was to be one of the final pair of radio mysteries to leave the air (the other, *Suspense*). "Amazing that a show with little budget and only brief periods of sponsorship could keep returning and actually be the final broadcast of the old era," a radio critic said.[29]

The radio documentary proliferated during the 1950s, realizing serious success as a program model. The verisimilitude experienced by the form may be directly attributed to developing uses and applications of tape recording. Even as the medium was rapidly ebbing from the commanding influence it enjoyed only a few years earlier, audiences remained for whom radio continued to be a primary means of information and entertainment. While the networks introduced several new anthologies each year of the decade, a couple of those debuting in 1955 had more than passing influence on their listeners: NBC's *Biography in Sound*, profiling contemporary greats in the words and voices of friends and acquaintances, and *X-Minus One*, a science fiction fantasy (introduced a few years earlier under another title). As documentaries went, they could be considered the cream of the crop that year and any year.

With its roots dating to 1949, *Biography in Sound* was the result of NBC journalist Joseph O. Meyers launching a tape library for the network. His first recorded bit: a statement by prize-winning boxer Joe Louis that he was giving up his career. Louis's piece became one of more than 150,000 declarations that Meyers would capture on tape and include in a storehouse of historic trivia he was acquiring. In time, having been indexed, this vast collection could be readily retrieved. The project was hailed not only by NBC staffers but also beyond that network's confines.

Such recognition surfaced when Meyers was requested to create a documentary on Winston Churchill to coincide with the British prime minister's 80th birthday on November 30, 1954. Meyers began the biography drawing upon file clips of Churchill's voice. But that was only the beginning. To it he supplied personal observations by friends, associates and adversaries of the great statesman. To sound effects and music he added anecdotes by American book publisher Bennett Cerf. Meanwhile Lynn Fontanne and Sir Laurence Olivier offered some British poetry.

This one-time feature was so well received by the public that a hue and cry went up for similar exploits in the future. Meyers answered a month later with a memoir on the life of American novelist and short-story author Ernest Hemingway. He subsequently provided another in January 1955 on Gertrude Lawrence. By then his experiment had gained such a determined following that the network provided a weekly time-slot for it. Meyers' hour-long anthology debuted on Sunday, February 20. It shifted variously between days and time periods before its cancellation three years later. It was most prominently aired as a Tuesday night entry on NBC's weekly agenda.

In each of the shows the famous were profiled in a series of sketches followed by interviews of people associated with the subjects. It was essentially the format that Meyers had adopted from the start. He continued throughout the run as its producer. Music was added by the Leith Stevens Orchestra.

A number of these programs have been preserved on tape. Members of vintage radio alliances often have access to them through their club lending libraries, and the tapes are also available for public consumption through multiple old time radio dealers. One source lists as many as 33 of the shows in current circulation. Even the passing of time has diminished very little of the series' interest and meaning.

The documentary subjects, in addition to those named earlier, include personalities such as Franklin P. Adams, Leo Durocher, F. Scott Fitzgerald, George Gershwin, Sinclair Lewis, Connie Mack, and Carl Sandburg.

The popular consumer magazine *Radio Life* cited Meyers' contributions not only to history but to his industry, claiming that "He had done the impossible: turned people's attention once more to radio." It was a thoughtful suggestion and there was some truth in it. Listeners were discovering programming on their radios that they simply could-n't find anywhere else. Tuning in *to Biography in Sound* was one of the constructive, upbeat things that large numbers did for themselves dur-ing the medium's days in decline.

In discussing the science fiction thriller *X-Minus One*, a media his-torian narrowed audible theater's field remarkably by stating: "The most interesting dramatic radio of the 1955 season was produced by two genre series, *Gunsmoke*, a western, and this space opera." (*Gunsmoke*, intro-duced in 1952, is profiled in the preceding chapter.) Claiming *X-Minus One* "blew through NBC like a breath of fresh air,"[30] the veteran observer suggested that it offered "some of the most creative melodrama the medium had yet heard."[31]

An updated version of *Dimension X*, radio's premier adult science fiction series, *X-Minus One* quickly exceeded the rave reviews earned by its predecessor. (Again see the preceding chapter.) *X-Minus One* left the air on January 9, 1958. But never say die. Fifteen years later, on June 24, 1973, long after the twilight passed for radio's golden age, these tran-scribed tales reappeared on NBC. That web offered the show on a trial basis to determine if a contemporary market existed for radio drama.

Regrettably the network made a colossal mistake in scheduling, offering it with little consistency or notice about air dates: *X-Minus One* was broadcast monthly, sometimes on Sunday evenings, sometimes on Saturday evenings. Even its most rabid fans had difficulty locating it on local outlets. Listeners had to contend with news bites, sporting events and other programming options. When announcer Fred Collins encouraged audiences to register their loyalty by writing to the network, few responded. The experimental test was at last called off on March 22, 1975.

Several other anthologies appearing in this period—*The NBC Radio Theater* (1955–56, 1959–60), *NBC Star Playhouse* (1953–54), *The Philco Radio Playhouse* (1953–54) and *Your Radio Theater* (1955–56) among them—indicated that if listeners weren't all that interested, the indus-try certainly was. These shows often "filled in the gaps" where traditional programming (comedies, quizzes, mysteries) faltered and disappeared.

As more and more comedians and other series left radio, a pro-liferation of lofty projects allowed the medium to appeal to greater num-bers of intellectuals. It was an interesting twist on the past when—with the exception of a few highbrow musical offerings and an occasional show like *Information Please*—most programming was aimed at more "middle of the road" tastes. In some ways it seemed that sagacity was finally getting its due, even as mainstream audiences went elsewhere. Those seeking a higher level of mental satisfaction were fortunate to find that radio had plenty to offer. It was something that really couldn't be said of television's typical fare in the 1950s.

The introduction of the transistor portable radio, coupled with more plentiful and affordable receivers installed in means of transportation, opened new frontiers for aural broadcasting. The number of automobiles equipped with radios in America increased by 10 million in the years between 1953 and 1957, to a total of 35 million vehicles, nearly 65 percent of all those on the road. For the very first time radio had become, in the 1950s, a truly mobile medium for many listeners.

As radio prices decreased, the number of sets per household rose. Simplified internal circuitry allowed small table-model receivers to sell for $15 or less. By the mid–1950s millions of American homes were equipped with multiple sets in bedrooms and kitchens, basements and garages, in addition to the larger sets that had occupied living rooms for many years. Fans could hear their favorite programs in virtually every corner of their domiciles.

Shows were available at work and at locales where people spent their leisure hours—playgrounds and ballparks, campsites, beaches, resorts and nearly everywhere else, even while they were in transit to and from these places. Indeed, people were, for the very first time, becoming accustomed to tuning in to the sensations of sound wherever they might be.

What was the experience of people living in rural America with electronic media during this epoch? Vintage radio collector Ted Kneebone, a South Dakotan, remembers that—by the mid–1950s—TV was still "sort of a novelty." The three major television networks shared a single channel in Sioux Falls, the state's largest city, though other channels were available "if you didn't mind snow!" Yet the good programs "were still on radio only," he maintained. Kneebone's assessment of how one family in the heartland tuned to aural broadcasts at the time is representative:

> The kind of radio we listened to was somewhat different. The big consoles were still with us, but many rooms in a typical home had table model radios. And if you didn't want to hear what mom and dad were listening to, you could go into your bedroom and listen to your own

radio. Portables were getting more common. Transistors made the sets smaller and easier to carry around. AM was our only kind of radio. FM didn't get to South Dakota until some time in the 1970s. There was at least one radio-phonograph in the house.[32]

Such portability encouraged new forms of programming to complement the more active lifestyles of people on the go. One theorist also observed it had become obvious by then that "if radio networks were to stay in business they would have to adjust to the needs of the stations."[33] Perceiving such changes, NBC leaped ahead of the competition in providing appropriate responses to the new demands and opportunities. It bode well for NBC in particular and radio in general, and was a reminder to listeners that it could perform certain things a visual medium couldn't do well.

As early as 1953 the network created a couple of series that favorably impacted the shifting patterns in American listening tastes—seeking to satisfy the tune-in, tune-out listening patterns of modern radio audiences. Beginning with four hours on Saturday afternoon (from 2 until 6 P.M.) and gradually increasing to six hours that day (10:30 A.M. to 12 noon and 1:30 to 6 P.M.) NBC offered its audience *The Road Show*. A stable of recognized broadcast talent presided over it, including names like Bill Cullen and Dave Garroway.

The Road Show provided music, snippets of comedy and drama, interviews, advice, news and games. A prominent feature focused on "Mr. Safety," an unidentified motorist who drove an unmarked car on the nation's highways. Each Saturday he sought out good drivers who were obeying the local traffic laws. On discovering one, he loaded that individual up with valuable prizes while the show was on the air. The object was an incentive for other drivers to remain alert as "Mr. Safety" might be in their own neighborhoods next.

On Sundays, initially at 4 P.M. and by 1954 at 3 P.M., NBC offered its listeners a similar two-hour marathon called *Weekend*. Sound bites, music and other vignettes typical of *The Road Show* were presented.

Perhaps as a result of NBC's experiment with the magazine format in these series, on October 10, 1954, CBS introduced *Sunday Afternoon*, obviously direct competition for *Weekend*. CBS's entry aired from 4:05 to 5 o'clock and 5:05 to 6 o'clock. Its thrust, however, was never as inclusive as that of *Weekend* with its multiple features; it focused almost entirely on live and recorded music. The program was an outgrowth of a 1950s summer-only CBS series, *On a Sunday Afternoon*. It featured Washington, D.C., disk jockey Eddie Gallagher playing classical recordings and show tunes. CBS's "magazine" entry could be labeled little more than a distant cousin of the new program form, though—a sort of restrained acknowledgment of it by the network. CBS had made a firm commitment to continue its established radio schedule for as long as possible, and *Sunday Afternoon* lasted two years, until November 4, 1956.

Unequivocally, the *greatest single development* in radio in the 1950s was NBC's innovative potpourri titled *Monitor*. Without question this omnibus of news and features rejuvenated a decaying medium by infusing it with energized animation up to 40 hours every weekend. Its significance could be seen in the transfer of millions of TV watchers to radio listeners as people found a source of audible interest and pleasure.

The brainchild of NBC president Sylvester L. (Pat) Weaver (1953–55), the architect of his network's successful *Today*, *Tonight* and *Home* TV series early on, *Monitor* was the ultimate in flexible programming. "Not a program but a continuous service format," Jim Fleming, the show's executive producer, cautioned local affiliates shortly before launch in midyear 1955. Fleming insisted it was to be "a complete departure from programming of the past."[34]

From the beginning, most of broadcasting had adhered to a prevailing pattern of set time periods that was now to be eliminated. *Monitor*, instead, would cover sporting events, rocket liftoffs, presidential announcements, world tragedies and entertainment specials "as long as necessary" and whenever necessary. It had an ingenious suppleness that brought about totally new ways of thinking and performing.

Monitor zealot Weaver shared his dreams for the new radio service with the network's affiliates a few weeks before its start date:

> You have a form now that merely says that from our communications center anything of interest or that can be made of interest to the people we'll bring to the people and in a form that has a vignette feel to it. In other words, if you don't like what's announced and what is going to play you know roughly what time it will take and you can come back.... Essentially we can once again have the whole American public know that any time in the weekend they need not be alone and they don't have to sit there looking at the television set: they can turn this service on and in will come the flow. It will be like having a personal editor who would go out and listen to everything, read everything, know everything and

Sylvester L. (Pat) Weaver (shown) was president of NBC in the mid–1950s and was largely responsible for introducing *Monitor*, the network's 40-hour weekend omnibus listening service that aired from 1955 to 1975. Weaver's ingenuity had earlier resulted in NBC-TV's popular *Today*, *Tonight*, and *Home* shows, concepts that continue to endure a half-century later. *Photofest*.

then be there as your little tame cap-and-bells jester with the whole range of moods telling you the very best of everything that's happening. You certainly can't ask us to do much more than that.... For the first time radio really looks at the whole field with no rules. The only rule is: is it interesting?; is it absorbing?; is it amusing? Will people say: "Did you hear that?"... The minute they say that we're in business.... The minute they say that we've got the big audience back and we're really rolling.... This show will have more people on it and more important people saying things of high interest and repeatable value than probably anything that has ever been attempted. It will even be able to top the original *Today* plans because of the fact tape on radio is perfect and film on television isn't—certainly isn't yet—with the result that we can do things in this show that we certainly couldn't on TV.[35]

Was Weaver pumped up or what?

Monitor premiered on June 12, 1955. It was impressive. (One reviewer called it "the ghost of radio-to-come," suggesting *Monitor* was radio's "final extravagant effort."[36]) Mixing news, features, music, comedy, advice, interviews and so forth, it provided programming for 40 hours over the weekend—from Saturday mornings through Sunday nights at its start, later beginning on Friday evenings. Remote pick-ups became a crucial part of the mix. Several traditional series such as *Meet the Press* and *The National Radio Pulpit* were integrated into the agenda but most of the material was new.

Some of the highlights included short improvisations by such well-

Dave Garroway was one of the first communicators, or hosts, "going places and doing things" on NBC's weekend marathon radio serivce, *Monitor*. He is flanked by some talent who appeared frequently at the series' start: (l–r) announcer Frank Gallop, melody girl Lorna Lynn, Garroway, "Miss Monitor" Tedi Thurman, and announcer Ben Grauer. *Photofest.*

known radio comedians as Bob and Ray, Goodman and Jane Ace, Fibber McGee and Molly, Bob Hope, Phyllis Diller, Henry Morgan, Mike Nichols and Elaine May. (McGee and Molly, among the more prolific, prepared 109 such spots.) Marlene Dietrich offered beauty tips while a vast number of professional gardeners shared their expertise with interviewers like Arlene Francis and others. *Monitor* was a true magazine cradled in the news and documentary styles that had origins in the 1940s.

The weekend radio service interviewed newsmakers and celebrities, aired live horse races from far-flung places, provided Broadway and movie production vignettes and even offered taped segments from popular TV shows. Frequently, the NBC orchestra and chorus would cut in with brief promotional refrains. One went like this:

> *Don't move, just leave your dial now ... here's Monitor...*
> *Lean back and stay a while now ... here's Monitor...*
> *On N ... B ... C...!*

There was an instrumental and vocal crescendo on the final line.

Even the weekend radio service's "theme" (referred to on the air as the *"Monitor beacon"*) maintained such a delightful resonance that it nearly defies description. Its instantly memorable notes were played often, typically at the beginning and end of segments, following the news, before and after commercial breaks and surrounding various special features.

Actually there were dual sets of sounds. The first, played repetitiously, might—to anyone unfamiliar with it—be best described as an old-fashioned calliope. The second reverberation, bass sounding notes, climbed up and down the scale. Its origins were in telephone "touch tone" technology that had been labeled by AT&T as "multifreq." "Even we at the phone company referred to 'multifreq' tones as 'Monitor tones,'" admits telephone technician Jim Wood, "showing that many of us were familiar with NBC's weekend service."[37]

Henry Brugsch attests that those multifreq tones "had an interesting musical cadence when mixed and played together." Brugsch observes: "Someone cleverly discovered the tonal relationships and made them work by juxtaposing recordings of them."[38]

Ken Piletic explains how it worked:

> Previously long distance calls were routed through manual switchboards. While pulse dial relays were involved several operators were required to route the calls. By the 1950s, however, advanced proficiency allowed tones to be coupled between circuits to perform switching operations. When the touchtones were tested they could be heard on the phone lines as the routing was taking place. Someone at NBC heard the tones and decided to record them, slow them down, speed them up, overdub them and mix them to produce the *Monitor* beacon. Those tones, incidentally, aren't necessarily those in use today. There were many problems with some of the frequencies then in use.[39]

Thus the *Monitor* beacon was born. It became one of the most identifiable sounds in radio and was promptly associated with the weekend radio service for 20 years. Henry Brugsch, who grew up with it, fondly remembers:

> My first encounter with Monitor was a sense of wonder and excitement. The future was now. We could get to the moon and radio could take us there. The beeps and tonal mixing of the Monitor beacon was a clarion call to a new dawn.... I was determined to listen to the whole thing. Every weekend I'd carry a radio with me, catching every word, awaiting the next unexpected event. What would it be? Up in the cockpit of the latest jet fighter? The sound of the sound barrier being broken? A man being launched aboard a rocket ship? It was all being promised to the attentive listener.[40]

The structure was set in four-hour segments with well-known "communicators" (later "hosts") officiating in each portion. Some of the most recognized voices among those presiders belonged to Red Barber, Frank Blair, Bill Cullen, Hugh Downs, Bob Elliott and Ray Goulding, Clifton Fadiman, Art Ford, Allen Funt, Frank Gallop, Dave Garroway, Ben Grauer, Ed McMahon, Henry Morgan, Leon Pearson, Gene Rayburn, John Cameron Swayze, J.B. Tucker and David Wayne.

The flexibility of the weekend radio service that Pat Weaver had espoused in the spring of 1955 was curtailed to an extent in its later years. By then Monitor evolved into a pattern of providing five minutes of network news at the top of every hour, as its leading competition was doing. That was followed by 25 minutes of music and the traditional features for which Monitor was well recognized. On the half-hour, NBC offered five minutes of music, some vocal, some instrumental. Local affiliates could opt to carry their own programming and commercials in those five minutes, or they could air the network music that was briefly introduced by the host of the hour.

At 35 minutes past, strains of the Monitor beacon wafted above the fading tunes. Another 25 minutes of archetypal Monitor interviews and music completed the hour. Near the midpoint every half-hour, five seconds of the beacon signaled the start of a break. There would be a 70-second instrumental melody—when local stations could air commercials or public service announcements if they chose—followed by five seconds of the beacon. Then the host would introduce more music and features. (In earlier years, during such breaks the beacon was preceded by this announcement from the communicator: "You're on the Monitor beacon. Take one." The latter reference was to the one minute that local stations were given to cut away from the network. Sometimes the host would substitute: "This is *Monitor*, going places and doing things. Take one." The latter phrase adroitly summarized what the service was about.)

Restructuring the show's multiple hours into specific time frames helped affiliates adapt the network offering to local scheduling preferences. With established breaks hourly at 00:00, 05:00, 30:00 and 35:00, stations had more options for integrating their own mix of local shows. This made the weekend service more attractive to the affiliates, of course, and kept many of them on board. Others discontinued the marathon altogether, preferring to air local programming exclusively that netted them larger amounts of cash.

The affiliates had earlier gained the upper hand in dealing with the network on many counts. The bottom line was that stations had far greater control than they had ever experienced over what they broadcast. Fortunately, a crucial number remained loyal to *Monitor* and its faithful audiences until the network at last withdrew the weekend radio service.

In observing NBC's enormously successful *Monitor*, a couple of competing networks jumped on the bandwagon. (One may recall that CBS was already programming *Sunday Afternoon*, two hours of live and recorded music. CBS made no further efforts to capitalize on the new form.) While applications of the magazine format by the other networks were never as bold or as well-received as the original, those webs gave it a try, albeit in limited doses.

Possibly sensing a developing trend, MBS was the first to attempt to emulate the model via a service termed *Companionate Radio* that it introduced in July 1955. Four months later ABC premiered its own weekday evening magazine called *New Sounds*. Neither experiment lasted; both never found substantial audiences. There may have been a lack of genuine commitment by their respective networks, too.

In the twilight years of *Monitor*, the show devoted multiple segments in tribute to such earlier epochs as the big band and rock 'n' roll eras. For a typical offering, on the evening of Sunday, August 19, 1973, from 7:35 to 8 P.M., host Art Ford—a former local New York disc jockey and one of the show's smoothest voices—introduced a popular vocalist special: "Crooners, Spooners and Rockers." It featured recorded excerpts by singers Jack Leonard, Frank Sinatra, Vaughn Monroe, Bob Eberle, Perry Como, Dinah Shore, Doris Day, and Peggy Lee. Recorded interviews with Como and Day were added. Several of the big bands—with headliners Tommy and Jimmy Dorsey, Ted Weems, Les Brown, and Benny Goodman among them—backed the singers or were featured in instrumental tunes.

On such occasions, host Ford frequently invited listeners to register their response to these musical feasts. Near the close of this one he expanded the marketing research: "If you're enjoying it [the show] why not drop me a line and tell me?" he inquired. "While you're at it, tell me what kind of radio you heard it on: a transistor, a car radio, a plug-in set at home. Tell me if you lived through the early days of popular music and the vocalists who sang it, or if you're just discovering them now. Write to me, Art Ford, care of *Monitor*, 30 Rockefeller Center, New York, New York 10020." Such opportunities were regularly presented in later years but if the replies were sparse that might have hastened the demise of *Monitor*.

The end finally arrived on the fourth weekend of 1975, nearly two decades after its inception, 14-plus years beyond what was generally considered radio's golden age. On Saturday, January 25, 1975, a day before *Monitor* signed off forever, host John Bartholomew Tucker asked Frank Blair to reminisce about the durable series' humble origins:

> It is sad.... I think *Monitor* was one of the greatest radio shows that was ever devised by our good friend and imaginative chairman of the board of NBC, Pat Weaver.... He thought radio should not be a static thing, that it should be on the move and I think that was what was behind *Monitor*. And I had the privilege of being the first voice heard on *Monitor* because I was assigned to the Saturday morning four-hour stint that started on June 12th. I was in here at ... oh, way before 8 o'clock in the morning and I did the eight-to-12 shift. What started out as an experiment turned out to be an institution.

Monitor may have begun as an experiment all right, but Blair was right on the money: it wound up becoming an institution. In what this protracted radio series did, none did better. It remained a viable option for those seeking knowledge and enjoyment long after old-time radio was dead. The mark *Monitor* made upon the medium was indelible; its achievements, lamely imitated but never equaled.

Can lightning strike twice in one place? Does a rose by any other name smell as sweet? Is imitation the highest form of flattery? For the answers to these and other questions, stay tuned.

The weekend radio series *Monitor* gained added respect for its network while raising the perception of the medium itself within the broadcasting industry. Before *Monitor* took to the airwaves, Pat Weaver claimed that he would never be satisfied with less than a cumulative rating of 50 after a reasonable start-up phase. He anticipated that half of all radio listeners would eventually tune to *Monitor*. In the meantime, NBC executives hoped to capitalize even more on their good fortune.

Could such heady success ever breed contempt?

With its weekend schedule showing promising signs of new life, the NBC brass turned its focus toward daytime programming, an area in which the network was sagging, according to critics. If the magazine format worked well on the weekends, the executives theorized, why wouldn't it be just the prescription for a faltering daytime agenda? Hoping to capitalize on their newfound momentum, they rushed to devise an omnibus extravaganza for daytime audiences that would emulate *Monitor*. Once readied, it was to be called *Weekday* and would be a virtual carbon copy of the advice, interview, comedy and dramatic vignettes, music and news features found on its only slightly older sibling. Perhaps its singular difference was that it would be cohosted by teams rather than individuals: Walter Kiernan and Martha Scott in the mornings, perhaps, and Mike Wallace and Margaret Truman in the afternoons, or maybe vice versa.

To free the time for *Weekday*, officials of the chain decided to discard the audience listening patterns that had been established for decades. As a result, the web cleared its deck of a trio of its four remaining audience participation quizzes: the venerable *Break the Bank* (1945–55), *The Phrase That Pays* (1953–55) and *Second Chance* (1954–55). Only *Strike It Rich* would survive (to late 1957).

There were other features that disappeared in the wake of preparing for NBC's new *Weekday* magazine, too. But no species experienced the full frontal attack as that suffered by the soap opera, the traditional daytime moneymaker of the major networks. The genre of serialized dramatic fare appealing primarily to women was instituted during the very first decade of network broadcasting. Several of those tales had been broadcast five times weekly for more than 20 years. Yet of seven still popular washboard weepers that NBC was airing in the first half of 1955—each one with a legacy of more than a decade and a half on the air—four had been canceled by the end of the year: *Backstage Wife* (1935–59—which would be fortunate enough to be rescued in 1955 and continued by CBS), *Just Plain Bill* (1932–55), *Lorenzo Jones* (1937–55) and *Stella Dallas* (1938–56).

With those vanishing, *Weekday* was launched on November 7, 1955, and soon filled four and three-quarter hours of the daily schedule: 10:15 to 11:45 A.M., 12 noon to 12:30 P.M. and 12:45 to 3:30 P.M. Aside from its early morning news programs and the human interest quiz *Strike It Rich*, NBC offered little else until late afternoon. *Fibber McGee and Molly* condensed its comedy routines into a quarter-hour at 11:45 A.M. and *Pauline Frederick* was permitted another quarter-hour at 12:30 P.M. for news and analysis. That was it until a half-dozen soap operas aired between 3:30 and 5 P.M.: *Hotel for Pets, The Doctor's Wife, The Right to Happiness, Young Widder Brown, Pepper Young's Family* and *The Woman in My House.*

Did the daytime transformation meet the anticipation of its ambitious creators? Did it perhaps exceed the success the network was enjoying on the weekend? Unfortunately, both questions merit a resounding "No!" The overall idea was little short of a disaster.

American housewives, the principal audience for daytime radio in the 1950s, weren't enamored by NBC's experiment at their expense. In fact, they turned away in droves. The NBC brass quickly realized that pinning its hopes on *Weekday* had been a colossal mistake. Though never admitting it publicly, management must have seen that tampering with listening patterns that had worked so well for decades contributed heavily to the debacle. By then it was too late: a trust with the fans had been irretrievably broken. Radio audiences were leaking like a sieve, and this would soon turn into a flood.

After 39 weeks, on August 3, 1956, NBC terminated *Weekday*. In its wake, the fiasco created utter carnage in place of a competitive daytime schedule. Missed opportunities and the dynamics of so little time left in the race against television doomed any hope of recovery. NBC lost the gamble for weekday audiences and would never regain them. In the interim, *Monitor* would continue to attract new listeners to a format that had proved a total disaster on weekdays.

Only in hindsight did the network's moguls fully appreciate the differences in the two audiences, their programming penchants, and the circumstances under which those listeners heard radio. In the latter years of the golden age, NBC could do little more than console itself with a final score of 1–1.

As noted, no program category was hit as hard in the dismantling of NBC's daytime agenda as the soap opera. Half of the network's six remaining dishpan dramas airing alongside *Weekday* were born in the 1950s, therefore were unable to proffer high percentages of listeners who were faithful followers for decades. By then NBC had lost or abandoned a score or more of its durable daytime narratives. Housewives spending their late afternoons doing housework, tending kids and preparing meals while longstanding favorite radio serials played in the background had suddenly become history in millions of homes.

Despite the axing of some eminent NBC mainstays, including the four washboard weepers that were swept aside to grant more time for *Weekday*, the end wasn't in sight: management at the oldest network wasn't yet satisfied. Before pulling the plug on its matinee magazine, on June 22, 1956, it canceled *Young Widder Brown* (1938–56); one week later, *The Right to Happiness* (1939–60) left NBC. (The latter was to be picked up by CBS, just as *Backstage Wife* had been salvaged the year before.) Meanwhile, it appeared to many as if masochistic sadism had taken the reins at the network of the chimes.

Serial producer Anne Hummert inquired: "What's to become of all my actors?" She and her husband Frank weren't interested in TV on whose channels they could never recreate their vast empire. Meanwhile, some of their actors had seen the handwriting on the wall and were exploring other opportunities.

Karl Swenson, who played Lorenzo Jones, and his spouse, actress Joan Tompkins, the actress who had the title role in *This Is Nora Drake*, found sustenance in New York TV. Then they left the Big Apple for Hollywood and many new roles came their way. Anne Elstner (Stella Dallas) and her husband Jack Mathews [sic] purchased an upscale diner at Lambertville, New Jersey, and fed their guests in plush surroundings when her series left the air. But as the radio soap operas ended, numerous actors faded into a void, petrified by cameras and live audiences — an environment many had never had to deal with in their professional careers.

Following the fall of *Weekday*, NBC rushed to fill many gaps in its daytime schedule. The web added a few self-contained dramas (those that told their stories in total in a single chapter). It also debuted a few new serials. On September 3, 1956, NBC added *Hilltop House*, a long-running serial that had left CBS 14 months earlier. Those protracted listening patterns were gone, however, and so was *Hilltop House* only 11 months later.

Meanwhile, an astute dramatic raconteur reported the competition's strategy:

> NBC's changeability, coupled with CBS Radio's loss in serial sponsorship in 1955, placed daytime serial drama in a critical position. To some, the death of radio soap opera seemed imminent. Yet CBS Radio held firm, presenting its serials in an unbroken two-and-a-half-hour block, whether sponsored or not, in the expectation that the regular listening patterns which always had sustained daytime drama would overcome the attractiveness of television. The network's trust was well placed. Not only did CBS Radio's serial sponsors return, but also the network gained new daytime listeners. In the spring of 1956 a CBS vice-president, John Karol, told the Wisconsin Broadcasters' Association that the preservation of the serial block had resulted in an 8 per cent increase in the daytime audience of his chain. At the same time, the major competitor, NBC, had lost more than half its daytime listeners, making the CBS daytime audience twice that of any other network. Karol pointed to the new $1.5 million contract with Colgate as an indication of the appeal of the daytime serial.[41]

Despite the optimism, a trio of casualties displaced CBS Radio's long-running serial agenda in 1956, although two continued in video form: *The Brighter Day* (1948–56, on CBS-TV 1954–62), *The Guiding Light* (1937–56, on CBS-TV from 1952 to the present) and *Aunt Jenny's Real Life Stories* (1937–56).

While ABC abandoned its single remaining open-ended soap opera *When a Girl Marries* (1939–57) a few months later, and NBC wiped its diminishing slate of them clean in early 1959, CBS persevered until the latter part of 1960. Finally it, too, caved in to mounting pressure from its local outlets that were demanding reduced network programming so they might sell time more profitably to local advertisers. That occasion will be visited in depth later.

In 1953 the Alfred Politz research firm reported findings from a study of radio listenership. It was of little consequence that program ratings were rapidly shrinking, inquisitors found; two out of every three American adults were still tuning in to their radios every single day.[42]

Yet by the close of 1955, not a single evening series remained in the top 10 radio shows, A.C. Nielsen Company ratings confirmed. Tied at 14th place, *Dragnet* was the most popular evening program, running well behind the soap operas and daytime variety shows. That same year researchers reported that nearly 47 million of the nation's households had at least one radio but only 786,000 of them were tuning in to a typical evening program.[43]

An insightful radio historiographer suggested that such statistics proved an obvious point: "Radio had lost its audience and now had to adjust to the new environment." He affirmed: "Radio on the network level was now a supplementary, secondary entertainment source. To survive, it had to do better those things which television could not do. It also had to find new means of obtaining sponsors."[44] A decade earlier NBC president Niles Trammell had stated that radio should derive a role "where it can best serve the public."[45]

Most radio stations not affiliated with one of the four major networks in the mid–1940s had already made the transition to a new climate. Programming that was generally not available on the networks—local interest features, music, sports and foreign language series—was being offered by these independents. In addition since TV couldn't replicate radio's portability very well, such radio stations also offered shows that were geared to audiences in their cars, while at work, in eating establishments, and in other places where listeners often spent their leisure hours.

Meanwhile, many local advertisers liked to collaborate with other firms in sponsoring part of an independent station's schedule. This was particularly true when a prospective client couldn't afford to underwrite a single program by itself.

This should be contrasted with what was transpiring at the affiliates, or the remaining 75 percent of U.S. radio stations. The four networks combined suffered a gross annual revenue loss of $32 million between the mid–1940s and mid–1950s.[46] As a result, they started testing programs that originated from various regions of the country, as well as having participating sponsorship (including more than one advertiser) on some programs. Surveying it decades later, it appears to have been a foretaste of things to come.

One of the most telling factors occurred when local stations were requested by their networks to sell time to local sponsors rather than expecting the webs to underwrite everything. Did this simple request open Pandora's box, allowing local stations to eventually gain the upper hand? From this vantage point it appears it could have.

At the time it seemed like a wise choice. The infusion of cash from time sales led to the affiliates becoming more demanding while enhancing their control of local broadcast schedules. A scholarly historian correctly argued: "Cut-backs in programs from the networks, and the ability to reach a wider local and regional audience than the weaker-signaled independent stations, soon allowed them [the affiliates] to become more profitable than ever."[47] For a while, at least, both the networks and their local outlets prospered under the relaxed modus operandi.

The CBS Radio Workshop was a last hurrah of sorts, "dedicated to man's imagination, the theater of the mind." In radio's final years some of its favored shows had found themselves sponsorless, stuffed with trite public-service announcements that had the effect of rubbing salt into open wounds. As no one was thought to be paying much attention anyway by then, the medium could loosen up and get away with some things it couldn't have before. In its infancy it had done this with *Escape* and *The Henry Morgan Show*. Now it pushed the envelope with *Dimension X*, *Gunsmoke*, *The Stan Freberg Show*, *You Are There* and—as of January 27, 1956—*The CBS Radio Workshop*. A network vice president assured director Elliott Lewis: "Do whatever you want. You have a half hour." A prominent author recalled what happened:

> For this unsponsored series, the network's finest talents rose to the occasion and produced a series of challenging, experimental, one-of-a-kind broadcasts, beginning with an ambitious rendering of Aldous Huxley's *Brave New World*. William N. Robson wrote some especially memorable shows, including an adaptation of Sinclair Lewis's "Young Man Axelbroad" and "An Interview with Shakespeare," moderated by Dr. Frank C. Baxter and featuring remarks by Christopher Marlowe, Sir Francis Bacon, Richard Burbage, and others who claimed to have written the Great Bard's plays. William Conrad was especially fond of "1,489 Words," which was simply a recitation of three great poems set to original music by Jerry Goldsmith. Top actors, writers, directors, musicians, and soundmen gave their best efforts to this show, which earned a fair amount of print publicity.[48]

The series signed off forever on September 22, 1957. It had employed cutting edge technology in writing, music and sound effects, a combination that often varied from the traditional to the bizarre. CBS vice president Howard Barnes told *Time*: "We'll never get a sponsor anyway, so we might as well try anything."[49] Some believe it may have outstripped its role model, *The Columbia Workshop* (on erratically from 1936 to 1947). It's a fact that *The CBS Radio Workshop* made full use of the audio techniques pioneered by its predecessor. When it ended, radio fans had again lost a valuable literary endowment that may have contributed eloquently to the fabric of society as well as to their own intellects.

What other series that strongly influenced the medium arrived and departed in the middle years of the 1950s? There were easily fewer shows debuting than leaving, a trend that would continue throughout the remainder of network radio's fading days. Three noteworthy series turned up for the first time in 1955: *The $64,000 Question*, which arrived and departed on radio within two months; *The Howard Miller Show*, a weekday morning deejay series, and definitely a foretaste of things to come in radio; and *Changing Times*, a business-oriented newspaper talk program of the air.

Meanwhile, no fewer than 59 light music or musical variety series premiered on the networks in the three years under study, yet failed to return for second seasons. They included shows headlined by Don Cornell, Johnny Mercer, Julius La Rosa, Mahalia Jackson, Rosemary Clooney, Ted Steele, and Tennessee Ernie Ford. A host of shows with orchestras can be incorporated as separate series to this grouping. They had maestros like George Shearing, Jerry Gray, Ralph Marterie, Skinnay Ennis, Tex Beneke, Woody Herman, and dozens more whose names are now less than familiar to most audiences.

Few of these musical diversions were sponsored, in whole or in part. Yet to the networks' credit, they remained stoical for most of the 1950s. Vainly they searched for winning formulas that could plug the recurring holes in their schedules. It was obvious to many, however, that the poor reception most of the no-name musical interludes received from the fans during the final days of network radio simply meant that the productions weren't what their listeners were hoping for. After repeated attempts to convert audiences with little signs of acceptance, some of the chains' valuable time would almost certainly be handed back to the affiliates. The webs would suffer a while longer, in desperation.

On the cancellation side, the numbers were already mushrooming. Here's a list of some of the more prominent ones, in addition to those mentioned previously, by year of cancellation, with their years of premiers in parentheses:

1954: *The Adventures of Ozzie and Harriet* (1944), *The Armstrong Theater of Today* (1941), *Breakfast in Hollywood*, et al. (1942), *Bulldog Drummond* (1941), *Can You Top This?* (1940), *The Cisco Kid* (1942), *Dr. Christian*

(1937), *Double or Nothing* (1940), *Escape* (1947), *The Falcon* (1943), *Father Knows Best* (1949), *Front Page Farrell* (1941), *Grand Central Station* (1937), *Junior Miss* (1942), *Let's Pretend* (1934), *Life Can Be Beautiful* (1938), *Lum and Abner* (1931), *The Molle Mystery Theater* (1943), *My Friend Irma* (1947), *The NBC Symphony Orchestra* (1937), *The Phil Harris–Alice Faye Show* (1948), *The Railroad Hour* (1948), *The Shadow* (1930), *Sky King* (1946), *The Vaughn Monroe Show*, aka *The Camel Caravan* (1942), *Welcome Travelers* (1947).

1955: *The Adventures of Rin Tin Tin* (1930), *The Amos 'n' Andy Show* (1929) [although *The Amos 'n' Andy Music Hall*, a separate series, aired from 1954–60], *Barry Craig, Confidential Investigator* (1951), *The Big Story* (1947), *The Challenge of the Yukon*, aka *Sergeant Preston of the Yukon* (1947), *The Dave Garroway Show*, aka *Dial Dave Garroway* (1949), *The Dinah Shore Show* (1939), *The Hallmark Hall of Fame*, aka *The Hallmark Playhouse* (1948), *Joyce Jordan, M.D.* (1938), *My Little Margie* (1952), *Perry Mason* (1943), *Rosemary* (1944), *The Roy Rogers Show* (1944), *Stop the Music!* (1948).

1956: *Gene Autry's Melody Ranch* (1940), *The Sammy Kaye Show* (1937), *Sherlock Holmes* (1930), *Truth or Consequences* (1940), *Twenty-First Precinct* (1953), *Wild Bill Hickok* (1951), *You Bet Your Life* (1947).

In some fashion, the network schedules still resembled the great days of the previous two decades in the mid–1950s. At no time, in fact, before or after the 1953–54 season did the radio networks offer as many programming hours per week. Yet by 1956 that number had begun to shrink acutely. (That was a year in which more hours were devoted to news broadcasts by the chains, incidentally, than any other type of programming.) Desiring to go their own ways, affiliates were by then deleting sustaining musical programming by the carloads. The remaining sponsored programs, except for news, were often next on the chopping block. Clearing time for network shows was no longer a guarantee to their webs. The local stations now possessed the whip hand, and fully realized that they could produce far more revenue by generating their own programming rather than automatically subscribing to whatever a chain was feeding.

The times, they sure had changed.

On May 19, 1954, CBS news correspondents participated with experts in foreign relations in a panel discussion of the future of Indo-China. The French colonial power had collapsed at Dien Bien Phu a short time earlier. With narration by one of the most widely respected voices in radio, Lowell Thomas, their hour-long conversation pondered:

• What is the nature of American involvement in the fighting there?

• What is the stake of the United States in the war?

• How can the United States contribute to resolving the situation?

Writing for *Variety*, a reviewer explained: "There were no pat answers, but for the listener it meant a new slant on that vast, far-off area."[50]

Current events programming like this one was another example of radio's continuing influence in education and understanding, highlighting the medium's ability to help Americans comprehend world events. It was a testimony to radio's acceptance of responsibility to the public it served, a trust it had often risen to across two prior decades. To its credit, it never abandoned that task.

An unmistakable derivative of the economic good times that many Americans experienced in the 1950s was reflected in an abundant increase in the birthrate. Actually, the baby boom had begun in the mid–1940s as millions of individuals returned to their homes from active military service in World War II. As more prosperous times enveloped the nation during the subsequent decade, the population increase showed little signs of abating.

Not surprisingly, yet another trend occurred: by 1956 the average marrying age had plunged significantly, to 20.1 years for women. Couples were starting their families earlier, too. Within a few months the boom maxed out as a record 4.3 million offspring were born in the U.S. in one year. "Of all the accomplishments of the American woman," boasted *Life* magazine, "the one she brings off with the most spectacular success is having babies."[51] In the decade of the 1950s, the nation's population increased by 29 million. Domesticity reigned supreme. By 1956, especially for white Americans, it appeared that the good times had arrived and would remain forever.

As their young families grew, Americans' desire for home entertainment expanded. Television had already made significant strides into their lives. The increased birthrate meant more and more individuals gathered around large black-and-white sets with rectangular 13-inch screens. Those oblong boxes dominated living rooms across the land, much as radios had done in the previous generation. A middle class society growing accustomed to the material wealth that it had been denied during the war offered a fertile environment for TV to thrive in.

Almost weekly more and more radio shows that, for years, had held listeners in rapt attention were dying in carload lots. Loyalties were swept aside in favor of the newfangled system that allowed people to witness live pictures with their sound. While the aural medium's last epitaph hadn't yet been written, a low gasp escaped from the lips of this old friend.

Radio time sales slipped to $453,385,000 in 1954, a 5 percent decline from the previous year, and the first dip in time sales since 1938. The handwriting on the wall was becoming clearer by the day. The purveyors of doom were onto something. The whole country would finally acknowledge the truth.

It was only a matter of time.

On August 16, 1954, CBS announced that its radio and television news operations, maintained separately until then, were being combined into a single corporate division. TV news chief Sig Mickelson would head it, and he was given the rank of vice president. Only four years earlier he had supervised 13 people. Now, he would command a staff of 376.

If anyone needed a sign of which way the wind was blowing, that was it, and a pretty ominous sign at that.

4

The Late Years:
1957–1960

A new term introduced into the lexicon of commercial radio broad-casting in the 1950s, "drive time," replaced "prime time" as the true attention-getter for many advertisers. As the decade neared its conclu-sion, more and more sponsor dollars were being spent on the hours that people were in transit to and from their occupations. Presumably they were listening to newly installed radios in their vehicles, in newly manufactured automobiles as well as in older models. Sponsors had discovered a preferable venue in the aural medium than longstanding or new nighttime series, which had effectively been displaced by tele-vision. While sunup and sunset commercial time had been available all along, its importance to radio sponsors increased significantly as evening series took a severe ratings nose-dive.

The "drive time" emphasis and jargon instituted then worked so well for advertisers that it continues to this day. Virtually every com-mercial radio station in America still earns its foremost revenues between 6 and 10 A.M. and 3 and 7 P.M. local time, charging peak fees for commercials aired in those hours due to significantly larger listen-ing audiences.

Programming in drive time may be more sophisticated today than then, depending on one's point of view, but it may have basically changed very little in the intervening years. In many markets on mul-tiple stations the fare consists of recorded music interrupted by news, the time, reports of weather and traffic conditions, commercials and banter by one or more local disk jockeys. A modern development has been the implementation of automated music services beamed from elsewhere across the country, eliminating a need for local deejays. With the advent of talk radio, some stations now devote much or all of their programming to call-in features, interviews, public forums and nationally syndicated talk shows.

In the nine-year period 1952–60, radio's total revenues rose from $624 million to $692 million, an increase of $68 million or 11 percent. Despite those impressive numbers, in the same time total advertising dollars spent dropped from 9 percent earmarked for radio in 1952 to only 6 percent directed to it in 1960. Other promotional tools were usurping radio's longstanding position as a formidable media advertising conduit. It shouldn't take rocket science to figure out where many firms' ad budgets were being placed.

As if this weren't enough bad news for radio industry executives, a growing trend had begun in which some influential and powerful affiliates had finally thrown up their hands and cried: "Enough!" Failing to renew venerable contracts with the national chains, they cut their losses and generated their own programming as independents. By the start of 1957, for instance, the Westinghouse Broadcasting Corporation, then a major group owner, had wrested four of its local outlets from the NBC lineup.

While the majority of stations remained identified with their webs, a large number dropped prime-time programming. Instead, they carried only news services and daytime features that continued to demonstrate holding power over listeners.

"Except in those cases where a new show was hosted by an attractive and dynamic personality, soap operas remained more popular with the daytime audience," claimed one media observer.[1] Only a handful of durable weekday shows that drew live studio audiences persisted: *Arthur Godfrey Time, Art Linkletter's House Party, The Breakfast Club* hosted by Don McNeill, and *Queen for a Day* hosted by Jack Bailey (which ended a 12-year radio stint on June 10, 1957).

A couple of innovative programming ideas occurred in this epoch. One might be considered a flop, given its brevity on the air; the other was likely the last truly popular series premiering in the dying embers of network radio.

The Stan Freberg Show, the last live, big-scale show of its kind to air on network radio, debuted on CBS on July 14, 1957. It was gone by

Orchestra leader Billy May suggested "we were kind of closing down a chapter of some sort of history" when, in mid–1957, CBS launched the final network radio series performed before a live audience. *The Stan Freberg Show* with its offbeat comic star of the title (shown) poked fun at individuals and institutions of many types. *Photofest*.

October 20. In between, listeners were treated to a brash (for that day) young performer whose satirical diatribes poked good-natured fun at mediocrity, complacency, stuffed shirts, censorship and other abominations that its star found annoying or, more likely, easy to spoof.

In this half-hour venue, Freberg—who had risen to prominence by way of some humorous Capitol Records releases and a brief CBS comedy sustainer in 1954 called *That's Rich*—appeared in a series of lampoon sketches. These played up the flaws, perceived or real, in the lives of some well-known personalities (Lawrence Welk, for example) and even some other radio shows. (Freberg's *Dragnet* parody, *St. George and the Dragonet*, [1953] was the first million-selling comedy recording.) If you can imagine it, it was *Saturday Night Live* a few decades early—although a squeaky-clean version—on Sunday night radio.

"It was an expensive show to do," Leonard Maltin recalls, "not the least because Freberg held out for musical director Billy May and a full-sized band. By this time, virtually all surviving network radio series were using canned music, so the presence of a live orchestra signaled that this show was something special indeed."[2]

Later, maestro May reminisced about the program's strategic spot in the annals of aural broadcasting: "I think everybody realized that we were kind of closing down a chapter of some sort of history."[3] That would become even more pronounced with the passing of time. The

15-week experiment, which had inherited Jack Benny's old studio, led Freberg to portray himself as the last network radio comedian. "One of my big thrills," said he, "was looking out in the audience one night before my show went off and there was Groucho [Marx] sitting in the third row."[4]

Freberg subsequently went on to host a syndicated hour, *When Radio Was*, subscribed to by 300 stations. It was a tribute to the vintage shows of early broadcasting and it, too, was all in good fun.

Have Gun, Will Travel, on the other hand, lasted longer—and arrived on radio by a most unlikely method. When this adult western premiered on CBS Radio on November 23, 1958 (with some dramatic parallel to *Gunsmoke*, a series that had been airing since 1952), it had also been appearing in video form for a little more than a year. The tube's rendering of *Have Gun, Will Travel* starred Richard Boone and debuted on CBS-TV September 14, 1957. There it continued as a Saturday night staple (and as a lead-in to CBS-TV's *Gunsmoke*) for six seasons, through September 21, 1963.

Travel became one of only a handful of televised series, albeit the most successful, making the jump to radio. This was, the reader will instantly recall, diametrically opposed to the route that most series made. It was one of the peculiarities that anyone seriously studying both radio and television in this era was bound to encounter, and deserves to be considered in some detail, having not been dealt with earlier. Let us digress momentarily.

TV shows that added radio versions are one of the incongruities in broadcasting of the 1950s. While their number wasn't large, the fact that they occurred at all seems to contradict what was happening widespread. The analysis we have presented thus far has repeatedly underscored the fact that—if the dual mediums were working in tandem—the one taking the lead almost invariably was radio. Prominent features broadcast there lent their talents to TV to assist the newer medium in becoming established. Radio favorites became TV favorites, carrying their audiences along with them as they jumped from audio to video. This was particularly true in the late 1940s and early 1950s.

Yet there were actually a number of programs surfacing on the tube throughout the decade of the 1950s that eventually produced either identical or entirely separate radio adaptations. Let us briefly focus on a few of the more notable shows to cross over from video to audio.

One of the more unusual was *The Original Amateur Hour*, the first series to originate on radio, leave the air and make a comeback on TV, then add a radio broadcast. It first appeared on a national radio hookup on March 24, 1935, running its course on NBC and then CBS until July 19, 1945. It left the air shortly before its creator and host, Major Edward Bowes, died. A Bowes' protégé, Ted Mack, revived it on Dumont TV on January 18, 1948. The show eventually made the rounds of all the TV networks until it left the air permanently on September 26, 1960. Meanwhile, its instant video popularity brought it back to ABC Radio on September 29, 1948, where it lasted until September 18, 1952.

Following a successful repackaging of his films from the 1930s and 1940s for early television, cowboy actor Bill Boyd debuted on NBC-TV March 13, 1949, in *Hopalong Cassidy*. A few months later, on January 1, 1950, a radio sequel was added over Mutual. That series continued on MBS and later CBS through March 15, 1952. The TV show had already ended on December 23, 1951.

The CBS-TV occupational game *What's My Line?* added an adaptation on *two* radio networks. Having succeeded on CBS-TV since February 16, 1950, it turned up on May 20, 1952, on NBC Radio, too. Following that, for 10 months in the 1952–53 season it aired on CBS Radio, through July 1, 1953. The live CBS-TV series remained to September 3, 1967, a 17-year run.

With the TV cast playing its leading roles, the juvenile adventure series *Tom Corbett, Space Cadet* aired a twice-a-week ABC Radio version between January 1 and July 3, 1952. Actor Frankie Thomas was heard in the series' title role, and the show eventually ran on all four television networks (ABC, CBS, Dumont, NBC), starting October 2, 1950, and ending June 25, 1955.

My Little Margie was another series that bucked tradition. Beginning on CBS-TV on June 16, 1952, it added a radio counterpart on CBS on December 7 that year. The aural series, which ran concurrently though was not simulcast (there were different original episodes for each medium) played through June 26, 1955, a couple of months before it left the tube (August 24), at that time on NBC-TV.

The $64,000 Question, in the meantime, launched on CBS-TV on June 7, 1955, was simulcast on CBS Radio from October 4 to November 29, 1955. Given what happened in the show's run later (to be considered in full presently) the fact that the radio version was abbreviated may have been just as well. It abruptly left TV on November 2, 1958.

There were only a handful of other TV-to-radio features.

Returning to *Have Gun, Will Travel*, the series was the "chief prototype of a rash of dapper heroes invented by TV to populate the Old West."[5] Who knows what effect it ultimately might have had on radio had it not appeared in the medium's fading days? Ironically, it surfaced there only two years and two days before the end of radio's golden age.

Paladin, its central figure, wasn't your illiterate run-of-the-mill gunslinger. Instead he was a man of culture, college-educated, preferring the finer things of life. Following a stint in the Civil War, he moved to San Francisco, became a high-priced gun for hire, and was able and willing to journey wherever his services were required. "He did the sometimes dangerous work that others would not or could not do for themselves," Dunning noted. "That he did these jobs for a hefty price did not diminish the fact that he was a man with a conscience."[6] Actor John Dehner was cast in the radio role of this soldier of fortune.

On the weekend that CBS Radio pulled the plug on most of its network dramatic series, November 25–27, 1960, *Travel* was canceled as part of audio theater. If the fans wanted to continue their love affair with the gunslinger with a conscience, they'd fortunately still have three more years to do so via the little screen in the rectangular box.

One thousand AM radio stations went on the air for the first time during the decade of the 1950s. If nothing else, even as network radio lay comatose, this was a strong indication that the stations themselves were still considered highly lucrative capitalistic ventures. One or more AM stations were located in practically every town of decent size in the nation by 1960. Outside major metropolises, suburban entities frequently became home to their own stations.

It was a contradiction of sorts. Network radio's energy was being sapped, yet the medium that carried it was poised for its next major role. Entrepreneurs and other enterprises were obviously optimistic about that future.

By the end of the 1950s virtually no room remained for any AM stations to be added in most U.S. cities. The only way then to establish a new radio signal, particularly one to carry nighttime programming, was to apply for an FM license.

It's a fact, as we noted previously, that in the 1950s more FM stations left the air than went on the air. More FM stations lost money than made money throughout the decade. Yet the trade weekly *Broadcasting* reported in its April 1957 issue that there was a turnaround then transpiring: for the first time since the late 1940s, applications for new FM stations were greater than the number of outlets going silent. By the summer of 1958, 548 FM stations were operating, reflecting the first increase in a decade. Within two years of that, there were about 750 commercial FM stations on the air, setting a new record in FM broadcasting.

Commensurate with the trend, in excess of one million FM receivers were sold between late 1958 and the end of 1959. The following year, 1960, Americans purchased almost two million FM sets, 10 percent of them imported largely from Germany and Japan. That was an indication that the electronics industries of the old Axis powers that had been devastated during the Second World War were up and running again, by then turned into highly efficient advanced technology operations.

While stereocasting had been practiced on AM stations since the early 1950s, it was not tried on FM until Boston outlets WBZ-FM and WCRB-FM launched a series of stereo experiments in May 1960.

The cost of a typical AM-FM receiver dropped to around $30 in this period. That was only $10–$15 above the cost of a radio equipped with AM reception only. Conspicuous, too, was the fact that AM sets in the 1950s were smaller than those made earlier. By the latter part of the decade, portability was unquestionably in vogue. While radio-phonograph combinations were still on the market, the demand was for table, clock, portable (with batteries) and other smaller sets. Plastic cases and tube sets were still around, but when lightweight transistor portables appeared at comparatively low cost in the final few years of the decade, they became an object of desire for millions of radio buffs.

In a sense, were Americans returning to their roots in broadcasting? Not if radio audiences are compared with those watching television. The picture tube and its accompanying sound still held enormous fascination for the majority, and sales of sets were steadily increasing. At the same time, TV was no longer a novelty. The excitement was over and video had slipped into something ordinary and familiar. A perceptive Edward R. Murrow warned his contemporaries during a 1958 address to the Radio-Television News Directors Association: "This instrument can teach, it can illuminate, yes, and can even inspire. But it can do so only to the extent that humans are determined to use it to those ends. Otherwise it is merely wires and lights in a box."[7]

Programs telecast during prime time simply weren't the sensation that they had been earlier in the decade when they were the primary topic of conversation around office water coolers every day. Granted, the small screen was something that dominated the living rooms in most U.S. households in the late 1950s. But it was still their radios that Americans tuned to in their kitchens and bedrooms and workshops and workplaces, and enroute between them.

There was no more *Your Hit Parade* on radio that late in the decade, but the popular feature was still carried on live television every week (through 1959). The nation continued to hum its favorite tunes, relentlessly played on the airwaves by radio deejays. In 1957, the number one melody was Debbie Reynolds' soft vocal, "Tammy"; 1958 brought in Domenico Modugno's version of "Volare (Nel Blu, Dipinto di Blu)"; and in 1959, Bobby Darin offered a hyper arrangement of "Mack the Knife."

This was an auspicious period when even a deserving woman who had been a broadcasting mainstay could be elevated to high elective office within the industry. Virginia Payne, the sole heroine of daytime's eminently popular *Ma Perkins* serial for almost three decades, was named president of the national organization the American Federation of Television and Radio Artists in 1958. She was the first of her gender to occupy that influential spot. Earlier, she had presided over local AFTRA unions in Chicago and New York. It was a crowning achievement for one who had labored tirelessly within the ranks, for both Payne herself and, in certifying the contributions of women to broadcasting, for all her gender.

This was also a period in which the network with the largest number of affiliates, Mutual, acquired some notoriety for discord and disgrace. In the years between 1956 and 1959 the chain was purchased and sold several times. A few of those transactions were tainted by scandal: stock manipulations by one owner gave the network a black eye, and favorable mentions on the air for a Latin American dictator in exchange for big payoffs occupied another administration. Immediately thereafter, 130 stations dropped their MBS affiliations, leaving the web that regularly boasted in its on-air promotions that Mutual was "the network for all America" as something decidedly less.

A comparison of changes in network affiliations across the decade is illuminating.

There were 2,086 commercial radio stations operating on the AM band in the United States in 1950. Of that number, 1,170 (56 percent) were affiliated with one of the four major national chains as follows: ABC, 282 (13.5 percent); CBS, 173 (8.3 percent); MBS, 543 (26.0 percent); NBC, 172 (8.2 percent).

Ten years later, in 1960, things had shifted dramatically. There were 3,456 AM stations in operation then, a net gain of 1,370. Yet only 1,153 (33 percent) maintained network affiliations. While this was a loss of but 117 outlets, it was a 23 percent decrease. By that time, the four networks claimed the following numbers of stations: ABC, 310 (9.0 percent); CBS, 198, (5.7 percent); MBS, 443 (12.8 percent); NBC, 202 (5.8 percent).

In the 10-year period ABC had suffered a net loss of 28 affiliates, CBS had gained 25, MBS was then down by 100, and NBC had picked up 30.

An encouraging sign turned up in all of these statistics, however. The dual chains (ABC and MBS) that had largely wiped their slates clean of most of their network programming—save news and sporting events and a few long-running features (e.g., *The Breakfast Club*)—witnessed significant losses in the number of affiliates still carrying the remnants of their former schedules.

On the other hand, CBS—with impressive vestiges of its traditional daytime, nighttime and weekend schedules, at least through late 1960— and NBC—with its flexible, attractive *Monitor* programming covering almost all of every weekend—were hanging on to most of their stations. The pair actually effected increases, a combined 55 more outlets than they attracted together in 1950. An NBC critic admitted: "In 1960 the network's radio business, as distinct from television, began to show substantial profits in the face of a contrary trend in the industry as a whole."[8]

NBC and CBS simply *had* to be doing something right. Such acknowledgment, and the increase in their number of outlets, was a silver lining in an era when so much seemed to be working against the aural medium. Surely this was welcome news to some fatigued and often maligned national radio executives.

It may have been fortunate for quiz shows on radio that they fell into decline in the late 1950s, based upon what was to transpire in television then. What happened there virtually made broadcasting such ventures anathema for years to come. It certainly would have tainted radio in the future, if only by association, had network radio persisted in the degree of popularity it had enjoyed in the past.

Game features had been introduced to radio audiences in the late 1930s, becoming more prevalent in the early 1940s. They failed to reach their potential then, however, due to wartime diversions. Yet in the postwar period they developed into a national phenomenon, instantly attracting the masses, being successful nearly everywhere they appeared on radio's schedules. A host of these diversions continued into the 1950s, including prominent features like *The Bob Hawk Show, Break the Bank, Can You Top This?, Double or Nothing, Give and Take, Grand Slam, Juvenile Jury, People Are Funny, Quick as a Flash, The Quiz Kids, The $64 Question, Stop the Music!, Strike It Rich, Take a Number, True or False, Truth or Consequences, Twenty Questions, Winner Take All* and *You Bet Your Life.*

One of their number, *The $64 Question,* launched on radio in 1940 under the banner *Take It or Leave It,* started a trend that would eventually lead to trouble. The radio program ended in 1952, several years before corruption visited the game show industry, yet it might be fairly easy from this distance to assume that the progenitor was tainted, too. It wasn't. There was no guilt by association then, nor should there be now. The radio series took itself far less seriously; after all, it dealt in a few dollars and not in thousands: "There were no isolation booths for contestants, and all the coaching was done onstage, in full view of the studio audience," noted one sage.[9]

Having projected a top cash prize of $64 throughout its existence, after 10 years—in 1950—with the catchphrase "the $64 question" regularly falling from the lips of scads of Americans, the show's producers decided to retitle their little quiz—what else?—*The $64 Question.* From March 18, 1951, until the program left the air forever on June 1, 1952, it was known under the new appellation without any format changes.

Sometime after its departure, Milton Biow, who had guided this little game show through the years, determined to disperse his advertising agency and retire. In 1955 he sold half his interest in what had been a profitable *Take It or Leave It*—including the right to use the figure 64—in a new quiz being readied for television by producer and packager Louis G. Cowan.

Cowan's quiz, an outgrowth of *The $64 Question,* was to be built on the same principle of doubling the initial amount, which was to start with $1,000 instead of $1. The ultimate prize would be $64,000, hence the title *The $64,000 Question.* A 1950s historiographer observed: "In the new age of television, ... everything had to be bigger and better.

Americans were not going to sit home, glued to their television sets, wondering whether some electronic stranger, who had briefly entered their living rooms, was going to be able to double his winnings from $32 to $64. In the postwar era that was pocket money."[10]

The new show was wildly anticipated even before its debut on CBS-TV on June 7, 1955. Hal March was master of ceremonies. No audiences of any previously broadcast competition had ever witnessed cash prizes at that level; the national response, as a result, was euphoric. After a player reached the $4,000 stratum she asked only a single question weekly, prolonging the attention span of viewers while adding to the show's mystique. Just as players had done on the radio version, one could quit at any time or risk everything already won by trying for the next level, each time doubling the earnings to a maximum of $64,000.

So successful was the TV venture that other mega-moneyed quizzes soon began appearing elsewhere, including *The Big Surprise, Twenty-One* and—on April 8, 1956—a spinoff of the original video series labeled *The $64,000 Challenge*. The latter involved contenders battling former winners of *The $64,000 Question*, contestants whose prize money totaled at least $8,000. Eventually, in an effort to maintain supremacy among the growing maze of giveaway shows, *The $64,000 Question* added three new plateaus, boosting its top prize to $256,000.

If it had all stayed clean and honest, who knows where it might have led?

But it didn't.

In their incessant drive to win higher ratings against the competition, the producers of several of these giveaways—among them, *The $64,000 Question, The $64,000 Challenge* and *Twenty-One*—tainted their genre by discussing potential questions and answers with some (but not all) of the players, in order to drive up the ratings. (Specifically naming those shows two decades later, genre interpreter Maxene Fabe attested: "Three of the best games ever were also the crookedest."[11])

Had not a disgruntled contestant in August 1958 on *Dotto*—a lesser-known TV quiz with daytime and primetime editions—spilled the beans, declaring the show was "fixed," the scandal that erupted and destroyed Americans' confidence in what they had been watching might never have transpired. It turned out that that initial revelation was but the tip of the iceberg.

In the ensuing investigation and subsequent trials, finger-pointing of many stripes took place involving a widespread number of shows and individuals. When other contestants testified that they had been prompted with answers, deep secrets that had been carefully tucked inside dark corners suddenly appeared in the light; and with those secrets, there was virtual banishment of a species for many years. *The $64,000 Challenge* abruptly departed September 7, 1958; *Twenty-One* was gone on October 16 of that year; and *The $64,000 Question* disappeared November 2.

Nearly two decades elapsed, in fact, before a syndicated revival of the original big-money quiz that doubled players' winnings surfaced under the title of *The $128,000 Question*. It featured Mike Darrow as the first host, in 1976, and a youthful Alex Trebek the following year. By 1978 it, too, was gone, having lacked both novelty and suspense. Its predecessor had been televised live, with contestants succeeding or failing in front of the whole country. The reprise, on the other hand—pretaped weeks in advance and shown by local stations at varying times and on different dates—missed the tension that the original had generated.

It would take *Twenty-One* even longer to make a comeback. In light of the eminently successful *Who Wants to Be a Millionaire?* that debuted on ABC-TV in August 1999, NBC-TV reintroduced a modern version of its former famous scandal-ridden show—complete with isolation booths—that autumn. It had been 41 years, and a couple of generations, since the model on which *Twenty-One* was based had left the air. Unfortunately, its reprise was short-lived; shifting days and timeslots and a less than enthusiastic greeting by viewers led to its cancellation a few months later.

Take It or Leave It may have spawned these shows but never the disgrace they became. Audience members, emcees and other staffers unhesitatingly supplied answers to the radio contestants, too. Yet none of it was done via the clandestine methods employed by those who later exploited the players in a feverish pitch to hype the ratings.

On the radio series, shouting out hints frequently made the outcome funnier, especially when a contestant didn't connect with the clues. It was done in jest, of course, and seldom resulted in the tense moments that the TV series with their isolation booths generated. Then again, the stakes weren't nearly as high.

On learning that some of the quiz shows had been rigged almost from the outset, Edward R. Murrow—an early advocate of impartiality, integrity and ethical standards, and still a force of some magnitude within the CBS organization—swallowed hard. He took his own superiors to task in a scathing diatribe before the Radio and Television News Directors Association at Chicago in October 1958. Chastising network executives who had, in his view, turned TV into little more than a medium of "decadence, escapism and insulation," he denounced staff slashes at CBS News in the interest of greater profits.[12] Needless to say, his speech was not well received by CBS officials in New York. His star, too, seemed to become tarnished within CBS from that point on.

Murrow had made his broadcast debut on March 13, 1938, as a CBS correspondent reporting on the Nazi takeover of Austria. That occasion was historic in the life of CBS not only from Murrow's point of view but also because it was the beginning of the network's *World News Roundup*. Critics noted that it became "the main force in popularizing on-the-spot reporting over just a studio announcer reading text items transmitted from the overseas correspondents."[13] The quarter-hour *CBS World News Roundup* at 8 A.M. ET was its chain's premier morning news program by the 1950s. It was anchored by Dallas Townsend from the late 1950s and into the early 1980s.

In autumn 1956 that web introduced *The World Tonight*, a weeknight equivalent of the *CBS World News Roundup*. The new report initially aired for 20 minutes and was later trimmed to 15 minutes starting at 6 P.M. ET; it reviewed the major national and global transactions of the day. As this book is written, *The World Tonight* continues, although it is now reduced to five minutes.

MBS premiered its own roundup of news in June 1958 called *The World Today*. Westbrook Van Voorhis, who had guided the popular earlier series *The March of Time*, anchored the 25-minute nightly news report.

As in the periods examined earlier, there were a number of significant features leaving the radio airwaves in the latter 1950s and in 1960. Some of the most prominent are given here, by year of departure, with their debuting years in parentheses:

1957: *The Cities Service Band of America*, et al. (1927), *The Crime Files of Flamond* (1952), *David Harding, Counterspy* (1942), *Dragnet* (1949), *The Fred Waring Show* (1933), *Gangbusters* (1935), *Hilltop House* (1937), *The Lawrence Welk Show* (1949), *Official Detective* (1946), *Our Miss Brooks* (1948), *Queen for a Day* (1945), *Romance* (1943), *Strike It Rich* (1947), *Walter*

Winchell's Journal, aka *The Jergens Journal* (1931), *The Voice of Firestone* (1928), *When a Girl Marries* (1939).

1958: *Arthur Godfrey's Talent Scouts* (1946), *The Bell Telephone Hour* (1940), *Big Jon and Sparkie* (1950), *City Hospital* (1951), *The FBI in Peace and War* (1944), *The Great Gildersleeve* (1941), *The Longines Symphonette* (1943), *The National Farm and Home Hour* (1929), *Wendy Warren and the News* (1947), *X-Minus One* (1955).

1959: *The National Barn Dance* (1933), *The Robert Q. Lewis Show* (1945).

1960: *People Are Funny* (1942).

Also in 1960, for the first time in 29 years, the weekly concerts of the Metropolitan Opera—airing since December 25, 1931, and originally hosted by Milton Cross—were discontinued over a major national network. The broadcasts initially played over NBC, then NBC Blue and ABC between 1940 and 1958 and finally on CBS from 1958 to 1960. When CBS bowed out, a special hookup of some 300 stations was strung together so the live Saturday afternoon performances could continue to reach millions of listeners all over the country. A media department within the opera organization coordinated the project. Texaco, the program's sponsor since 1940, continued to underwrite the broadcasts for many years beyond the passing of radio's golden age. As of this writing, those weekly performances are still being aired, still one of the medium's most time-honored and cherished traditions.

Of Milton Cross, dubbed "Mr. Opera" and "The Voice of the Met," a critic observed: "His resonant voice was an instrument in itself, one that produced a burnished announcer-profundo sound. Cross was a veritable talking playbill who synopsized convoluted plots and provided biographical notes, between-acts trivia, and an intermission quiz with celebrity opera buffs."[14] Cross presided over more than 800 weekly concert broadcasts in 43 years between 1931 and 1974.

A foursome departing network radio during this epoch is deserving of special treatment for the enormity of the impression they left not only on radio but on entertainment in general: the *Grand Ole Opry*, *One Man's Family*, *The Amos 'n' Andy Music Hall* (and, in particular, its long-running predecessor, *The Amos 'n' Andy Show*) and *Ma Perkins*. We'll survey them individually in that order. Each could be considered to have reached the zenith of its individual classification. Together, these series brought into American homes 102 years of pleasurable listening via network radio—and 155 years when local and network broadcasts of the quartet are combined.

In 1925 on a fledgling Nashville, Tennessee station, the insurance company that owned WSM made a conscientious decision to offer its listeners the strongest programming it possibly could. WSM thus generated its own schedule. The station predating the National Broadcasting Company—a chain with which it would later affiliate—by a year. One of the most popular features launched that year was a hillbilly music hoedown on Saturday nights.

Tom DeLong recalls it this way: "The tranquil atmosphere of the old South was suddenly shattered by lowbrow foot-stomping mountain music from a few fiddle, guitar, and banjo players, pouring forth from the radios. The group of players were introduced by a soft-spoken Indianian, George Hay, who believed that rustic folk deserved a chance to hear music closest to their roots; not merely accept programs that were shaped to please city folk and urban-oriented individuals. For his programs, George Hay sought local talent, chiefly nonprofessional, who were familiar with the homespun music dear to the hearts of people in rural and mountain areas; especially farmers, ranchers, and woodsmen."[15] Originally called the WSM *Barn Dance*, the entry was renamed the *Grand Ole Opry* two years later as it immediately followed the concert broadcasts of the Metropolitan Opera Company.

History was born then and has been made ever since. This shindig has never missed a Saturday night broadcast since it began on November 28, 1925. When this volume is published, the show could be within striking distance of 4,000 consecutive weekends. The *Opry* continues to play to sellout crowds at two performances every Saturday night, currently broadcast on radio, television and the internet. There are also performances on Friday nights, with Saturday and Sunday matinees in summertime and other shows added to meet the demands.

Some of the music has changed across the years. While it could truly be considered little more than hillbilly and folk tunes in the initial decades of the *Opry*, the show later adapted to country and western. In contemporary times it welcomed pop stars crossing over to country, and vice versa, diversifying and embracing those with more sophisticated tastes.

A host of stars have played the *Opry*. Among the better known are Roy Acuff, Eddy Arnold, Chet Atkins, Garth Brooks, Johnny Cash, Jerry Clower, Floyd Cramer, Little Jimmy Dickens, Lester Flatt and Earl

Scruggs, Red Foley, Vince Gill, Ferlin Husky, The Jordanaires, Loretta Lynn, Barbara Mandrell, Dolly Parton, Minnie Pearl, Jim Reeves, Marty Robbins, Hank Snow, Ernest Tubb, Porter Waggoner, Kitty Wells, Hank Williams, and Tammy Wynette.

From October 14, 1939, through December 28, 1957, NBC carried a half-hour portion of the live four and a half hour stage show every week. The full lineup aired over clear channel 650 via WSM's powerful 50,000 watts transmitter, and reached 38 states and Canada. Yet the only segment that was timed and followed a script was the half-hour broadcast over NBC.

While the *Opry* is considered the ultimate of its form (industry insiders refer to it as "the mother church of country music"), and few country music pickers and singers have hit the big time without playing it, WSM was but one of several stations in the Eastern U.S. offering similar country music bashes on Saturday nights. Other notables included the *Big D Jamboree*, KRLD, Dallas; *Carolina Hayride*, WBT, Charlotte; *Hayloft Jamboree*, WCOP, Boston; *Louisiana Hayride*, KWKH, Shreveport; *Louisville Barn Dance*, WHAS, Louisville; *Midwestern Hayride*, WLW, Cincinnati; *National Barn Dance*, WLS and WGN, Chicago; *Old Dominion Barn Dance*, WRVA, Richmond; *Renfro Valley Barn Dance*, WLW, WHAS and WCKY, Renfro Valley, Kentucky; *Tennessee Barn Dance*, WNOX, Knoxville; *WJR Barn Dance*, Detroit; *WSB Barn Dance*, Atlanta; and the *WWVA Jamboree/Jamboree USA*, Wheeling, West Virginia.

Bill Knowlton, host of a bluegrass show airing on WCNY-FM, Syracuse-Utica-Watertown, New York, who has devoted his life to hillbilly-folk-country-bluegrass music, reported: "Sad to say, only *Jamboree USA* remains a shadow of its former self. WWVA airs it early on Saturday night for only two hours, before clear channel output sets in. It's extreme modern country and they suspend it in deep winter, ironically when it was most popular in a snowy northeast and eastern Canada."[16]

The *Grand Ole Opry* is distinguished as the longest-running continuing series of any kind on the air, beating durable features like *The Guiding Light* by 12 years and *Meet the Press* by 20. The *Opry* celebrated its 75th anniversary in late 2000 with accompanying national acclaim, to which it has become not only accustomed but also entitled. The celebration was aired over WSM Radio, cable TV's TNN network, the internet and as the focus of a couple of two-hour birthday specials, on CBS-TV and the A&E cable network. The foot-stomping binge that

Actress Mary Lou Harrington helps author Carlton E. Morse, who created radio's quintessential prestige family drama, *One Man's Family*, steady a stack of scripts from the durable series. Harrington played Joan, the firstborn of Barbour daughter Claudia, in the NBC narrative that aired uninterrupted for over a quarter of a century. *Photofest.*

George D. Hay created in 1925, as of this writing, shows no sign of abating in the foreseeable future.

One Man's Family doubtlessly was radio's quintessential prestige family drama. None other of its breed could boast of the longevity (27 years), awards for fine writing, acting and producing, and its genuinely heartwarming—some would say *inspiring*—tale of several generations of one ancestral tree. From the time it was launched on San Francisco's KGO on April 29, 1932, and moved to the full NBC network on May 17, 1933, until its cancellation on May 8, 1959, it drew a supremely devoted following.

Unquestionably among the best literary efforts radio produced, One Man's Family was a profound statement of life as it unfolded in an upper-middle class American tribe. The serial debuted during the depths of the Great Depression and became a listening ritual in millions of households. Although the drama's central figures, the Barbours of San Francisco, had few financial worries, they were not without cares. Their concerns were universal—love, adolescence and a ceaseless amazement over the succeeding generations they nurtured.

Unlike most other serialized tales of the time, theirs celebrated the positive aspects of living, abhorring stock formulas and devices (like amnesia) so typical elsewhere. More a novel than a soap opera, the narrative's structure was built on "books" and "chapters" rather than typical subplot story lines.

It was the crowning achievement of Carlton E. Morse, an adroit and creative individual who wrote, directed and produced the program for most of its years. (Other Morse broadcast creations were: *His Honor the Barber, I Love a Mystery, I Love Adventure, Adventures by Morse, Family Skeleton* and *The Woman in My House*.) One Man's Family championed Morse's own philosophical view, that the family was unparalleled in providing moral fiber for the nation. It was, to Morse, absolutely imperative that the family be honored and preserved for generations yet unborn.

For 18 years the series aired as a weekly half-hour drama. Then it moved to a five-night-a-week format (on June 5, 1950), similar to that of the sudsy daytime washboard weepers. Even then its focus on daily life in one extended family's home remained, along with its literary and production superiority. The serial played out its final years in a daytime quarter-hour (from July 22, 1955). (The show attempted a couple of NBC-TV runs, at night from 1949 to 1952 and in the day from 1954 to 1955.)

Failed tries on both large and small screens never thwarted Morse and his associates; they routinely acquired virtually every decoration given for radio drama, including the celebrated Peabody Award, earned by only one other serialized drama (*Against the Storm*). *Family* won more awards for its scholarly contributions to radio than any other fictionalized tale of domestic life.

Principals in the cast included J. Anthony Smythe as father Henry Barbour, Minetta Ellen followed by Mary Adams as mother Fanny Barbour, and their five children—Paul played by Michael Raffetto and later by Russell Thorson; Hazel by Bernice Berwin; Claudia by Kathleen Wilson, Floy Margaret Hughes, Barbara Fuller, and Laurette Fillbrandt; Clifford by Barton Yarborough; and Jack by Page Gibson. More than 100 supporting players contributed.

Performances of the show were introduced with: "*One Man's Family*, a Carlton E. Morse creation, is dedicated to the mothers and fathers of the younger generation and to their bewildering offspring." When it ended in 1959, Morse told a Los Angeles newspaper reporter: "My own sorrow is not so much in the cessation of the show as such as in the thought that one more happy, sober beacon to light the way has been put out. One more marker has been torn down.... The signposts for sound family life are now few, and I feel the loss of *One Man's Family* is just another abandoned lighthouse."

For a man who believed in the preeminence of the family, and for others like him, thinking otherwise would have been unconscionable. Morse died at 91 on May 24, 1993.

The *Amos 'n' Andy Music Hall* was but a method of extending the broadcasting lives of two great performers who predated the formation of the first nationwide radio hookup, NBC. The pair, white Southern comics who went North to perform in a sketch as blacks transplanted from deep in the heart of Dixie, were initially introduced to radio audiences as *Sam 'n' Henry* over Chicago's WGN on January 12, 1926. Freeman Gosden (Amos Jones) and Charles Correll (Andrew H. Brown) would soon become an American institution.

Loved by members of all races, they developed an instant following. Soon afterward they moved to Chicago's WMAQ under new appellations and were offered $100,000 annually to broadcast a quarter-hour six nights a week on NBC Blue. Their network performances were launched on August 19, 1929.

Radio historiographer John Dunning has designated the series "the

Freeman Gosden (left) and Charles Correll assumed the roles of blacks from the South who moved North and kept the nation laughing for 35 years, largely in *Amos 'n' Andy*. The pair consistently earned the highest ratings in broadcast history. When their sitcom departed the air in the mid–1950s, they had already launched a successor DJ series. *Photofest.*

most popular radio show of all time." At its peak, said he, the program "held the hearts and minds of the American people as nothing did before or [has] since."[17]

By 1931 it reached an all-time ratings high of 53.4. Movie houses interrupted their screenings for 15 minutes nightly, piping the radio series into local theaters so their patrons wouldn't miss it. When there were just over 100 million Americans alltogether, *Amos 'n' Andy* drew 42 million as listeners every night. No other broadcast series before or since has sustained that high percentage of response.

Amos was "the most priceless" of men and Andy was "the most worthless," a comedy critic assessed.[18] Andrew Brown's egotism, lack of knowledge and lethargy was in direct opposition to the rational intellect, work ethic and family esteem displayed by Amos Jones. The clash between the two was classic. "It was the guy who knows all the angles (and how to cut the corners) out to take the square."[19]

In later years, when George (Kingfish) Stevens dominated the dialogue, it was he (Kingfish) who played a crook, although he was never clever enough to make a success of being a confidence man. Ever the honest one, Amos seldom fell victim to the Kingfish. Andy, on the other hand, was a totally selfish individual. He'd easily succumb to the Kingfish's scheming, as when the Kingfish unloaded a gold watch "at a sacrifice, son, a powerful sacrifice." As longtime listeners heard it, payback time had arrived for Andy for all of the one-sided deals he had long plotted against Amos.

For years the show played in serialized form but by 1943 it became a half-hour situation comedy with a live audience, orchestra and chorus. The cast was expanded to include Sapphire, the Kingfish's wife; Mama, his mother-in-law; Shorty the Barber; Miss Genevieve Blue, secretary at the Fresh Air Taxi Company which the boys operated; Amos's juvenile daughter Arbadella; shyster lawyer Stonewall; and more. The half-hour show continued through May 22, 1955. (A Gosden/Correll-produced stint on CBS-TV, 1951-53, featuring black actors in the leading roles simply didn't work out, and was considered a poor substitute for the radio original.)

The end was not yet, though.

On September 13, 1954, about eight months before their durable comedy series vanished from the airwaves, these humorists were transported to a new venue: five nights a week they would spin popular recordings on a turntable, interspersing them with commercials and banter sometimes involving a celebrity guest. The new series was billed as *The Amos 'n' Andy Music Hall* and lasted more than six years, through November 25, 1960, a monumental date in radio's life (as we shall soon see).

Reviewers of their final aural "act" were basically disparaging. One referred to it as a "watered-down disc jockey show," but claimed the "embarrassing" *Music Hall* didn't negate the fact that they had at one time been "a great show."[20] Another depicted the *Music Hall* as "sterile, stilted.... It was sad."[21]

Interestingly, the same pair of highly distinguished voices resurfaced on October 3, 1961, in the parts of *Calvin and the Colonel*, an animated cartoon of that name carried weekly by ABC-TV. They appeared as noncontroversial humanized animals, avoiding charges of racial stereotyping, which had been an issue with the earlier televised version of *Amos 'n' Andy*. Gosden was the voice of Colonel Montgomery J. Klaxton, a fox, and Correll was heard as a bear, Calvin Burnside.

It was reminiscent of their career success; the animals from the deep South had taken up residence in a large city in the North. Cast regulars included the Colonel's wife Maggie Belle (the voice of actress Virginia Gregg), her sister Sue (Beatrice Kay) and Oliver Wendell Clutch (Paul Frees), a lawyer who was a weasel. The Gosden- and Correll-created cartoon lasted until September 22, 1962, giving the boys opportunities to ply their basic theme well into a fourth decade in broadcasting.

Charles Correll died on September 26, 1972, in Chicago at age 82. Freeman Gosden died on December 10, 1982, in Los Angeles at 83.

A reviewer of the clever, comical characters summarizes them thusly:

> Both Amos and Andy had a certain innate innocence for they were in reality ... universal human character types, the back-country provincials who come to the big city and find themselves in conflict with the ways of that city.... In reality, Amos and Andy were all of us, reluctantly leaving the rural unsophistication of the first half of the twentieth century for our inevitable trip into the urban mechanization of the second half of the century. As we traveled farther into awareness, we left behind *Amos 'n' Andy*. Theirs was a time when everybody in America, rich or poor, black or white, was too innocent not to love *Amos 'n' Andy*.[22]

Only one drama would air more radio episodes than *Ma Perkins*. *The Romance of Helen Trent* broadcast 7,222 chapters while *Ma Perkins* was heard 7,065 times. Both soap operas lasted roughly 27 years: *Trent* debuted on CBS on October 30, 1933, and never left that web, offering its final performance on June 24, 1960. *Perkins* was introduced to Cincinnati area listeners over WLW on August 14, 1933; thence it was beamed to a nationwide audience via NBC starting December 4, 1933. While not aired continuously, that dishpan drama played at varying times on all four chains, and concurrently for years on both NBC and CBS. At its peak, it was carried on stations in Hawaii, Canada and Europe, the latter through Radio Luxembourg. Only a TV pilot in the 1940s failed to turn into reality. *Ma Perkins* departed the airwaves forever on Novem-

For 27 years the show was dubbed "Oxydol's own" *Ma Perkins*, even after soapmaker Procter & Gamble withdrew from the tale of Rushville Center four years before it left the air in 1960. Actress Virginia Payne (sitting), who played the title role, never missed a performance. Support players Murray Forbes (Willie Fitz) at left and Charles Egleston (Shuffle Shober) surround her. *Photofest*.

ber 25, 1960. Clearly it had been America's most beloved daytime serial drama.

Protagonist Ma Perkins was an affable widow blessed with the wisdom of Solomon. Like most of her contemporaries, she was situated in a rural, closely knit community marked by pathos and heartache. Such factors combined to distinguish her story as the most enduring and heartwarming of radio's golden age. Ma's convivial spirit, her love for humanity and her concern that reason must prevail and decency be practiced were hallmarks that endeared her to those in the narrative and to millions of fans listening at home.

As the unassuming conscience of mythical Rushville Center (and perhaps the nation), she was sought by the local citizenry for her advice in solving moral and ethical dilemmas. More often than not, the dilemmas involved her own little enclave—three children (including one who died in the Second World War), their mates, her grandchildren and Ma's closest friend and business associate.

Actress Virginia Payne, age 23, highly cultured and bearing two earned master's degrees when she began the part, went all the way in the title role. Fans held her and the figure she played in exalted esteem. Head writer Orin Tovrov had the good fortune of molding the characters and interrelating the principals for more than two decades. While all of it was purely make believe, to those who welcomed it for a daily shot of adrenaline across the decades the tale appeared exceptionally believable.

In its earliest days a note on an NBC file card cautioned that Virginia Payne's identity was never to be released to the public. That suggested that a certain perception might be destroyed if people knew who she really was—and, perhaps, just how young she really was. With the passing of time, however—as Payne advanced in age—the rule was relaxed. In response to the demands of her fans, CBS wrapped the young blonde actress in a gray wig, steel-rimmed glasses, low-heeled Oxfords and dowdy dresses, and sent her out to make public appearances. Local audiences absolutely adored it.

Two principals in the *Perkins* drama were with the broadcast from beginning to end: Payne, and Murray Forbes, who played Ma's faithful son-in-law Willie Fitz. A third actor, Charles Egleston, playing Ma's confidant and business partner Shuffle Shober, was with the washboard weeper for 25 years, until his death in 1958. Multiple thespians were cast in other roles of the durable drama, which included Ma's daughters

Evey and Fay and son John, along with several grandchildren and other residents of Rushville Center.

Scholars studying radio drama coined phrases for Ma Perkins, more than adequately conveying the serial's and the heroine's places in soap opera history. One referred to her as the "mother of all soap opera," hardly a misnomer, while the program itself designated her as the "mother of the air."[23]

Another observer labeled her the "den mom of our dreams," describing Ma Perkins as a "pie-baking Sherlock Holmes with an I.Q. of about one hundred and eighty."[24]

Virginia Payne later returned to the city of her birth, Cincinnati, where she died on February 10, 1977. She was 66.

More than four decades have elapsed since this author was privileged to participate in a series of exchanges with daytime heroine Vivian Smolen. For at least a dozen years, Smolen played in the title role of *Our Gal Sunday*. For many of those same years she also appeared as Laurel Grosvenor, the beloved daughter of *Stella Dallas* in the show of that name, and was familiarly known by serial lovers as "Lolly Baby." Smolen, who was to be of great assistance to the author in preparing an earlier volume, *The Great Radio Soap Operas*, supplied behind-the-scene anecdotes on how *Sunday* got on the air—insights that those outside the industry couldn't possibly acquire without a direct pipeline.

Little did either the actress or the writer realize at that juncture (late 1958) that just six weeks hence on January 2, 1959, the network airing *Our Gal Sunday* (CBS) would pull the plug on her 22-year-old serial. That same day it would banish three peers of *Sunday* to never-never land: *Backstage Wife*, *Road of Life* and *This Is Nora Drake*. Together, the foursome had aired about 78 years. (Earlier, when General Foods announced the cancellation of two late-afternoon washboard weepers, *When a Girl Marries* and *Portia Faces Life*, the venerable Virginia Payne observed: "I feel as though the main pillars had been knocked out of the house." Colbee's Restaurant at CBS, where many heroes and heroines of daytime drama gathered socially, was "Forest Lawn without the flowers," according to another soap star.[25])

A scholar in the field epitomized the environment:

> Even as the form [soap opera] was being pushed from radio,... the sales appeal of the daytime serial remained strong.... The cost per thousand impressions could be as low as forty-nine cents....

But the belief of a network and its advertisers in daytime serials mattered little to local affiliates.... The fees stations received for carrying the network's offerings were much less than those they could obtain by selling the same time locally. Accordingly, CBS Radio's affiliates asked, then demanded, that network offerings be reduced substantially to free more hours for local sales. That, at last, was the death sentence for radio's serials. It was not that they as a form were not wanted. Listeners as well as advertisers still loved them.... No, network radio itself, at least as it survived from the golden days, was the entertaining, but now unwelcome guest.

During December, 1958, CBS Radio announced that in January, 1959, it would cut its network programing from sixty-three to thirty hours a week.[26]

Vivian Smolen told the author in April 1998 that she was informed of her show's fate when she read it in the newspaper along with everyone else. It seemed a shabby way to treat an employee who had helped to generate millions in profits for the corporation.

Aside from news and a few features like *The Breakfast Club* and *My True Story*, ABC Radio had already overhauled and largely cast aside its program offerings. MBS had done the same, although it continued offering reruns of *Family Theater*, a half-hour inspirational anthology drama that it had carried since 1947 (with original programming through July 4, 1956). Father Patrick Peyton was host of the nonsectarian play; repeats aired through January 31, 1962. Another MBS staple, *Hawaii Calls*, lingered in places. Hosted by Webley Edwards and featuring live island music, the show had debuted on Mutual's West Coast–Don Lee hookup in 1935. From 1945 to 1956, the full MBS network picked up its Waikiki-based performances. It was reputedly broadcast over more stations than any other radio series, reaching a pinnacle of 600 outlets in 1953 via MBS and the AFRS, Australian and Canadian Dominion networks, the Voice of Freedom to Europe and by shortwave to Asia, Oceania and South Africa. *Hawaii Calls* reverted to regional status in 1956, airing weekly through 1975. Regional broadcasts were resumed on October 3, 1992. Neither ABC nor MBS showed many signs of resuscitation beyond these few features. Both chains were mere illusions of their former selves by the end of the 1950s.

At the same time NBC Radio was facing the twilight of its broadcast operation, too. Not a lot beyond *Monitor* and news on the hour would constitute programming at the network of the chimes. Its longest running serial—*Pepper Young's Family*, airing under various monikers since October 2, 1932—was yanked, coincidentally, on the same day (January 2, 1959) that CBS discarded the four soap operas previously named. Carlton E. Morse's pair of daytime dramas still airing on NBC had surely woken up and smelled the coffee then: *The Woman in My House* vanished on April 24, 1959, and *One Man's Family*, last of the breed on NBC, bit the dust two weeks later (May 8).

Virtually all the web had left on its weekday matinee slate, aside from news and short features, was a new anthology produced by Himan Brown titled *NBC Radio Theater*. Actors and writers could still ply their crafts there for a little while longer: the dramatic series ran for 55 minutes daily at 11:05 A.M. ET from April 27, 1959, through January 1, 1960. Brown called it "the last gasp of quality daytime drama."[27]

It included a distinguished band of actors: Eddie Albert, Madeleine Carroll, Gloria DeHaven, Celeste Holm, and more. "It was really *Inner Sanctum* in disguise.... Great writers writing in the Gothic mode," Brown recalled.[28]

Then—beyond *Monitor*—not much else at NBC.

Over at CBS, meanwhile, in addition to news, weekday features comprised half or more of the total output that chain fed to its affiliates—then limited to 30 hours of network-generated programming a week. In addition to six quarter-hours of drama each day, there was *Art Linkletter's House Party* and *Arthur Godfrey Time* (the latter reduced from 90 to 30 minutes), and the comedy of *The Couple Next Door* and *Bob and Ray* (the latter from June 19, 1959, through June 24, 1960) each weekday. While some of the serials fluctuated—*Best Seller*, five-part dramatizations of popular novels, entered the fray on June 27, 1960 after *The Romance of Helen Trent* departed June 24 after 27 years, and a few others shifted time periods—by midsummer all had settled down again.

Since the last major cutback on January 2, 1959, in practice, serials represented a greater fraction of CBS hours following the network time reduction than before it—a fourth of all hours then as opposed to about 15 percent previously. To the end the web had unmitigated credence in its daytime serials. John Karol, vice-president in charge of sales, called the hours devoted to serials "the biggest audience-attracting block of programing in all network radio." A lavishly produced promotional piece in 1959 indicated that serials were audience leaders in their time periods in almost all of CBS's major markets.

Then came what might have been a startling—though not entirely unexpected—announcement, given what had transpired elsewhere. In mid–August 1960, CBS Radio President Arthur Hull Hayes publicly declared that radio must shift from entertainment forms "which can be presented more effectively by other media."

The other shoe, it appeared, was about to drop.

Hayes scheduled a public execution for the remaining handful of serials still being aired by CBS, along with most of the web's other continuing series running in prime time. These sweeping orders would encompass *The Amos 'n' Andy Music Hall* and *Have Gun, Will Travel*. Undisturbed for a while, at least, would be the daytime Godfrey and Linkletter shows, a quarter-hour weeknight Bing Crosby and Rosemary Clooney musicale (which had premiered as recently as February 28, 1960), and a trio of weekend dramas: *Gunsmoke*, *Suspense* and *Yours Truly, Johnny Dollar*.

In addition, the network's five minutes of news on the hour would expand to ten minutes starting November 28. (In a well-researched work, Sterling and Kittross allowed that the new plan was "intended to preserve the physical network for prestige, emergency, and news."[29]) All of the cuts were to take effect between November 25 and 27, 1960.

The announcement was timed to give serial writers several weeks to tie the loose ends of their story lines together, some of them dangling for decades. While not unexpected, it was still a shock that reverberated through the industry. The network that appeared most concerned about its listeners had finally caved in, just as its peers had done earlier. While television would be repeatedly cited as the culprit for much of its fall, the affiliates had actually provoked and won the final battle.

On Friday, November 25, 1960, the last vestiges of the radio serials died, leaving the air in this order: 12:30 EST, *The Couple Next Door*; 12:45, *The Right to Happiness*; 1:05, *Whispering Streets*; 1:15, *Ma Perkins*; 1:30, *Young Doctor Malone*; 1:45, and *The Second Mrs. Burton*. As they departed, several actors stepped out of character roles they had played for years to bid a fond farewell to their faithful listeners. Typical for these farewells, as unraveled ends were secured, were the action and monologue on *Ma Perkins*.

In the concluding episode, announcer Bob Pfeiffer suggested that listeners turn back the clock to the day before. The Perkins clan had gathered for its traditional Thanksgiving meal at Ma's house. As the turkey and dressing and cranberry relish were passed, over the babble of conversation the organist played a rendition of the hymn "Faith of

Our Fathers." Ma turned to the microphone and softly reflected, to no one in particular:

> I look around the table at my loved ones and to me the table stretches on and on. Over beyond the other end past Shuffle I see faces somehow familiar and yet unborn, except in the mind of God....
>
> Someday, Fay will be sitting here where I'm sitting, or Evey, or Paulette, or Jamie or Anushka's child. They'll move up into my place and I'll be gone, but I find right and peace in that knowledge....
>
> I give thanks that I've been given this gift of life, this gift of time to play my little part in it.

The music went up and faded, and another commercial came on. Following it, the organist struck up the theme song, a variation of "My Old Kentucky Home," one last time. Virginia Payne addressed her audience directly:

> Ma Perkins again. This was our broadcast 7,065. I first came to you on December 4, 1933. Thank you for all being so loyal to us these 27 years....
>
> Ma Perkins has always been played by me, Virginia Payne. And if you'll write to me, Ma Perkins, at Orleans, Massachusetts, I'll try to answer you.
>
> Good-by, and may God bless you.

Pfeiffer reiterated: "And so, after more than 7,000 broadcasts—27 years—we say 'good-by' to *Ma Perkins*. This is Bob Pfeiffer speaking." Then an unidentified announcer's voice broke in to laud CBS's daytime schedule changes: "Remember," he chortled, "Monday, CBS News goes double to ten minutes an hour weekdays on the hour on the CBS Radio Network." The expanded concept wouldn't survive long. But the vain attempt to pump up an audience that was losing a friend who had visited in their homes daily for nearly three decades fell on deaf ears. Few saw the personal benefit to themselves in ten minutes of news in the face of pulling the plug on *Ma Perkins* and its peers.

So outraged were they, in fact, that the CBS switchboard lit up like a Christmas tree. Angry callers and letter writers gave the network a piece of their minds, sparing no words in the process. Such offense had not been taken at this drama's producers and executives since the early 1940s. Only when Ma's son, John, was allowed to die on a lonely battlefield overseas did such abuse occur. Through tears of anguish, writers and callers vented their hostilities toward the network, some practically unable to write or speak due to extreme emotional states.

Deeply embedded in the very nature of the serials had been the implied trust that they would go on forever. On November 25, 1960, that trust evaporated. Rushville Center and its inhabitants were swept away without a trace of their ever having existed in Radioland. The characters whom audiences had come to know so well disappeared, forgotten by the medium, never to be met again. It was too much for some of the faithful to comprehend; they had lost some of their very best and most dependable, albeit fictional, friends.

This author penned the following lines in an epilogue for *The Great Radio Soap Operas*. They seem pertinent here:

> When the Thanksgiving feast was over at Ma Perkins' house in 1960, millions of faithful listeners felt utterly dispossessed. Soap opera had extended the promise of immortality and eternal return—on the same station, at the same time, tomorrow. Now it was reneging on its covenant pledge. Rushville Center and Three Oaks and Simpsonville and Fairbrooke and dozens of other mythical hamlets disappeared as if they never existed. Worse, their inhabitants—who for many listeners seemed more like friends, neighbors and relatives than mere acquaintances—also evaporated into thin air. In fact, their existences wouldn't be acknowledged ever again on the very stations that had aired them for so long!
>
> How could any justification be made to those legions of fans who had composed the audiences of their local stations for all those years? And how could anyone responsible for this debacle be trusted again with any real sense of credibility? Such lingering questions must have filtered through the agony and anger that the disenfranchised felt on that awful day when radio drama died.
>
> Actor Les Tremayne would note in 1988 that the unfortunate part was that the end didn't have to come. Radio drama in other countries, he observed, continued broadcasting after the advent of TV. Vast audiences, including convalescents, the aged, the blind and all who get starry-eyed when they talk about "those days," were simply left mired in an abysmal swamp....

Nevertheless, what happened that day—though it may have been the end of an era—was not the end of a genre. The radio serial died. In its place the successful medium, television, carried on a tradition that had begun in the 1930s and that continues today. A newspaper account totally misinterpreted the demise of the radio serials when it announced that they "along with their longsuffering relatives and friends were sent to the Valhalla of soap operas with the blessings of the network."[30] It simply didn't happen.

Soaps would remain an enduring part of American popular culture for decades into the future, on television. Radio had created an entertainment form that would not be dissolved—at least, not anytime soon.

November 25, 1960 was definitely a watershed in broadcasting. Often referred to by aficionados as "the day radio drama died," the occasion was perhaps more aptly marked by a reviewer as "the date traditional radio died."[31] One should recall that *Amos 'n' Andy* bowed out that same evening, and *Have Gun, Will Travel* journeyed no more following its broadcast that weekend. The golden age of radio—in the main—was silenced forever in just two days. What it had provided to American listeners could be passed forever into the sphere of national folklore.

Nearly a quarter-century later, a TV commentator reflected on the fifties:

> The decade had begun with the sounds of the big bands. It ended with rock and roll at full volume....
>
> So much had changed by the time the decade ended. The cities were starting to fall apart, the suburbs were filling up, and the countryside was being emptied.
>
> America was becoming a different nation, tied no longer to the certainties of the past.... Before we got to the Fifties, we had lived in one kind of country. When the decade ended, we were on our way somewhere else.[32]

Radio, it seemed, could easily have been exhibit A.

5

The Postgolden Years: 1961–Present

Network radio, particularly after 1960, was an altogether different entertainment and information service from what it had been three—two—even one decade earlier. No longer was the aural medium America's foremost mode of instantly linking millions of households for dramatic announcements of great import, or for amusement. While the national chains offered updated news bulletins once or twice an hour on a regular basis, plus a few companion features to attract listener segments tuning in to local stations, in no way could they be compared with the powerhouses that were the webs only a short time before. By 1961, at best, they had mere remnants of formerly proud programming departments supplying regional affiliates with some of their daily schedules.

Yet the medium certainly was not dead. Not by any means. It would continue to be a part of the setting in which succeeding generations of Americans lived. It had, instead, experienced a metamorphosis. "Just as it had always reflected the values and realities of its environment," observed one analyst, "radio by this date was reflective of a mobile, affluent, and commercialized America, solidly committed to television for its creative amusement, but still requiring radio for music and instantaneous information. Radio in the 1960s would be the realm of the disk jockey and the newscaster."[1]

Local stations, for the most part, would provide the disk jockey; the networks would supply most of the national and international current events.

Actually, ABC Radio had instituted a five-minute hourly news update on weekends in 1954, the first net to do so. That web suggested that such informative reports blended well with the gradually increasing mood of local stations for flexible programming agendas. Rival networks obviously agreed, for by the end of the decade all four national chains scheduled capsule bulletins once hourly.

Some of the chains tried to tweak their newscasts to gain greater listener advantage while distinguishing themselves from competitors. Instead of programming their newscasts exclusively at the top of the hour as the others were doing, ABC attempted to gain audience margin by offering many of its news bulletins at five minutes before the hour. Sometimes news flashes appeared on various networks at 25 or 30 minutes past the hour. NBC incorporated the news into its 40-hour *Monitor* service on weekends. CBS, the reader will recall, boosted its emphasis by offering ten minutes of news on the hour instead of a limited five-minute capsule as the others were doing.

CBS would also become the first network to provide news on the hour 24 hours a day, in five-minute portions, starting April 2, 1973. Until then that web had programmed its daily news from 6 A.M. (7 A.M. Saturdays and 8 A.M. Sundays) through 1 A.M. only. NBC followed suit, offering bulletins 24 hours daily beginning January 1, 1974.

"In a changing and frightening world," wrote a couple of media critics, "special news events were to remain radio's forte, as it could deliver flash or bulletin stories faster than television or any other medium.... Radio networks became vestigial. Stations without network affiliations offered a minimum of 'rip 'n' read' or 'yank 'n' yell' newscasts, composed of wire services' five-minute summaries read by a disc jockey. However, in times of great stress or national disaster the networks often allowed independent stations free use of their coverage."[2]

In addition to news, after 1960—for a while, at least—there were a few long-running staples still carried by the networks, some of which will be discussed further (e.g., *Arthur Godfrey Time, Art Linkletter's House Party, The Breakfast Club* and a few anthologies and dramatic features). The preponderance of programming offered by the national chains from then on beyond news, however, was event coverage, recorded music and informative presentations on a diverse selection of special-interest topics.

Radio was no longer in demand as a comprehensive entertainment source. Television supplied that. The aural medium turned the bulk of its time back to local stations to concentrate on substance that TV couldn't provide faster, more conveniently or more efficiently. An NBC Radio vice president, Matthew J. Culligan, declared as much, as the golden age passed, while addressing a cluster of advertising agency executives: "Radio didn't die. It wasn't even sick. It just had to be psychoanalyzed.... The public didn't stop loving radio despite TV. It just started liking it in a different way—and radio went to the beach, to the park, the patio and the automobile.... Radio has become a companion to the individual instead of remaining a focal point of all family entertainment. An intimacy has developed between radio and the individual. It has become as personal as a pack of cigarets."[3]

Thus, for the first time since the 1920s, radio stations were relying upon their own resources for the lion's share of their daily agendas. Most followed the networks by offering a music and news package. This was initially referred to as a *standard* format, although it was later termed middle-of-the-road (MOR). Stressing instrumental and vocal melodies at least 50 percent of each day, such stations attempted to appeal to audiences of sundry persuasions. Specialty and local talk features were frequently thrown into the mix. The ultimate goal was to attract and maintain the widest and largest potential number of listeners available.

It was a new day for radio. Almost everything that had gone before was over. The transformation that had taken place with its strong emphasis on hourly news and recorded music was to predominate for several decades on the majority of stations, large and small, in most markets. In fact, until talk radio gained a foothold in the 1970s, music and news was the dominant pattern virtually everywhere.

While the tune-in, tune-out approach seemed to agree with the tastes and habits of most on-the-go American radio listeners beyond 1960, there would always be a contingent that would never be sympathetic to the new format. Those for whom radio had been an inescapable part of every day as a literal companion—who depended upon it markedly for its contributions to their lives, and profoundly missed their favorite programs of the past—may have found it difficult to reconcile the new state of affairs. Some in this disenfranchised minority likely held out hope that they might witness a reversal of the current programming trends some day.

While many of these individuals have since passed, some are still alive and their memories haven't dulled. Legions hold membership in vintage radio clubs and attend a myriad of old time radio (OTR) conventions annually. The hobby attracts students, teenagers, twenty- and thirtysomethings, too—people who weren't alive during the golden age but who have been exposed to it through the magic of recording tape and printed matter and online web sites. Many were introduced to vintage radio by adherents who were never able to let it go. These individuals trade, buy and sell memorabilia—books, magazines, scripts, CDs, tapes, recordings, photographs, autographs, and a plethora of premiums that were originally offered on the air and are still in circulation—while subscribing to OTR newsletters and other publications that maintain the spirit of fascination with all things nostalgic.

Each year tens of thousands of dollars' worth of recorded programs change hands. Entire firms exist to supply this market, while individual hobbyists participate in selling and trading on smaller scales. A single firm in the industry reportedly maintains a mailing list of 200,000 actual and potential customers. All of this fervor generates new enthusiasts. For every identified radiophile, perhaps there are dozens more who are like-minded, yet unaware that they could connect with individuals with similar tastes; indeed, that such activity even exists. It does, and can be unequivocally claimed as a direct descendant of the legacy of network radio.

In the late 1940s Charles Hull Wolfe, director of the broadcast testing bureau of one of the nation's premier advertising agencies, compiled a comprehensive treatise on current radio advertising practices. Calling amplitude modulation (AM) the "conventional method" of broadcasting, Wolfe cited three other "air-borne media" that appeared ready to displace it in communications transmissions: frequency modulation (FM), facsimile (FAX), and television (which he also labeled TV, video or tele). (FAX, as envisioned at that time, was an electronic process by which the content of a newspaper could be transmitted by radio waves from a central source and reproduced in a receiving unit in the form of an endless roll of news sheet to be torn off. This function, introduced in 1946, was touted as a means for radio sponsors to transmit pictorial advertisements to expand their broadcast commercials. Furthermore, it was perceived as a method for nonradio advertisers to employ as a promotional scheme in and of itself.) With that background in mind, Wolfe offered seven personal predictions for the application of these devices which he anticipated would be met by 1970, then more than two decades away. Here they are:

1. Television will be the greatest instrument for entertainment, advertising, and education in the world.

2. Television transmitters, at least five hundred of them, will be serving most of the country, and most of these TV stations will be linked in national video networks. International television may also be in operation.

3. Color television will be as common as technicolor movies were in 1949; and three-dimensional television may also be available.

4. Radio facsimile will give many American families, particularly those in somewhat inaccessible areas, newspapers in color delivered while they sleep; and these facsimile papers will carry advertising.

5. The consumer demand for straight sound will still exist, and sightless radio will continue to be an effective advertising medium even though television will cut into radio listening, especially during choice tele-viewing periods.

6. Radio stations will still be linked in chains, but they will consist of FM outlets for intense urban and suburban coverage, supplemented by strategically located, high-powered AM transmitters to serve vast rural areas.

7. The advertising end of TV and radio will be conducted on a scientific, tested basis that will make 1949 methods look like the guesswork of amateurs.[4]

Since several of Wolfe's predictions came true by his appointed deadline, just think what the great prognosticator might have foretold had he been exposed to *computers!*

Until the late 1960s the trend in AM radio progressed toward increased format specialization, and near the close of that decade an all-news format enveloped the largest markets. While those stations generally showed strong ratings performances, their personnel requirements made sustaining them costly ventures.

Seeking alternatives, some stations in virtually every major urban market ditched the news-music format in favor of all talk. Such outlets boasted programming schedules that were characterized by call-in programs, public affairs, interviews, panel discussions, and the like. While brief news updates were retained, they were no longer the centerpieces of each hour's broadcast day.

AM stations founded upon music continued to flourish, however, even though those that were programming Top 40 hits were beginning to alter their tunes. Among those focusing on musical formats, a great deal of specialization could be witnessed: some outlets were exclusively black-oriented (although mostly controlled by white licensees) while others zeroed in on country and western, rock, middle-of-the-road, or golden oldies sounds. (The latter group played hit songs from the past, taken from six months to a decade or two earlier. Such stations were most often directing their play toward adults who had listened to that music on radio in their teens and were now in the all-important sponsor-preferred age range of 18 to 35.)

A couple of factors in the mid–1960s undoubtedly influenced and ultimately shifted the kinds of sounds that Americans were hearing on their radios: the Beatles, whose international rise to fame occurred in 1964; and in 1965–66, songs of protest arising from collegians' folk music. Vocalists were by then recognized more for causes than tune types. As a consequence, greater significance was placed on the lyrics than on the sound and beat. (Curiously, a New York City station, WMCA, affected the release date of the soundtrack album of the Beatles' first movie, A Hard Day's Night—about which the nation seemed to be going bonkers—by acquiring a copy and airing it in its entirety on June 25, 1964, ten days before its scheduled release. United Artists, responding to the clamor of other radio stations as well as the public, shipped copies to retail stores on June 26, several days earlier than it had planned.)

Black pop artists became increasingly established on the airwaves in this era. While rhythm and blues music had originated among African-Americans in and prior to the 1950s, white Americans predominated in performing the style thereafter. By the mid–1960s, however, a number of widely accepted black vocalists and ensembles emerged to turn rhythm and blues into soul music. Detroit's black-dominated Motown Record Company (named for the city's acknowledged status as the motor vehicle capital of the world) became the center of soul productions. The firm engaged several artists (e.g., Diana Ross and the Supremes) who gained enormous popularity with both races.

Some stations tailored their programming still further to appeal to even smaller diverse groups, including ethnic or religious factions, listeners with classical music tastes, and other specialty interests. Inconsistent advertising revenues were often the result of such fragmentation, however, and automated formats—comparatively inexpensive to produce—soon appeared and increasingly supplanted local radio staffs.

When this happened, these local outlets were once again linked by connections to far off places (albeit for canned music and talk), something they had fiercely resisted only a few years earlier. What had gone around had finally come full circle.

Most FM stations, in the meantime, were affected by a 1967 Federal Communications Commission decree: a minimum of half of their programming must now be original if they were partnered with AM stations under joint ownership in markets with more than 100,000 residents. All FM stations fell under this edict in the 1970s. Previously, most dual stations had carried only a simulcast of their AM signal. Mandating that independent programming be offered for AM and FM, the FCC now forced owners to create fresh material.

As a result, FM outlets began to specialize their formats, too, concentrating on country and western, progressive jazz, beautiful music, or classical music. One diversification FM stations were rapidly enamored with was eclectic "underground" rock music. This alternative offered schedulers relatively inexpensive programming combined with long stretches of time filled by obscure album tracks. Just beyond the mid–1960s, New York City outlets WOR-FM and WNEW-FM were among the first in the nation to adapt to progressive rock formats. (The FCC edict requiring noncompetitive programming for jointly owned AM and FM stations, incidentally, was later abolished, in 1977.)

Widespread acceptance of the changes instituted by FM broadcasters in this epoch generated a positive by-product for radio manufacturers: there was a massive increase in sales of radios capable of receiving FM transmission.

A startup radio network was developed by RKO and launched on October 1, 1979. RKO distributed most of its shows in novel fashion. While airing three-minute newscasts by way of land cable every half-hour 14 hours daily, it taped and mailed longer features, shipping them by the U.S. Postal Service. RKO was able to expand its broadcast day to 24 hours when satellite distribution was accomplished in February 1980 and the net became the first to offer dual overnight satellite network services, effective September 1, 1981.

As early as July 1962 station WMIN, Minneapolis-St. Paul, had fostered the first U.S. all-news format, running 18 hours daily for a couple of months. (Even WMIN wasn't the first broadcaster to attempt such a course, however; Tijuana, Mexico's XTRA pursued that route earlier with a signal that extended to metropolitan San Diego and Los

Angeles.) Subsequently, Chicago's WNUS instituted round-the-clock news in September 1964 and New York City's WINS adapted to that form effective April 19, 1965. Philadelphia's KYW followed suit in September of that year while New York City's WCBS adopted the plan on August 18, 1967. The innovations kept arriving and some outlets were quick to add them.

As more and more stations converted to an all-news lineup, predictable casualties followed. Something of a tradition was broken when the six-hour *Music Till Dawn* was eliminated in January 1970. Its soothing sounds had been aired weeknights over CBS's handful of owned-and-operated stations since April 1953. Most of the outlets carrying it shifted to a round-the-clock news-weather-sports programming pattern.

There were other factors that appreciably impacted radio in the decade of the 1960s. Edward R. Murrow, who for years was CBS's most recognized news analyst and an early public affairs strategist (yet of late was its senior whipping boy) resigned after a 25-year tenure. In January 1961 he accepted the invitation of newly elected President John F. Kennedy to become director of the U.S. Information Agency. His wife, Janet, called it "a beautiful and timely gift."[5] Four years later, on April 27, 1965, Murrow was dead, a victim of cancer, at age 57. Communications had lost one of its most effective, outspoken, and heralded champions.

Earlier we observed that none of the Murrow Boys (those loyal professionals who worked alongside the admired news chief at CBS for years, and considered him their mentor) readily embraced TV. Especially was this true of Eric Sevareid, who, ironically was to spend the bulk of his career in the newer medium. Until the mid–1950s, though, Sevareid did not even bother to purchase a television receiver. Before he really overcame a fear of the radio microphone, Murrow's biographers noted, Sevareid was thrust before the video cameras. "It was a miracle that he not only survived in TV news but actually became a figure of some consequence," said they.[6]

The adventure tale of Marshall Matt Dillon and of the citizens of Dodge City, Kansas, opening the early West to settlers moving across the Plains—*Gunsmoke*—ended on CBS Radio on June 18, 1961. It had begun there on April 26, 1952, and a separate version had been added on CBS-TV in 1955 and ran to 1975, making it one of the longest runs in the history of video drama. Meanwhile, after virtually all audio drama died in November 1960, a trio of surviving CBS Radio narratives soon went down to two: *Suspense* and *Yours Truly, Johnny Dollar.* Both were to continue another 15 months.

On September 4, 1961, CBS debuted a weeknight 20-minute variety series, *The Carol Burnett–Richard Hayes Show.* Comedienne Burnett was then a popular member of *The Garry Moore Show* on CBS-TV and she would launch her own comedy series there later. Vocalist Hayes, a *Talent Scouts* winner, wound up as Arthur Godfrey's perennial crooner, remaining with the durable entertainer as his last permanent semi-regular vocalist.

Also in 1961 ABC Radio divested itself of its long-running *My True Story* anthology that had featured daily dramatizations from *True Story* magazine since 1943. A few more months of melodrama were squeezed out when MBS extended the series through February 1, 1962.

On March 25, 1962, a syndicated quarter-hour anthology series, *Guest Star,* produced for the U.S. Treasury Department since March 23, 1947, ended. It had touted the purchase of U.S. Savings Bonds while offering a celebrity appearing in brief narratives with dramatic or musical themes.

The venerable CBS dramatic series *Suspense* and *Yours Truly, Johnny Dollar,* the last of their breed, held over from the golden age, reached the end of the line together on September 30, 1962. Their unique position in the annals of network radio seems to qualify them for some further comment instead of merely a marking of their passing.

At its peak *Suspense* was one of radio's high-profile dramas. Reviewer John Dunning attributed its success in its heyday to producer William Spier "who personally guided every aspect of the show, molding story, voice, sound effects, and music into audio masterpieces."[7] Spier was the series' head honcho between 1943 and 1948 and again from 1949 to 1950. Dunning noted that top stars loved to play the show: "If I ever do any more radio work, I want to do it on *Suspense,* where I get a good chance to act," said movie idol Cary Grant in 1943.[8]

Audiences obviously loved its spine-tingling chillers each week, too, for the series otherwise never would have achieved the longevity it acquired. Those 30-minute "tales well calculated to keep you in suspense" introduced listeners to spine-tingling drama with just the right edge for it to be believable. In its most memorable episode, reprised a total of eight times by popular request, Agnes Moorehead played an invalid housewife in Lucille Fletcher's play "Sorry, Wrong Number."

Overhearing a murder being plotted for an unknown victim, too late she realizes that the killer is coming for her. The gripping tension that subsequently develops is marvelously portrayed through her own agonizing realities and the superb background noises provided by an inspired sound technician. The radio play, typical of the caliber of fare regularly offered on *Suspense*, won numerous awards for its achievements. Dunning, given to hyperbole but to some extent justified in his description here, wrote that the performance was "the most effective radio show ever."[9]

Suspense, first introduced to listeners on June 17, 1942, became a showcase for luminaries, attracting stars from the legitimate stage, screen, and broadcasting. The series hit on the idea of inviting actors to play against type in their celebrated exhibitions. Among their number: Desi Arnaz and Lucille Ball, Jack Benny, Milton Berle, Humphrey Bogart, Jimmy Cagney, Eddie Cantor, Ronald Colman, Ralph Edwards, Henry Fonda, Judy Garland, Phil Harris, Lena Horne, Jim and Marian Jordan (*Fibber McGee and Molly*), Danny Kaye, Peter Lorre, Fredric March, Herbert Marshall, Henry Morgan, Ozzie and Harriet Nelson, Donald O'Connor, Gregory Peck, Mickey Rooney, Dinah Shore, Red Skelton, Jimmy Stewart, Orson Welles, Richard Widmark, and legions more.

Quality scripting and directing as well as the acting contributed heavily to the success of *Suspense*. Following its demise, one of its sharpest minds, writer Ray Bradbury, adroitly observed: "When *Suspense* died, part of my creative soul died with it."[10]

The other superdrama that was a casualty that same day in 1962, *Yours Truly, Johnny Dollar*, had been running with little interruption since February 11, 1949. It featured seven of the East Coast's better actors starring as the private insurance investigator with the action-packed expense account: Dick Powell, Charles Russell, Edmond O'Brien, John Lund, Bob Bailey, Bob Readick, and Mandel Kramer. Its initial reviews were less than promising but given a little time, plus better scripts and acting, the critics were more benevolent.

For a portion of the gain from repossessed merchandise, Dollar pursued goods and villains with a vengeance. "He had an analytical mind, a nose for trouble, and the brawn to take care of himself when the going got dirty," one analyst asserted.[11] Dollar was often impatient with people and situations, and adept at shamelessly padding his expense account. Though a confirmed bachelor, he kept a romantic interest on the string, respected the police (not all sleuths did), and called on stoolies and tipsters for information as needed. He also reported the details of his escapades in the first person to his radio listeners, a penchant that several private eye investigative types embraced in radio.

At the end of every episode, he'd total up his expenses for submission to the insurance company paying his fee, then add his signature: "Yours truly, Johnny Dollar." It was a familiar line that the faithful came to anticipate. On September 30, 1962 he expressed it for the final time and with it "vintage radio drew its last breath."[12] Not precisely, of course; yet his departure left a void that has never been filled by an ongoing dramatic series that focuses on a single character. It was, with absolute certainty, the end of the age.

A few years later, in 1965, a milestone of another type occurred in radio: for the first time in 11 years all four national radio chains made money. Their earnings had spiraled appreciably downward since the onset of TV. Yet by the mid–1960s, with the programming fat trimmed to the bone, MBS and the aural divisions of ABC, CBS and NBC again began to turn a profit.

In 1966, Clayton (Bud) Collyer, a durable dramatic actor, announcer and game-show host during radio's golden age, who was the voice of *Superman* in the 1940s radio series of the same name, reprised his role. Introducing the man of steel to a new generation, Collyer delivered his lines for a smash hit CBS-TV Saturday morning cartoon series, *The New Adventures of Superman*. Coincidentally, the dialogue was recorded in one of the old studios used for the radio series two decades earlier.

Radio has frequently been the backdrop of choice for TV sitcoms. In 1967 CBS-TV offered its viewers *Good Morning, World* starring Dave Lewis and Larry Clarke as a couple of A.M. disk jockeys ("Lewis and Clarke") on a Los Angeles radio station. In 1978, the same network premiered a more successful *WKRP in Cincinnati* with offbeat characters improving a low-rated station's fortunes by turning it into a Top 40 rock 'n' roll outlet. The following year McLean Stevenson played a radio call-in host living in Portland, Oregon, on NBC-TV's *Hello, Larry*. Of these only *WKRP* lasted beyond one season; that one stuck around for four.

Radio actors, writers and directors continued to find a few places to parade their talents after the golden age passed, although opportunities were quite limited. In addition to the handful cited already, in

1964 ABC introduced a 25-minute anthology series, *Theater Five*, which ran until June 1965.

The major networks carried five-minute topical reports throughout the day in the 1960s: CBS titled its segments of this nature *Dimension* and they began in 1962. NBC named its features *Emphasis* and they started in 1963. ABC, meanwhile, had premiered a 55-minute weekday afternoon disk jockey and feature show, *Flair*, on October 3, 1960, with comedian Dick Van Dyke as host. By July 1963 he was gone, leaving to become the star of his own TV sitcom. The radio show he left was renamed *Flair Reports* and was patterned after the peer series on NBC and CBS; it aired five-minute capsule features throughout each weekday.

On December 31, 1963, CBS added advice columnist Abigail Van Buren to its weekday lineup—she meddled in people's personal lives for 11 years, through December 27, 1974. On another front, CBS carried former New York Yankees shortstop Phil Rizzuto in a 19-year run of *It's Sports Time*, from 1957 to 1976. That chain also devoted a quarter-hour to *World Wide Sports* weeknights starting on May 28, 1962, which was hosted by Chris Schenkel. When Schenkel defected to ABC in late 1964, CBS replaced him with Frank Gifford. In autumn 1965, CBS began airing a weekly 25-minute interview series called *Mike Wallace at Large*. In the early 1970s, the show was revamped into five segments, each one of five minutes' duration, and aired on weekdays. In January 1979, Wallace's five-minute features moved to weekends, broadcasting twice on Saturdays and Sundays. Meanwhile, *Vietnam Update*, which had premiered on ABC on November 19, 1965, was the first news weekly on the air devoted solely to the conflict in Vietnam.

Beginning in October 1966 and continuing through December 1982, NBC offered its listeners *Second Sunday*, a 55-minute documentary. The program aired monthly on the date in its title. Meanwhile, in 1967 ABC launched *Perspective*, a commentary-feature series broadcast in dual 25-minute segments, broken by a five-minute newscast. Stations preferring less than an hour of public affairs programming aired a single portion of the show. It confused listeners, however, who often heard references to preceding or successive reports without actually having heard those sequences.

Near the end of the decade, in 1968 ABC Radio—seeking to accommodate the interests of its affiliates after the programming cutbacks of a decade earlier—subdivided itself into a quartet of separately fashioned webs, each one geared to a specific format: Information (for all-news stations), Entertainment (for middle-of-the-road operations), Contemporary (for rock outlets) and FM (for classical music programmers). (On January 4, 1982, the chain diversified still further, expanding with two added formats: Direction [for adult-oriented operations] and Rock [for album-oriented rock stations.])

ABC's new plan reflected a "narrowcasting" preference for stations aimed at particular listener segments. Local outlets had rejected certain program types because they didn't blend with the dedicated formats the stations had selected. A Federal Communications Commission tenet prevented a chain from providing separate and competing services. To avoid running afoul of this rule, ABC supplied a chain with various programs from its four services, thus technically remaining in compliance because programs from a common supplier could not be in competition with each other. Touting its multiple webs in the trade press, ABC ballyhooed the fact that it needed "84 percent to 196 percent less time than any other major network today" to fulfill its agenda.

On May 1, 1972, MBS inaugurated the Mutual Black Network, the nation's first ethnic-oriented web. In September 1979, MBS sold its controlling shares in the venture to the Sheridan Broadcasting Corporation, which promptly renamed it the Sheridan Broadcasting Network. In the meantime, an independent competitor, the National Black Network, began operating on July 2, 1973.

MBS would eventually offer its subscribers a choice of seven networks by satellite, starting October 17, 1982. One of those program services was for Spanish-speaking stations. Following a trial period of seven months, that experiment was abandoned.

A couple of durable daytime series that survived the golden days finally came to a close in the late 1960s: *Art Linkletter's House Party*, a staple since January 15, 1945, principally airing on CBS, faded from the aural medium on October 13, 1967; and *The Breakfast Club*, almost entirely an ABC venture that by then had been *renamed The Don McNeill Show* for its seemingly ageless host, which had debuted on June 23, 1933, departed on December 27, 1968. These two audience-participation series contributed immeasurably to the prestige of their respective networks.

After overwhelming success with the nighttime stunt show *People Are Funny*, which bowed on NBC April 10, 1942, Hollywood broadcasting producer John Guedel sought a daytime vehicle for that series'

For a quarter of a century *Art Linkletter's House Party*, on radio and TV, a potpourri of human-interest abstractions, allowed its host, Art Linkletter (shown), to interact in unrehearsed exchanges with a live audience. Linkletter's gregarious personality and spontaneous repartee never failed to win vigorous approval from the fans at home as well as in the studio. *Photofest.*

ebullient master of ceremonies, Art Linkletter. When an opportunity to submit ideas for just such a show turned up, Guedel and Linkletter literally thought up the format for *House Party* in one night: a potpourri of human-interest abstractions that allowed Linkletter to interact totally unrehearsed with a live audience.

According to Guedel, the original concept positioned the onstage action in the various rooms of a house. Hints for the housewives comprised a major portion of the show—how to dress, how to look one's best, how to cook, and how to solve menial but thorny issues at home. Gags were another aspect of the commotion with Linkletter's curiosity being checked only within limits of acceptable taste.

Later, a video version of the show debuted on CBS-TV in 1952 and continued through 1969, known in its latter years as *The Art Linkletter Show*. For a while it was simulcast; however, a tape-edited edition was replayed for the radio audience during much of the run.

Occasional guests may have become celebrities in their own right stemming from their casual appearances on *House Party*. Fashion expert Edith Head kept fans apprised of what should be in milady's wardrobe and considered chic for each upcoming season. Dr. James A. Peterson, a marriage counselor at the University of South Carolina, entertained questions from the studio audience in his area of expertise. By 1964 an America then gradually turning to health awareness received exercise tips from trainer Bonnie Prudden. Occasional law enforcement agents and social service reps warned fans about scams operating across the nation.

There were hints for missing heirs: in its lifetime the show found descendants whose estates exceeded a million dollars.

There were also contests galore!

The most frequent, "What's in the House?," included the visual effect (for the benefit of studio and television audiences) of a child's doll house held by announcer Jack Slattery. A series of clues led players to guess specific objects that it contained.

There were frequent searches among the studio audience for the oldest and youngest ladies, mothers, grandmothers, fathers and so forth. Honorees carried home prizes like mixmasters, waffle irons, toasters, roasters, hand irons, and scads of other small appliances. More challenging contests might reward an occasional lucky winner with a kitchen range, refrigerator, or laundry machines. By the final radio broadcast in 1967, the grand prize for identifying the object in "What's in the House?" was an Oldsmobile Cutlass automobile.

When Linkletter went "peeking in some lady's purse," he probably provoked more sustained laughter than during any other exchange with the studio audience. Jubilantly he'd withdraw a set of dentures from the handbag of a guest, hold them high for everyone to see, then ask the giddy contestant to tell why she had them in her purse. In addition to "normal fare" he'd find in women's handbags—mirrors, eye shadow and lipstick tubes—he gleefully acknowledged to everyone those rare occasions when he found a small flask of rum or a roll of toilet tissue or a pair of ladies' "unmentionables" tucked in the hidden recesses of a guest's carry-all.

Invariably he'd inquire, "Why on earth would you have such-and-such in there?" as a dumbfounded interviewee stuttered while attempting to offer some plausible defense. Of course that generated more guffaws from an audience already reeling from the indelicacy of it all. Finally, Linkletter—having picked through several items that could subject an owner to red-faced embarrassment—asked the "victim" if she had a specific object in her purse, such as a pack of chewing gum. If she could produce it she received a gift; if she failed, she got a "consolation prize" for her good sportsmanship and for the humiliation she had endured.

Unquestionably the best remembered feature over the years was Linkletter's talks with kids—precocious preschoolers through precipitous preteens. Four or five little ones were transported to the CBS studios each day from Los Angeles–area public and parochial schools. There they'd participate in on-the-air exchanges with the program's host. After years of practice Linkletter knew how to prompt responses that mommies and daddies couldn't possibly have wanted to hear over radio and television: "Who's the most beautiful woman in the world?" a rambunctious lad was asked. "My mama used to be," came the reply, "but now that she's 35 that's all finished."

Such spontaneous repartee never failed to win vigorous approval from the audiences at home and in the studio. "*Of course* I egged them on," Linkletter admitted. "I was always a straight man for kids or anyone I talked to.... I'd never let on that I thought what a kid said was funny, because they weren't trying to be funny. So I would just listen."[13]

After 23,000 such interrogations with the younger set, Linkletter included some of the better responses in a couple of books that sold well.

Sometimes Linkletter took the show on the road, playing to vast audiences across the nation who had only witnessed it from afar—broadcasting from whatever city the cast happened to be in. It was a novelty genuinely welcomed in the hinterlands across 22-plus years on radio. For all of that time, *House Party* became a delightfully rewarding interruption in the afternoon melee and humdrum routines that America's typical homemakers experienced in the 1940s, 1950s, and 1960s.

The Breakfast Club, which debuted over 56 stations in 1933, advanced to 352 outlets by its peak in 1953. When the show was finally canceled 15 years beyond that it was still beamed over 224 stations to two million households every morning. In its halcyon days, it generated

"A get together time for all of us who smile before breakfast and then can't break the habit all day long," *The Breakfast Club* was America's durable lift-off every weekday morning for 35 years. Genial master of ceremonies Don McNeill (shown) left the show's legions of fans each day with the optimistic motto: "Be good to yourselves!" *Photofest.*

more revenue for its network, ABC, than anything else that web offered throughout the day. At one point that hour maintained an annual budget of $4 million, boosting host Don McNeill as the chain's prime money earner in the late 1940s and early 1950s.

McNeill's personal philosophy *permeated The Breakfast Club* and helped create a strong bond between the show and its loyal following. He frequently and joyously exclaimed that the show was "a get together time for all of us who smile before breakfast and then can't break the habit all day long—the place to come when a feller needs a friend."[14]

A snooze alarm gently rousing Americans from their slumber every morning between 9 and 10 o'clock Eastern Time (even earlier in westward time zones), *The Breakfast Club* supplied the corn that put smiles on the faces of millions of early risers during most of radio's golden age and beyond. To many nonMidwestern ears, Don McNeill's Chicago-based program was an authentic, yet acquired taste of middle Americana. The silly gags, instrumental and vocal music, inspirational poetry and prose, humorous skits, amusing monologues, contests, assists for common causes, special guests, exchanges with studio audiences, and mail supplied by tens of thousands of listeners became a warm-up for the day ahead.

Like some of his broadcast peers, McNeill applied a vast arsenal of resources to encourage unified efforts in support of U.S. servicemen, especially during World War II. He also backed copious numbers of other worthy drives. Fans of the genial master of ceremonies viewed him as principled, clean and wholesome, staunchly standing for love of God and country while espousing classic family values.

Most of his audience bought stock in his accepted wisdom. For 3½ decades they carried on a love affair with the emcee and the program he headlined. As McNeill waved good-by each morning at the close of their daily "love-in," he offered admirers an optimistic "Be good to yourselves!" While *The Breakfast Club* never became a success on the tube, its audio version acquired a supremely devoted bunch to whom McNeill literally dedicated his career. Early risers from the plains to the mountains, the beaches and the valleys beyond—in the big cities and rural hamlets—soon discovered that, at that hour, his show was the best radio had to offer.

A wave of nostalgia surfaced on radio in the 1970s. By then more than a decade had elapsed since most longstanding listener favorites had departed. TV was no longer a commanding influence in many people's lives, and some within the broadcasting industry believed that an appreciable number of Americans would be ready to welcome back a portion of what they had previously heard on their radios.

According to Christopher Sterling and John Kittross, a few specialty companies bought up broadcast rights to old series like *The Lone Ranger*, *The Shadow* and some comedies. They were syndicated on tape to local stations that often discovered sustained listener interest.

Fifteen years following its previous success, the science fiction anthology *X-Minus One* resurfaced on NBC on June 24, 1973. Unfortunately the chain made colossal mistakes in scheduling, offering the series with little consistency or advance notice in very fluid dates and times. These repeats were broadcast monthly, sometimes Sunday evenings, sometimes Saturday evenings. Even the series' most rabid followers had difficulty keeping abreast of it, however. When announcer Fred Collins asked fans to register their allegiance by writing the network, few did. The show was permanently dumped on March 22, 1975.

As the decade progressed, a conscientious effort was made on several fronts to reprise the genre of the dramatic anthology. Not only did this have the effect of turning back the clock for millions of listeners, it also produced the added benefit of introducing scads of new listeners to the theater of the mind. A group born after the aural narrative had faded, therefore, was hearing their first broadcast narratives. Today many of those who participate in vintage radio organizations claim they were first attracted to the hobby as a result of the programming they listened to coming out of their radios in the 1970s. In essence, yet another generation was produced to carry on the traditions of those who lived through the golden age.

A couple of syndicated carry-overs appeared early in the decade: the Salvation Army–produced *Heartbeat Theater* (1956–77) and repeats of the popular *Lights Out* thriller (which had originally aired between 1934 and 1947), then renamed *The Devil and Mr. O* (1971–72). Arch Oboler hosted the latter fantasy.

During the 1970s (sources disagree on exact dates, some claiming 1972–73, others 1975–76), *The National Lampoon Radio Hour* made a 30-minute satirical appearance by syndication. Sponsored by the publication of the program's title, it poked fun at anything and anybody. Among its cast members were John Belushi, Chevy Chase, Billy Crystal, Bob Dryden, and Gilda Radner.

Meanwhile, MBS offered its listeners a suspenseful narrative titled *The Zero Hour*. Hosted by Rod Serling, it appeared in two distinct sections, from September 10 to December 7, 1973, and from April 29 to July 26, 1974. Each half contained 13 complete stories in five 30-minute segments.

CBS premiered the twice-weekly *General Mills Radio Adventure Theater* on February 5, 1977, a 55-minute Saturday and Sunday series produced by Himan Brown. The show was retitled the *CBS Radio Adventure Theater* on August 6, 1977, and it continued to air through January 29, 1978.

On February 5, 1979, CBS launched a 55-minute five-times-a-week *Sears Radio Theater* broadcasting original dramas through August 3. It was produced by Elliott Lewis with music supplied by Nelson Riddle's orchestra, Each night a different host introduced a specific diversion: Monday, Lorne Greene with a western; Tuesday, Andy Griffith with comedy; Wednesday, Vincent Price with melodrama; Thursday, Cicely Tyson with a love and hate drama; Friday, Richard Widmark with adventure. Repeats were aired from August 6 through February 11, 1980. At that juncture the series transferred to MBS, becoming the *Mutual Radio Theater* and ran from February 14 through December 19, 1980. It was a weeknight 55-minute anthology throughout the run.

Without any doubt, however, the single most noteworthy production of the 1970s, which drew legions of faithful fans back to their radios for 55 minutes five nights a week, was *The CBS Radio Mystery Theater*. Created and produced by a master of the art in the medium's golden age, Himan Brown, the series debuted on January 6, 1974, and was indisputably a masterpiece in its day. One critic described it as "a nightly mix of original and classic creep shows."[15]

With distinguished actor E.G. Marshall as its host, this sometimes eerie series borrowed the creaking door Hi Brown had created for *Inner Sanctum Mysteries* during the earlier network radio era. It further adapted a famous line attributed to Raymond, the host of *Inner Sanctum*, in bidding farewell to its listeners each evening—"This is E.G. Marshall inviting you to return for another tale in the macabre ... until next time, pleasant dreams"—which was followed by the creaking door's closing shut.

The series boasted a coterie of New York actors, many of them holdovers from the golden age, who returned to the sound stage to pick up where they had abruptly left off a couple of decades earlier. Unfortunately, as one reviewer noted, "It was still a poor man's version of what radio once was, an echo of its unfulfilled promise. CBS gave the time but precious little money, and the affiliates felt free to tape-delay or drop it from the schedule at will."[16]

The CBS Radio Mystery Theater lasted until December 31, 1982, some of it in reruns. It was broadcast seven nights a week through 1979; beginning January 1, 1980 it reverted to weeknights only.

"There is no reason that radio can't accommodate drama now," a discerning Hi Brown told an interviewer in the late 1990s. Then in his late eighties, he continued to praise radio as a "still-vibrant form."[17] It may have been wishful thinking; he had been one of the last of the old guard capable of pulling it off, after all.

On December 18, 1971, CBS ended one of its last connections to radio's golden age by discontinuing a once-popular musical programming service—remote broadcasts of band concerts. Before recorded music was considered appropriate for radio, in the 1930s the networks and local stations filled much of their schedules with live pickups of bands performing at sundry locations. While most of these broadcasts ceased during the 1950s, CBS continued to feed them to a diminishing handful of stations that still requested them. Only 40 outlets were carrying the Saturday morning concerts when CBS made the decision to delete them from its weekend agenda.

A trio of durable talents extending from radio's golden age brought their long runs to a close in the 1970s.

Arthur Godfrey Time left its daytime stand at CBS on April 30, 1972, precisely 27 years to the day after the old redhead debuted before a live national audience offering so much promise. Godfrey was able to persevere with the program that had originally made his name a household word in millions of homes, despite airing some dirty linen and falling from his lofty perch. His daily half-hour series was broadcast by transcription in its latter half, devoid of studio audience and the formidable contingent of "little Godfreys" (performers and other cast members) who surrounded him when the show was performed live for 90 minutes every weekday. By the 1970s a victim of falling ratings and fewer outlets on which to display his witty pronouncements and occasional diatribes, the aging showman removed his seven-day-a-week feature from the airwaves himself. At one time he had been the biggest name in broadcasting but by the 1970s he attracted very little attention. Godfrey died in New York City on March 16, 1983, at the age of 79.

Through January 26, 1975, NBC virtually devoted its entire weekend schedule to *Monitor*, the omnibus entertainment form created by Pat Weaver that had begun on June 12, 1955. It was one of radio's most important series ever, and filled more hours of airtime than any other single broadcast effort. It departed when fewer and fewer affiliates cleared the time for it. But while it lasted, *Monitor* fulfilled a promise of "going places and doing things" by providing instant coverage of events around the globe, all the while employing sparkling personalities to accomplish it. Nothing else was as successful at its game or did it for nearly as long.

On May 14, 1976, the very eloquent, distinguished, readily recognized voice of CBS newscaster Lowell Thomas said "so long" for the final time. He had been broadcasting almost continually since September 29, 1930, and was one of the most admired commentators in radio. His standard opening was "Good evening, everybody" and his closing was "So long until tomorrow." A published article assessed his contributions: "He neither views with alarm like [Walter] Winchell nor views with gaiety like [Gabriel] Heatter ... he doesn't offer social messages or uplift; he never gives the impression that he has inside information like Drew Pearson, yet his rating as a newsman has consistently been either first, second, or third over the years."[18] Thomas left NBC for CBS in 1947, continuing a weeknight quarter-hour newscast at 6:45 ET that he had maintained for years. He remained in that time period until retiring at age 84. In addition to his radio work Thomas was a

"So long until tomorrow" was the familiar phrase that identified popular newscaster Lowell Thomas (shown) as he departed the airwaves each day. Thomas, whose reportage was approaching five decades, quit his long-running nightly newscast over CBS on May 14, 1976. Much earlier he had achieved added fame as a prolific writer and movie newsreel commentator. *Photofest.*

prolific writer, producing more than 40 books and countless magazine articles. He traveled widely and was frequently on the lecture circuit, while also becoming the voice of Fox Movietone Newsreels, completing two such assignments weekly for years. He died on August 29, 1981, at Pawling, New York. It was the same city in which a venerated colleague, Edward R. Murrow, had succumbed 16 years earlier.

A formidable competitor of the traditional radio networks emerged in 1971. That year a loosely organized chain of noncommercial radio stations, then known as National Educational Radio, was replaced by a stronger National Public Radio. The resulting communications system was to become the net of choice for millions of American listeners in the years ahead.

NBC launched an all-news radio network on June 18, 1975, over 33 stations. The web claimed it needed 150 outlets in order to turn a profit. When the decision was made to kill the service effective May 29, 1977, it was being carried in only 62 markets. Meanwhile, National Public Radio had premiered a successful 90-minute evening news-and-features program, *All Things Considered*, on May 3, 1971, via a hookup extending to 112 markets. In 1979, the same network added *Morning Edition*, an equivalent companion to its evening series.

Just about everybody remembers Lucille Ball, even those who weren't alive when she was a madcap comic in sitcoms on radio and television, thanks to audio- and videotape. Ball's daughter Lucie followed in her mom's acting footsteps, though she was less inclined toward comedic roles. She, too, flirted with radio briefly when she hosted a five-minute syndicated interview show in 1978, *Tune in with Lucie Arnaz*. S.C. Johnson and Sons, the makers of Johnson's Wax, sponsored Ms. Arnaz. For many years that firm brought radio listeners of the golden age the memorable comedy series *Fibber McGee and Molly*.

On February 9, 1979, NBC instituted a youth-oriented radio network with a one-hour taped Willie Nelson concert. It followed a similar success from the mid–1970s when ABC broadcast some live-on-tape music specials aimed at young people. "The Source," NBC's name for the new service, was expanded on May 28, 1979, to include more musical concerts and two minutes of youth-oriented reports per hour in a six-hour time span daily. The youth news feeds were stretched to run 24 hours daily on September 1, 1979.

President Jimmy Carter appeared in a CBS national call-in radio show broadcast for two hours on a Saturday afternoon in March 1977. *Ask President Carter* was hosted by news anchorman Walter Cronkite. A video version of that show was repeated later the same evening over the Public Broadcasting Service television network. Carter participated in yet another call-in show over National Public Radio on October 13, 1978.

The Mutual network was the last of the majors to purchase its own radio stations. In June 1979, it bought Chicago's WCFL for $12.5 million from the Chicago Federation of Labor. Six months later, it added New York's WHN, buying it from Storer Broadcasting for $14 million.

In 1979, *Music and the Spoken Word* "from the crossroads of the West" featuring the Salt Lake City Mormon Tabernacle Choir became the first network program to reach the milestone of its 50th year. The half-hour series had debuted over NBC Blue in 1929 and switched to CBS in 1932.

Less music and more talk was characteristic of radio by the 1980s. The deejay had definitely been deemphasized on many stations and in many markets, especially in urban areas. In keeping with this theme, CBS introduced its popular TV star *Captain Kangaroo* (in real life, Bob Keeshan) to radio audiences for a five-minute commentary each weekday. Keeshan's *The Subject Is Young People* debuted on January 21, 1980. Then there was National Public Radio's *Star Wars* from January to April 1980. The science fiction fantasy was a 13-week adaptation of the first movie production by the same name. On radio it starred Mark Hamill as Luke Skywalker. This radio version was produced by Richard Toskin, directed by John Madden, and written by Brian Daley.

The nation's first all-night network call-in program, *The Herb Jepko Show*, had debuted on MBS on November 3, 1975. The show had previously aired on Salt Lake City's KSL for a dozen years under the moniker *Nightcap*. In the early 1970s, an ad hoc network resulted when the show was extended to outlets in Baltimore, Denver, Los Angeles, Louisville, and Seattle. Jepko rarely invited celebrities to appear on his program. Rather than dealing with controversial issues as successor talk series hosts would, he encouraged callers to engage in person-to-person dialogue about the events transpiring at that moment in their individual lives.

Long John Nebel succeeded Jepko on MBS as the master of all-night conversation. But it was not until Larry King took over the 5½-hour post-midnight marathon on January 30, 1978, that the series gained serious national acclaim. King had previously hosted a popular call-in feature on Miami's WIOD. Within two years, his MBS show grew from a handful of stations to more than 200. This eventually led him to a widely acclaimed weeknight televised call-in show on the Cable News Network that included frequent guests chatting about current events.

On May 4, 1981, a live national call-in show, *Rockline*, originated over ABC's KLOS-FM in Los Angeles and aired by a hookup of 17 stations nationwide. Aimed directly at teens and twentysomethings, the 90-minute diversion was hosted by veteran disc jockey B. Mitchell Reed.

In late May 1981, Dick Clark hosted a three-hour musical history of the Beach Boys over MBS. Out of that came *Dick Clark's National Music Survey*, a three-hour weekly marathon in which Clark conducted celebrity interviews and played recordings of hit albums and singles on the air.

CBS became the last of the original quartet of national webs to diversify from a unitary program concept. On April 26, 1982, it launched Radioradio, which was also aimed at a youth-oriented market.

RKO got into radio talkathons when it created *America Overnight* on September 1, 1981. Ed Busch in Dallas hosted three hours of programming followed by Eric Tracy in Los Angeles with another three hours. A year later Tracy was gone, succeeded by Mitch Carr, who was also based in Dallas. Only 40 stations were carrying the show when RKO pulled the plug on it in December 1982.

NBC jumped into the all-night world of words with *Nighttalk* on November 2, 1981. For two hours starting at 10 P.M. ET, Bruce Williams addressed the financial concerns of callers. This was followed by three hours of banter concerning listeners' psychological issues from Sally Jessy Raphaël. Raphaël's segment would lead to her own daytime TV series. *Nighttalk* led NBC to form Talknet in September 1982, featuring these same personalities airing their shows via satellite distribution.

ABC, not to be outdone, aired an all-talk series linking a couple of ABC West Coast outlets starting May 3, 1982. A week later WABC in New York joined the fray and by June 18 a network of 22 stations carried the service named Talkradio. Its conversational format occupied the daily schedule between 10 A.M. and 4 P.M. and again from midnight to 6 A.M. ET.

Early in 1981, CBS's *Walter Cronkite Reporting* was bumped in favor of *Dan Rather Reporting*. Cronkite retired after his long-running anchor stint on the *CBS Evening News* on television and was superseded by Rather again at that juncture.

The following year (1982), at the Cable News Network, CEO Ted Turner developed his own all-news radio web by allowing local radio outlets to broadcast the aural portion of the televised CNN *News Headlines*.

December 31, 1982, was something of a defining moment for NBC Radio. On that date it ended the news-and-features approach it had pursued since the end of the 1950s. In one fell swoop the chain scrubbed nearly all of its daily features and weekend public affairs programming including: *Ask Dr. Brothers* with Joyce Brothers, *Here and Now* with Roger Mudd, *The Jensen Report* with Mike Jensen, *Man About Anything* with Gene Shalit, *Willard's Weather* with Willard Scott, and its long-running *Second Sunday* documentary series.

At that point all that was left of NBC Radio was the hourly news, several two-minute weekday *Comment on the News* bits and *Meet the Press*, an audio rebroadcast of the popular TV discussion series which aired every Sunday. Nothing more. It was a decidedly distasteful loss for old-time radio buffs. To think, too, that just 14 months earlier, on October 31, 1981, NBC boasted that it was airing the first live network radio drama in a quarter of a century. The occasion was its broadcast of "A

Halloween Story" for a special *All Star Radio Theater* performance. It appeared clearer with each passing season that there would be an unavoidable end to it all one day.

In the summer of 1983, Ringo Starr, a former member of the Beatles, began hosting a series of weekly one-hour shows over the ABC FM network tracing the history of that vocal group. The program was affectionately titled *Ringo's Yellow Submarine: A Voyage Through Beatles Magic.*

Also in 1983, the duo of Bob and Ray resurfaced on National Public Radio after a 23-year absence from appearances before nationwide audiences. The 1950s offbeat comics hadn't been heard by most Americans since their daily CBS Radio show folded on June 24, 1960. Featuring Bob Elliott and Ray Goulding, the team had been making merry in the interim via commercials (1960–62) followed by a local afternoon show on New York's WHN (1962), onstage in the Broadway production *Bob and Ray: The Two and Only* (1970), and again locally in New York over WOR Radio (1973).

They continued advertising and promotion work and occasionally turned up as guests on somebody else's TV shows. NPR introduced them to a new generation in a trio of stereo series airing sporadically across the nation in 1983, 1984 and 1987. Ray Goulding died at 68 on March 24, 1990, at Manhasset, New York. He and Elliott had been together since forming a comedy alliance at Boston's WHDH in 1946.

One of the obvious accomplishments of this period was the fact that satellite technology and the added competition of a growing number of stations changed forever the way most programs were distributed. To illustrate this, American Public Radio and National Public Radio were among the early and most successful customers of satellite technology for their program distribution. Applying TV's example, a radio program service could reach hundreds of potential subscriber outlets (by then many of them fully automated) without expensive wired interconnections, simply by relying upon a satellite transponder. More than a score of such services were operational by the late 1980s. Satellite Music Network and Transtar Radio Network, two instances of the trend, produced a total of 15 different 24-hour music formats combined.

The old method of sending voices across the ether was gone for good.

It may have been inevitable, given the bottom-line mindset of business, for the national radio networks to eventually pass into oblivion, much as their programming was abandoned earlier. Profits, after all, have nearly always been the pièce de résistance in U.S. commercial affairs, with little room left for sentiment.

Only to die-hard radio fanatics, perhaps, with their passionate tendencies approaching idolatry for their beloved medium and their intrinsic recollections linked to it (who seldom allowed themselves to clearly view corporate America), only to them did the inevitable become a shock. To an objective individual, however, it should have come as no surprise when the modern owners of the network licenses made hard-nosed, bite-the-bullet decisions to drastically reduce or even cease their aural operations.

Thus, the proud traditions of two of the four major players among the radio networks that served the nation for nearly three-quarters of a century have, as of this writing, been effectively curtailed. MBS, that great "network for all America," has actually been silenced completely while NBC Radio is little more than an echo of its former self. The general public, which lost them both, seems oblivious to their loss.

While the decisions to end them were purely business in nature, the reality is that little thought was given to their significant histories or to their contributions in informing and entertaining multiple generations. The bottom line—as it almost always is in business—is: "What have you done for me lately?"

The Mutual Broadcasting System originated in the summer of 1934 when a quartet of radio stations in the Midwest and East signed a pact that would allow each of them to create some dynamic programming and share it with each other. Interconnecting their operations by wire lines, they would offer their services to advertisers at a group rate. The foursome included WOR (Newark), WGN (Chicago), WLW (Cincinnati), and WXYZ (Detroit). On September 29, 1934, the foursome altered their designation from an earlier provisional Quality Network to the Mutual Broadcasting System, a name that stressed their unique new organizational structure. These were the humble beginnings of what was to become a fourth national network.

Unlike CBS and NBC, at its start Mutual had no central ownership, no owned-and-operated stations, or contractual affiliates. It was a cooperative venture instead, theoretically operated equally by its four partners, although only WGN and WOR technically owned its nominal stock. The following year (1935) when WXYZ left Mutual for NBC, Windsor, Ontario's CKLW—in the same territory—replaced it. A year later Mutual became a true national enterprise by expanding to 23 additional stations: 13 members of the New England–based Colonial Network and 10 members of the West Coast–based Don Lee Network affiliated with the original four. Soon the Texas Network added a further 23 more members to Mutual's number.

In less than five years MBS was linked with more than 100 local stations but this was only a start. The chain increased to 245 stations in its first decade. By 1952, in less than two decades, it had reached 560 outlets, nearly three times as many affiliates as either of the most listened to networks: NBC had 191 and CBS had 194. It should be noted, however, that most MBS affiliates maintained low power and therefore had smaller audiences. Not surprisingly, MBS also lagged behind NBC and CBS in advertising revenues.

While MBS suffered some casualties along the way, and some reasons for those have been considered earlier in this text, for the most part the network continued as a viable competitor to the big three. By 1979 it reached a peak of 950 affiliated stations, then in second place behind ABC's 1,561 (with its highly successful multiple webs under a single corporate umbrella). Mutual was still well ahead of NBC's 268 and CBS's 278 outlets.

Over the years the ownership of the Mutual Broadcasting System frequently changed hands. In September 1985, a California-based syndicated program service, Westwood One, purchased MBS from then owner, Amway Corporation, for $39 million. Two years later, on August 26, 1987, NBC Radio was also acquired by Westwood One. The buyer's stated objective was "to broaden its role as a provider of middle-of-the-road features and music services."[19] Westwood, then the second largest network, continued to operate as NBC, Mutual, and its original Westwood One program service.

In further developments, Westwood One later acquired the brand names of CBS Radio News, CBS MarketWatch.com Radio Network, Fox News, and CNNRadio, all of them radio news services. In the 1990s, therefore, three of the four radio chains that had served the nation since networks were first formed—all highly competitive for most of their histories—were under the same ownership. Only ABC, which had begun as the Blue network of NBC, the reader will recall, was continuing to operate totally independently of the other three.

Finality arrived for MBS in a terse announcement appearing in the April 12, 1999, issue of *Broadcasting & Cable:*

Owner Westwood One says Mutual will quit operating Sunday, April 18. The reason for the network's demise was not immediately made known. In its last days, Mutual primarily produced newscasts. But the network is perhaps best remembered for its shows and personalities, including The Lone Ranger, Dick Tracy, Queen for a Day, decades of the World Series, Dick Clark and Larry King. Westwood One now reportedly will deliver Mutual news under its CNN Radio brand.... CBS and Westwood One were not available for comment.

A former newscaster, recalling the cessation, wrote: "Official time of Mutual Radio's death was Midnight 4/17/99. No tribute, no mention it was the last newscast ... it just died." Meanwhile, another insider reported that the Mutual name remains in Westwood One's possession, actively used as a corporate trademark even though there is no on-air programming currently under that name. The Mutual legacy, it would seem, is over.

The National Broadcasting Company had existed since September 9, 1926, with its original ownership split three ways: 50 percent by the Radio Corporation of America, 30 percent by General Electric Corporation, and 20 percent by Westinghouse Corporation. The network era of radio broadcasting was actually christened by NBC on November 15, 1926, during a four-hour $50,000 extravaganza carried live by 25 stations, received as far west as Kansas City. Originating in the grand ballroom of the Waldorf Astoria Hotel in New York City, the event drew a crowd of 1,000 guests and featured appearances by numerous celebrities.

NBC was soon widely recognized for programming dual competitive operations that became popularly known as the Red and the Blue networks. In larger markets the chain maintained two affiliates to carry its separate schedules. The arrangement continued into the early 1940s when the Federal Communications Commission compelled NBC to sell one of its webs; it dispatched the Blue chain in mid–October 1943. Edward J. Noble, the buyer, magnate of the Life Savers candy manufacturing concern, paid $8 million for it. In 1945 that network's name was changed to the American Broadcasting Company.

In late 1986, the Radio Corporation of America, parent firm of NBC, was wholly acquired by General Electric in a $6.28 billion transaction. The sale represented an ironic twist, for GE had created RCA in 1919. RCA suffered an early indignity when GE promptly sold its consumer electronics division to a French firm, leaving only a single major

American manufacturer, Zenith, to produce TV receivers in the United States. But that was only the beginning of the new parent's divestitures.

One of the first actions of Robert Wright, a GE insider who ascended to the NBC presidency shortly thereafter, was to sell the NBC Radio network in July 1987 to Westwood One for $50 million. Continuing to dismantle decades of history, he followed up by a piecemeal selling of the NBC-owned and -operated radio stations. Wright fully intended for the business to concentrate on its more profitable TV operation.

Under Westwood One, the once-great NBC Radio network initially continued to provide news services to its affiliated stations, but it has since nearly disappeared, save for morning drive-time news reports prepared by Westwood's other news services and fed to a handful of outlets, plus a few features. To all intents and purposes, the world's pioneering radio service was no longer in the radio business, leaving the field to its old competitors. An informed source noted that while GE continues to license the NBC name to Westwood, "it is not promoted heavily."

What of CBS Radio? It would appear, on the surface, at least, that this is one of Westwood's more successful operations. Early in 2001, Westwood listed all of the following as regular programming on CBS:

- "CBS News on the Hour"
- "World News Roundup"
- "World News Roundup—Late Edition"
- "Newsbriefs"
- "Dan Rather Reporting"
- "What's in the News with Correspondent Christopher Glenn"
- "In the Marketplace"
- "Business Minutes"
- "Internet Daily with Frank Barnako, CBS Marketwatch"
- "Consumer Headline Report with Betsy Karetnick, CBS Marketwatch"
- "Capital Ideas"
- "Face the Nation on the Radio"

In addition, CBS Radio currently offers its affiliates two dozen 60- or 90-second features twice daily spread under four categories: lifestyles, health, money, and science and technology.

While Murrow and Thomas and Sevareid and Townsend are long gone, regular contemporary listeners of CBS's news reports are probably familiar with some of the following anchors and correspondents' names: Howard Arenstein, Barry Bagnato, Bob Fuss, Christopher Glenn, John Hartge, Mark Knoller, Sam Litzinger, Peter Maer, Cami McCormick, Lou Miliano, Dan Raviv, Dan Scanlan, Frank Settipani, and Cynthia Weber. In their day, they uphold the traditions that have characterized CBS Radio for the last four decades.

What of this modern age? Is the aural medium fulfilling its utmost potential for the American listener? Gerald Nachman summarized modern radio possibly as well as it has ever been:

> Radio today [is] killing airtime with words that make use of only radio's most basic forms of news, music, sports, and talk. Maybe the saddest part is that nobody seems to notice, much less care, primarily because few listeners under fifty-five realize that radio was ever anything more—that it once throbbed with theatrical life and exploded with laughter. People in their twenties, thirties, and even forties are scarcely aware that radio flourished with as much variety and vitality as TV does now, throwing its wide net over the full spectrum of human experience, knowledge, and entertainment.
>
> Radio today, stuck on a relentless treadmill of news-music-sports, interrupted for warmed-over weather, commute, and stock updates every ten minutes, has once again shrunk the medium to a single-cell, one-dimensional organism. Hapless stations employ their listeners to entertain themselves with a babble of opinion, most of it mindless and mean-spirited, whipped on by shrill talk-show hosts. Even in its current distorted state, however, radio remains more the people's medium than television.... While all of this goes on, as radio is reduced to a wisp of its once robust self, the Federal Communications Commission applauds with apparent satisfaction the idea that radio is serving the public.[20]

It's a sad commentary on an institution that was, in the halcyon days, a potent, formidable mode of communication with mass audiences—the first such medium in the nation's history. However, no less an esteemed scribe than Thomas Wolfe reminds each of us "You can't go home again." Radiophiles, like everyone, can identify with that dictum—we cannot retrace the steps we have pursued in life.

At the same time, for all of those with fond recollections of radio's golden age, the psalmist may have expressed our individual feelings better than anyone: "The lines have fallen for me in pleasant places; ... I have a goodly heritage."[21]

Our memories are among our most priceless possessions. When all is said and done, those treasures, unlike the programs ... and entertainers ... and networks, can never be taken away.

Appendix: Personalities Who Impacted Radio in the Fading Days

While this list is not offered as all-inclusive, it is illustrative of the major figures who heavily influenced the scope of American radio at the middle point of the 20th century and the decade that followed.

ARMSTRONG, EDWARD H., enterprising American innovator whose accomplishments included perfecting frequency modulation (FM) radio, recognized for its reduced static interference.

BANKHEAD, TALLULAH, dubbed herself the "Queen of the Kilocycles." She was an aging actress who presided over a glitzy revue in the early 1950s—*The Big Show*—that was erroneously christened "radio's last gasp," yet had profound impact on the medium and drew legions of glamorous stars.

BENNY, JACK, held a lock on a single timeslot for more than two decades; could perhaps be voted the most beloved comedian of the golden age.

BERLE, MILTON, considered by some critics a flop on radio, but early TV and his comedy video show happened at the same time, making both a success. His triumph was acutely instrumental in drawing other radio stars to transfer their loyalties to the cameras.

BROWN, HIMAN, produced the daily *NBC Radio Theater* in 1959 that he dubbed "the last gasp of quality daytime drama." He attempted, successfully for a while, to recreate OTR with *The CBS Radio Mystery Theater* (1974–82) and *General Mills Radio Adventure Theater* (1977–78).

CORRELL, CHARLES, played Andrew H. Brown in *Amos 'n' Andy*; with Freeman Gosden, he continued to find new ways to extend their characters' lives (film, TV, radio sequel).

CROSS, MILTON, originated the Metropolitan Opera broadcasts, and presided over 800-plus weekly concerts between 1931 and 1974, a legacy that continues to the contemporary era.

FREED, ALAN, brought a rock 'n' roll format to New York radio in 1954 and soon became a recognized exponent of the genre nationally. He was fired in 1959 in the payola scandal.

GODFREY, ARTHUR, an entertainer who most singularly impacted broadcasting in the early 1950s. He lost his dominance due to an autocratic style, yet was able to survive on radio well beyond the golden age.

GOSDEN, FREEMAN, played Amos Jones in *Amos 'n' Andy*; with Charles Correll, he continued to find new ways to extend their characters' lives (film, TV, radio sequel).

HARVEY, PAUL, newscaster debuting on ABC December 3, 1950, who celebrated 50 years at his post in 2000, an unparalleled achievement.

HAYES, ARTHUR HULL, CBS president who announced drastic programming cutbacks in late 1960, signifying the end of radio's golden age.

HELLER, GEORGE, guided the American Federation of Television and Radio Artists for 18 years, noticeably upgrading working policies and compensation for members. He met an untimely death at 49 in 1955.

MACDONNELL, NORMAN, producer-director who introduced a successful adult-oriented western, *Gunsmoke*, to radio, then TV, creating in effect a new broadcasting genre.

MCCARTHY, JOSEPH R., took his duty as chairman of a Senate investigations subcommittee to extremes, and ended up largely responsible for creating powerful blacklists which prevented many in broadcasting gaining employment. People were blacklisted based on innuendo and suspicions never proved about Communist and fascist sympathies.

MCLENDON, GORDON, Dallas multiple station owner who helped introduce a Top 40 recording format. He launched the Liberty Broadcasting System in 1948, which attracted 400 affiliates at its peak before the regime self-destructed in 1952.

MESTON, JOHN, skilled head writer on *Gunsmoke*, who assisted immeasurably in bringing the adult-oriented western genre to life.

MEYERS, JOSEPH O., collected more than 150,000 pieces of recorded historic trivia for NBC. He created *Biography in Sound*, a documentary that returned millions to their radios from 1954 to 1958.

MURROW, EDWARD R., the nation's most authoritative electronic journalist in the 1940s and early 1950s, delivered world news at pivotal moments in the nation's history. With strong ethics, he corralled a team of protégés with similar traits. In the mid–1950s, he confronted Joseph McCarthy on the air over his tactics, which led to McCarthy's public disgrace.

PALEY, WILLIAM S., owner-chairman of CBS. One of two major players in the industry, he was extremely competitive, and fought tenaciously to maintain radio's viability in the early days of TV.

PAYNE, VIRGINIA, first woman elected national president of the American Federation of Television and Radio Artists, in 1958. She completed 27 years in the title role of *Ma Perkins* in 1960, having never missed a performance.

SARNOFF, BRIGADIER GENERAL DAVID, highly competitive RCA chairman and chief NBC strategist whose moves turned TV into reality.

STANTON, FRANK, CBS president who guided the network into TV despite the ambivalence of owner-chairman Bill Paley.

STORZ, TODD, Omaha multiple station owner who helped introduce a Top 40 recording format.

TRAMMELL, NILES, NBC president who championed TV. Perhaps taking a cue from David Sarnoff, in 1949 he boasted "within three years, the broadcast of sound or ear radio over giant networks will be wiped out."

TRENDLE, GEORGE W., owned Detroit's WXYZ, a key station in forming MBS in 1935. His genius led to the acquisition of a cadre of talent which developed such important series as *The Lone Ranger, The Green Hornet,* and *The Challenge of the Yukon.*

TRUMAN, HARRY S, prevailed on the Federal Communications Commission to freeze the awarding of new TV station licenses in 1948. The ban, extended to July 1, 1952, delayed the inevitable surge of audiences from radio to video.

WEAVER, SYLVESTER L. (PAT), NBC president, 1953–55, whose numerous innovations included the *Monitor* flexible weekend programming service.

WEBB, JACK, starred in radio's most influential police drama in the 1950s, *Dragnet,* which ushered in a more mature, hard-nosed style than audiences had earlier encountered.

WOLFE, CHARLES HULL, an insightful advertising executive whose provocative ideas accurately projected some of the future of communications.

Bibliography

Arnold, Eve, et al. *The Fifties: Photographs of America*. Foreword by John Chancellor. New York: Pantheon, 1985.

Benny, Jack, and Joan Benny. *Sunday Nights at Seven: The Jack Benny Story*. New York: Warner, 1990.

Brooks, Tim, and Earle Marsh. *The Complete Directory to Prime Time Network TV Shows, 1946–Present*. New York: Ballantine, 1988.

Business Week, July 21, 1951.

Buxton, Frank, and Bill Owen. *The Big Broadcast, 1920–1950*. New York: Viking, 1972.

Castleman, Harry, and Walter J. Podrazik. *505 Radio Questions Your Friends Can't Answer*. New York: Walker, 1983.

Cloud, Stanley, and Lynne Olson. *The Murrow Boys: Pioneers on the Front Lines of Broadcast Journalism*. Boston: Houghton Mifflin, 1996.

Cox, Jim. *The Great Radio Audience Participation Shows*. Jefferson, N.C.: McFarland, 2001.

_____. *The Great Radio Soap Operas*. Jefferson, N.C.: McFarland, 1999.

DeLong, Thomas A. *The Mighty Music Box: The Golden Age of Musical Radio*. Los Angeles: Amber Crest, 1980.

_____. *Radio Stars: An Illustrated Biographical Dictionary of 953 Performers, 1920 through 1960*. Jefferson, N.C.: McFarland, 1996.

Dunning, John. *On the Air: The Encyclopedia of Old-Time Radio*. New York: Oxford University Press, 1998.

_____. *Tune in Yesterday: The Ultimate Encyclopedia of Old-Time Radio, 1925–1976*. Englewood Cliffs, N.J.: Prentice Hall, 1976.

Editors of Time-Life Books. *Our American Century: The American Dream, the 50s*. Alexandria, Va.: Time-Life, 1998.

_____. *This Fabulous Century: Volume VI, 1950–1960*. Alexandria, Va.: Time-Life, 1970.

Edmerson, Estelle. Quote from John Asher appearing in "A Descriptive Study of the American Negro in United States Professional Radio, 1922–1953." Master's thesis, University of California at Los Angeles, 1954.

Fabe, Maxene. *TV Game Shows: A Behind-the-Screen Look at the Stars, the Prizes, the Hosts and the Scandals!* Garden City, N.Y.: Doubleday, 1979.

Goldin, J. David. *The Golden Age of Radio: The Standard Reference Work of Radio Programs and Radio Performers of the Past.* Larchmont, N.Y.: Radio Yesteryear, 2000.

Grams, Martin, Jr. *Radio Drama: American Programs, 1932–1962.* Jefferson, N.C.: McFarland, 2000.

Halberstam, David. *The Fifties.* New York: Villard, 1993.

Harmon, Jim. *The Great Radio Comedians.* Garden City, N.Y.: Doubleday, 1970.

_____. *The Great Radio Heroes.* Garden City, N.Y.: Doubleday, 1967.

Harvey, Rita Morley. *Those Wonderful, Terrible Years: George Heller and the American Federation of Television and Radio Artists.* Carbondale: Southern Illinois University Press, 1996.

Havig, Alan. *Fred Allen's Radio Comedy.* Philadelphia: Temple University Press, 1990.

Hickerson, Jay. *The Ultimate History of Network Radio Programming and Guide to All Circulating Shows.* Third Edition. Hamden, Conn.: J. Hickerson, 1996.

Higby, Mary Jane. *Tune in Tomorrow; or, How I Found The Right to Happiness with Our Gal Sunday, Stella Dallas, John's Other Wife, and Other Sudsy Radio Serials.* New York: Cowles Education Corp., 1968.

Hyatt, Wesley. *The Encyclopedia of Daytime Television.* New York: Billboard, 1997.

Lackmann, Ron. *Remember Radio.* New York: G.P. Putnam's Sons, 1970.

_____. *Same Time ... Same Station: An A–Z Guide to Radio from Jack Benny to Howard Stern.* New York: Facts on File, 1996.

LaGuardia, Robert. *From Ma Perkins to Mary Hartman: The Illustrated History of Soap Operas.* New York: Ballantine, 1977, p. 6.

Lyons, Eugene. *David Sarnoff: A Biography.* New York: Harper & Row, 1966.

MacDonald, J. Fred. *Don't Touch That Dial!: Radio Programming in American Life from 1920 to 1960.* Chicago: Nelson-Hall, 1991.

Maltin, Leonard. *The Great American Broadcast: A Celebration of Radio's Golden Age.* New York: Penguin Putnam, 1997.

Modern Language Bible, The: The New Berkeley Version. Grand Rapids, Mich.: Zondervan Publishing House, 1969.

Nachman, Gerald. *Raised on Radio.* New York: Pantheon Books, 1998.

New York Times, The, September 13, 1925.

New York Times, The, November 26, 1960, p. 43.

Paley, William S. *As It Happened.* Garden City, N.Y.: Doubleday, 1979.

Perkins, Jack, host of a video biography. *Arthur Godfrey: Broadcasting's Forgotten Giant.* Originally shown in 1996 on the Arts & Entertainment cable network program "Biography."

Personal communication with the author from Bill Knowlton, November 30, 2000. Used by permission.

Personal communication with the author from Henry Brugsch, February 24, 2000. Used by permission.

Personal communication with the author from Jim Wood, February 25, 2000. Used by permission.

Personal communication with the author from Ken Piletic, February 24, 2000. Used by permission.

Personal communication with the author from Laura Leff, November 28, 2000. Used by permission.

Personal communication with the author from Ted Kneebone, February 14, 2000. Used by permission.

Schwartz, David, Steve Ryan, and Fred Wostbrock. *The Encyclopedia of TV Game Shows*. Second Edition. New York: Facts On File, 1995.

Settel, Irving. *A Pictorial History of Radio*. Second Edition. New York: Grosset & Dunlap, 1967.

Siepmann, Charles A. *Radio Television and Society*. New York: Oxford University Press, 1950.

Sies, Luther F. *Encyclopedia of American Radio, 1920–1960*. Jefferson, N.C.: McFarland, 2000.

Singer, Arthur J. *Arthur Godfrey: The Adventures of an American Broadcaster*. Jefferson, N.C.: McFarland, 2000.

Slide, Anthony. *Great Radio Personalities in Historic Photographs*. Vestal, N.Y.: Vestal Press, 1982.

Smith, F. Leslie. *Perspectives on Radio and Television: An Introduction to Broadcasting in the United States*. New York: Harper & Row, 1979.

Smith, Sally Bedell. *In All His Glory: The Life of William S. Paley, The Legendary Tycoon and His Brilliant Circle*. New York: Simon and Schuster, 1990.

Stedman, Raymond William. *The Serials: Suspense and Drama by Installment*. Norman: University of Oklahoma Press, 1971.

Sterling, Christopher H., Advisory Editor. *Telecommunications: Special Reports on American Broadcasting, 1932–1947*. New York: Arno Press, 1974.

Sterling, Christopher H., and John M. Kittross. *Stay Tuned: A Concise History of American Broadcasting*. Second Edition. Belmont, Calif.: Wadsworth, 1990.

Stumpf, Charles K. *Ma Perkins, Little Orphan Annie and Heigh Ho, Silver!* New York: Carlton, 1971.

Summers, Harrison B., Editor. *A Thirty-Year History of Programs Carried on National Radio Networks in the United States, 1926–1956*. New York: Arno and The New York Times, 1971.

Swartz, Jon D., and Robert C. Reinehr. *Handbook of Old-Time Radio: A Comprehensive Guide to Golden Age Radio Listening and Collecting*. Metuchen, N.J.: Scarecrow, 1993.

Terrace, Vincent. *Radio Programs, 1924–1984: A Catalog of Over 1800 Shows.* Jefferson, N.C.: McFarland, 1999.

Time, February 21, 1949.

Time, 1996, p. 108.

Transcription of live closed-circuit preview presentation to NBC Radio affiliates, April 1, 1955.

Variety, January 9, 1946, pp. 7, 120.

Variety, July 28, 1948, p. 41.

Variety, December 19, 1948.

Variety, March 30, 1949, p. 53.

Variety, July 18, 1951, p. 1.

Variety, December 16, 1953, p. 28.

Variety, May 26, 1954, p. 48.

Variety, March 30, 1955, p. 28.

Variety, May 11, 1955, p. 29.

Variety, December 21, 1955, p. 20.

Willey, George A. "End of an Era: The Daytime Radio Serial." *Journal of Broadcasting.* Spring, 1961, pp. 97–115.

Wolfe, Charles Hull. *Modern Radio Advertising.* New York: Funk & Wagnalls and Printers' Ink, 1949.

Writers and Photographers of the Associated Press. *Twentieth-Century America: The Eisenhower Years, 1952–1960,* Vol. 5. Danbury, CT: Grolier Educational Corp., 1995.

Notes

1. The Fifties: An Introduction to the Fading Days of Radio's Golden Age

1. Ecclesiastes 3:1. *The Modern Language Bible: The New Berkeley Version.* Grand Rapids, Mich.: Zondervan Publishing House, 1969.

2. Arnold, Eve, et al. *The Fifties: Photographs of America.* Foreword by John Chancellor. New York: Pantheon Books, 1985, p. iii.

3. Writers and Photographers of the Associated Press. *Twentieth-Century America: The Eisenhower Years, 1952–1960,* Vol. 5. Danbury, CT: Grolier Educational Corp., 1995, p. 125.

4. Editors of Time-Life Books. *Our American Century: The American Dream, the 50s.* Alexandria, Va.: Time-Life Books, 1998, p. 26.

5. Writers and Photographers of the Associated Press, p. 125.

6. Arnold, pp. iii, iv, vi.

7. Smith, F. Leslie. *Perspectives on Radio and Television: An Introduction to Broadcasting in the United States.* New York: Harper & Row, 1979, p. 69.

8. Cloud, Stanley, and Lynne Olson. *The Murrow Boys: Pioneers on the Front Lines of Broadcast Journalism.* Boston: Houghton Mifflin Co., 1996, p. 285.

9. Editors of Time-Life Books. *This Fabulous Century: Volume VI, 1950–1960.* Alexandria, Va.: Time-Life Books, Inc., 1970, p. 250.

10. MacDonald, J. Fred. *Don't Touch That Dial!: Radio Programming in American Life from 1920 to 1960.* Chicago: Nelson-Hall Inc., 1991, p. 323.

11. *The New York Times,* September 13, 1925.

12. Halberstam, David. *The Fifties.* New York: Villard Books, 1993, p. 185.

13. Smith, p. 52.

14. *Variety,* July 28, 1948, p. 41.

15. MacDonald, p. 84.

16. Buxton, Frank, and Bill Owen. *The Big Broadcast, 1920–1950.* New York: Viking Press, 1972, p. ix.

17. Nachman, Gerald. *Raised on Radio.* New York: Pantheon Books, 1998, p. 347.

18. Fabe, Maxene. *TV Game Shows: A Behind-the-Screen Look at the Stars, the Prizes, the Hosts and the Scandals!* Garden City, N.Y.: Doubleday & Co., Inc., 1979, p. 117.

19. Editors of Time-Life Books. *This Fabulous Century,* p. 250.

20. Halberstam, p. 180.

21. *Ibid.,* p. 183.

22. *Ibid.*, p. 182.

23. *Ibid.*

24. MacDonald, pp. 76–77.

25. *Ibid.*, p. 81.

26. Sterling, Christopher H., and John M. Kittross. *Stay Tuned: A Concise History of American Broadcasting*, Second Edition. Belmont, Calif.: Wadsworth Publishing Company, 1990, p. 158.

27. MacDonald, p. 89.

2. The Early Years: 1950–1953

1. Siepmann, Charles A. *Radio Television and Society*. New York: Oxford University Press, 1950, pp. 82–83.

2. Nachman, Gerald. *Raised on Radio*. New York: Pantheon Books, 1998, pp. 117, 266, 486.

3. DeLong, Thomas A. *The Mighty Music Box: The Golden Age of Musical Radio*. Los Angeles: Amber Crest Books, Inc., 1980, p. 284.

4. *Variety*, December 19, 1948; *Time*, February 21, 1949.

5. Smith, Sally Bedell. *In All His Glory: The Life of William S. Paley, the Legendary Tycoon and His Brilliant Circle*. New York: Simon and Schuster, 1990, p. 266.

6. *Ibid.*, pp. 290–291.

7. *Ibid.*, p. 268.

8. *Ibid.*, pp. 268–269.

9. *Business Week*, July 21, 1951.

10. Smith, Sally Bedell, p. 269.

11. *Ibid.*

12. Lyons, Eugene. *David Sarnoff: A Biography*. New York: Harper and Row, 1966, p. 275.

13. Smith, Sally Bedell, p. 269.

14. Lyons, p. 277.

15. Smith, Sally Bedell, p. 281.

16. Nachman, p. 487.

17. DeLong, Thomas A. *Radio Stars: An Illustrated Biographical Dictionary of 953 Performers, 1920 through 1960*. Jefferson, N.C.: McFarland & Co., Inc., 1996, p. 21.

18. *Ibid.*, p. 486.

19. Slide, Anthony. *Great Radio Personalities in Historic Photographs*. Vestal, N.Y.: The Vestal Press, Ltd., 1982, p. 14.

20. Reported in Dunning, 1998, p. 86.

21. Nachman, p. 487; comments by newsjournalist John Crosby.

22. Maltin, Leonard. *The Great American Broadcast: A Celebration of Radio's Golden Age*. New York: Penguin Putnam Inc., 1997, p. 300.

23. Nachman, p. 489; comment by Jack Gould.

24. Maltin, p. 301.

25. Dunning, John. *On the Air: The Encyclopedia of Old-Time Radio*. New York: Oxford University Press, 1998, p. 86.

26. Lyons, p. 286.

27. *Ibid.*

28. *Ibid.*

29. Maltin, p. 302.

30. Dunning, 1998, pp. 199–200.

31. Maltin, p. 58.

32. MacDonald, p. 220.

33. Nachman, p. 196.

34. MacDonald, p. 216.

35. Nachman, p. 203.

36. Dunning, 1998, pp. 304–305.

37. Nachman, pp. 465–466.

38. *Ibid.*, p. 305.

39. *Ibid.*

40. MacDonald, pp. 228–229.

41. *Ibid.*, p. 183.

42. Brooks, Tim, and Earle Marsh. *The Complete Directory to Prime Time Network TV Shows, 1946–Present.* New York: Ballantine Books, 1988, p. 219.

43. Paley, William S. *As It Happened.* Garden City, N.Y.: Doubleday & Co., 1979.

44. Harvey, Rita Morley. *Those Wonderful, Terrible Years: George Heller and the American Federation of Television and Radio Artists.* Carbondale, Ill.: Southern Illinois University Press, 1996, p. 98.

45. Smith, Sally Bedell, p. 306.

46. *Ibid.*

47. *Ibid.*, pp. 305–306.

48. *Ibid.*, p. 307.

49. Cloud, Stanley, and Lynne Olson. *The Murrow Boys: Pioneers on the Front Lines of Broadcast Journalism.* Boston: Houghton Mifflin Co., 1996, p. 260.

50. *Ibid.*

51. *Ibid.*

52. Nachman, p. 405.

53. *Ibid.*, p. 261.

54. *Ibid.*, p. 262.

55. *Ibid.*, p. 292.

56. *Ibid.*, p. 287.

57. *Ibid.*

58. Nachman, p. 404.

59. *Ibid.*, p. 297.

60. Edmerson, Estelle. Quote from John Asher appearing in "A Descriptive Study of the American Negro in United States Professional Radio, 1922–1953." Master's thesis, University of California at Los Angeles, 1954, p. 349.

61. *Variety*, July 18, 1951, p. 1.

62. Smith, F. Leslie. *Perspectives on Radio and Television: An Introduction to Broadcasting in the United States.* New York: Harper & Row, 1979, p. 48.

63. Siepmann, p. 52.

64. Smith, F. Leslie, p. 50.

65. Editors of Time-Life Books. *Our American Century: The American Dream, the 50s.* Alexandria, Va.: Time-Life Books, 1998, p. 150.

66. Sterling and Kittross, p. 262.

67. *Ibid.*

68. *Ibid.*, p. 271.

69. *Ibid.*, p. 262.

70. Halberstam, David. *The Fifties.* New York: Villard Books, 1993, p. 181.

71. Halberstam, pp. 184–185.

72. Siepmann, pp. 343, 346.

73. Sterling and Kittross, p. 277.

74. DeLong, 1980, p. 4.

75. Slide, Anthony. *Great Radio Personalities in Historic Photographs.* Vestal, N.Y.: The Vestal Press, Ltd., 1982, p. 52.

76. Singer, Arthur J. *Arthur Godfrey: The Adventures of an American Broadcaster.* Jefferson, N.C.: McFarland & Company, Inc., 2000, p. 1.

77. DeLong, 1996, p. 107.

78. Jack Perkins, hosting a video *Biography*, *Arthur Godfrey: Broadcasting's Forgotten Giant*, originally shown in 1996 on the Arts & Entertainment cable network.

79. Singer, *Ibid.*

80. Dunning, 1998, p. 43.

81. Lackmann, Ron. *Remember Radio.* New York: G.P. Putnam's Sons, 1970, p. 94.

82. Nachman, p. 355.

83. Dunning, 1998, p. 47.

84. *Time*, quoted without specific reference in DeLong, 1996, p. 108.

85. Nachman, p. 354.

86. Singer, p. 3.

87. *Ibid.*, p. 2.

88. *Ibid.*

89. Dunning, 1998, p. 46.

90. Singer, p. 160.

91. Dunning, 1998, p. 47.

3. The Middle Years: 1954–1956

1. *Variety*, December 21, 1955, p. 20.

2. *Variety*, January 9, 1946, p. 120.

3. MacDonald, J. Fred. *Don't Touch That Dial!: Radio Programming in American Life from 1920 to 1960.* Chicago: Nelson-Hall Inc., 1991, p. 86.

4. *Ibid.*

5. Singer, Arthur J. *Arthur Godfrey: The Adventures of an American Broadcaster.* Jefferson, N.C.: McFarland & Company, Inc., Publishers, 2000, p. 164.

6. *Variety*. March 30, 1955, p. 28.

7. MacDonald, p. 366.

8. Harvey, Rita Morley. *Those Wonderful, Terrible Years: George Heller and the American Federation of Television and Radio Artists.* Carbondale: Southern Illinois University Press, 1996, p. 173.

9. Nachman, Gerald. *Raised on Radio.* New York: Pantheon Books, 1998, p. 198.

10. *Ibid.*, p. 200.

11. Dunning, John. *On the Air: The Encyclopedia of Old-Time Radio.* New York: Oxford University Press, 1998, p. 416.

12. Nachman, pp. 436, 438.

13. MacDonald, p. 92.

14. *Ibid.*, pp. 93–94.

15. *Ibid.*, p. 94.

16. *Ibid.*, p. 145.

17. Nachman, p. 67.

18. Dunning, p. 362.

19. Benny, Jack, and Joan Benny. *Sunday Nights at Seven: The Jack Benny Story.* New York: Warner Books, Inc., 1990, p. 72.

20. *Ibid.*, pp. 97, 98.

21. *Variety*, January 9, 1946, p. 7.

22. Halberstam, David. *The Fifties.* New York: Villard Books, 1993, pp. 202–203.

23. *Ibid.*, p. 203.

24. Nachman, p. 68.

25. DeLong, Thomas A. *Radio Stars: An Illustrated Biographical Dictionary of 953 Performers, 1920 through 1960.* Jefferson, N.C.: McFarland & Company, Inc., Publishers, 1996, p. 30.

26. Harmon, Jim. *The Great Radio Comedians.* Garden City, N.Y.: Doubleday & Co., Inc., 1970, p. 26.

27. *Variety.* March 30, 1949, p. 53.

28. MacDonald, pp. 153–153.

29. Dunning, 1998, p. 743.

30. *Ibid.,* p. 729.

31. *Ibid.,* p. 730.

32. Personal communication with the author from Ted Kneebone, February 14, 2000. Used by permission.

33. Smith, F. Leslie. *Perspectives on Radio and Television: An Introduction to Broadcasting in the United States.* New York: Harper & Row, 1979, p. 68.

34. Transcription of live closed-circuit preview presentation to NBC Radio affiliates, April 1, 1955.

35. *Ibid.*

36. Nachman, p. 489.

37. Personal communication to the author from Jim Wood, February 25, 2000. Used by permission.

38. Personal communication to the author from Henry Brugsch, February 24, 2000. Used by permission.

39. Personal communication to the author from Ken Piletic, February 24, 2000. Used by permission.

40. Henry Brugsch, February 24, 2000.

41. Stedman, Raymond William. *The Serials: Suspense and Drama by Installment.* Norman, Okla.: University of Oklahoma Press, 1971, pp. 372–373.

42. *Variety.* December 16, 1953, p. 28.

43. *Variety.* December 21, 1955, p. 20; May 11, 1955, p. 29.

44. MacDonald, p. 86.

45. *Variety.* January 9, 1946, p. 120.

46. MacDonald, p. 87.

47. *Ibid.,* pp. 87–88.

48. Maltin, Leonard. *The Great American Broadcast: A Celebration of Radio's Golden Age.* New York: Penguin Putnam Inc., 1997, p. 304.

49. Dunning, p. 144.

50. *Variety,* May 26, 1954, p. 48.

51. Editors of Time-Life Books. *Our American Century: The American Dream, the 50s.* Alexandria, Va.: Time-Life Books, 1998, p. 28.

4. *The Late Years: 1957–1960*

1. MacDonald, J. Fred. *Don't Touch That Dial!: Radio Programming in American Life from 1920 to 1960.* Chicago: Nelson-Hall Inc., 1991.

2. Maltin, Leonard. *The Great American Broadcast: A Celebration of Radio's Golden Age.* New York: Penguin Putnam Inc., 1997, p. 279.

3. *Ibid.,* p. 280.

4. *Ibid.,* p. 304.

5. Brooks, Tim, and Earle Marsh. *The Complete Directory to Prime Time Network TV Shows, 1946–Present.* 4th edition. New York: Ballantine Books, 1979, p. 329.

6. Dunning, 1998, p. 311.

7. Sterling, Christopher H., and John M. Kittross. *Stay Tuned: A Concise History of American Broadcasting.* Second Edition. Belmont, Calif.: Wadsworth Publishing Co., 1990, p. 370.

8. Lyons, Eugene. *David Sarnoff: A Biography.* New York: Harper & Row, 1966, p. 313.

9. Dunning, 1998, p. 652.

10. Halberstam, David. *The Fifties.* New York: Villard Books, 1993, p. 643.

11. Fabe, Maxene. *TV Game Shows: A Behind-the-Screen Look at the Stars, the Prizes, the Hosts & the Scandals!* Garden City, N.Y.: Doubleday, 1979, p. 191.

12. Cloud, Stanley, and Lynne Olson. *The Murrow Boys: Pioneers on the Front Lines of Broadcast Journalism.* Boston: Houghton Mifflin Co., 1996, p. 337.

13. Castleman, Harry, and Walter J. Podrazik. *505 Radio Questions Your Friends Can't Answer.* New York: Walker and Co., 1983, p. 119.

14. Nachman, p. 156.

15. DeLong, Thomas A. *The Mighty Music Box: The Golden Age of Musical Radio.* Los Angeles: Amber Crest Books, Inc., 1980, p. 172.

16. Personal communication to the author from Bill Knowlton, November 30, 2000. Used by permission.

17. Dunning, 1998, p. 32.

18. Harmon, Jim. *The Great Radio Comedians.* Garden City, N.Y.: Doubleday & Co., Inc., 1970, p. 70.

19. *Ibid.*

20. Dunning, 1998, p. 15.

21. Nachman, p. 295.

22. Harmon, p. 86.

23. Stumpf, Charles K. *Ma Perkins, Little Orphan Annie and Heigh Ho, Silver!* New York: Carlton, 1971, p. 17.

24. LaGuardia, Robert. *From Ma Perkins to Mary Hartman: The Illustrated History of Soap Operas.* New York: Ballantine, 1977, p. 6.

25. Higby, Mary Jane. *Tune in Tomorrow; or, How I Found the Right to Happiness with Our Gal Sunday, Stella Dallas, John's Other Wife, and Other Sudsy Radio Serials.* New York: Cowles Education Corporation, 1968, p. 213.

26. Stedman, Raymond William. *The Serials: Suspense and Drama by Installment.* Norman, Okla.: University of Oklahoma Press, 1971, p. 393.

27. Nachman, p. 317.

28. *Ibid.,* p. 318.

29. Sterling and Kittross, pp. 337–338.

30. *The New York Times.* November 26, 1960, p. 43.

31. Willey, George A. "End of an Era: The Daytime Radio Serial." *Journal of Broadcasting.* Spring, 1961, pp. 97–115.

32. Arnold, Eve, et al. From a foreword by John Chancellor appearing in *The Fifties: Photographs of America.* New York: Pantheon Books, 1985, p. vi.

5. The Postgolden Years: 1961–Present

1. MacDonald, J. Fred. *Don't Touch That Dial!: Radio Programming in American Life from 1920 to 1960.* Chicago: Nelson-Hall Inc., 1991, p. 88.

2. Sterling, Christopher H., and John M. Kittross. *Stay Tuned: A Concise History of American Broadcasting.* Second Edition. Belmont, Calif.: Wadsworth Publishing Co., 1990, p. 338.

3. *Variety,* February 12, 1958, p. 49.

4. Wolfe, Charles Hull. *Modern Radio Advertising.* New York: Funk and Wagnalls and Printers' Ink Publishing Co., Inc., 1949, pp. 655–656.

5. Cloud, Stanley, and Lynne Olson. *The Murrow Boys: Pioneers on the Front Lines of Broadcast Journalism.* Boston: Houghton Mifflin Co., 1998, p. 339.

6. *Ibid.,* p. 331.

7. Dunning, John. *On the Air: The Encyclopedia of Old-Time Radio.* New York: Oxford University Press, 1998, p. 647.

8. *Ibid.*

9. *Ibid.,* p. 648.

10. Nachman, Gerald. *Raised on Radio.* New York: Pantheon Books, 1998, p. 315.

11. Dunning, 1998, p. 742.

12. Nachman, p. 502.

13. Nachman, p. 341.

14. *Don McNeill and the Breakfast Club Celebrate 20 Years of Corn,* p. 6.

15. Nachman, p. 318.

16. Dunning, p. 143.

17. Nachman, p. 318.

18. Dunning, 1998, p. 502, from a *Coronet* article by Maurice Zolotow.

19. Sterling and Kittross, p. 476.

20. Nachman, pp. 497–498.

21. Psalms 16:6. *The Holy Bible: Revised Standard Version.* New York: Thomas Nelson & Sons, 1959.

Index

199

Index

Index